Chinese Business in Southeast Asia

Although ethnic Chinese capital has contributed greatly to the post-colonial development of Southeast Asia, scholars and politicians paid scant attention to it until the early 1990s when it became fashionable to assert that Chinese entrepreneurs from Southeast Asia, Taiwan and Hong Kong were collaborating in business ventures responsible for a huge flow of investments into China. Today it is widely assumed that Chinese capitalists in the region will have an enormous impact on the global economy in the 21st century. Studies allege that they run extensive ethnically based business networks that add hugely to their collective muscle. Some say that they will emerge even stronger from the Asian financial crisis that occurred in 1997 and are destined to become a global economic force.

The paucity of empirical studies on the formation and development of even the largest Chinese-owned companies calls into question many of the sensational claims made about ethnic Chinese business. Does a handful of deals by a tiny number of leading capitalists add up to a 'global tribe'? Does the popular notion of a dynamic 'Chinese capitalism' and a proliferation of intra-ethnic corporate ties among Chinese businesses stand serious examination in the wider Chinese communities of Southeast Asia?

This volume contests the fashionable thesis that the institutions, norms and practices of ethnic Chinese help explain the dynamics and growth of Chinese enterprise in Southeast Asia, and challenges the notion that Chinese entrepreneurs have depended primarily on business networks based on shared identities to develop their corporate ideas.

Chinese Business in Southeast Asia

Contesting Cultural Explanations, Researching Entrepreneurship

Edmund Terence Gomez and
Hsin-Huang Michael Hsiao

Routledge
Taylor & Francis Group

LONDON AND NEW YORK

First published 2004 by Routledge
2 Park Square, Milton Park, Abingdon, Oxon, OX14 4RN

Simultaneously published in the USA and Canada
by Routledge
270 Madison Ave, New York NY 10016

Routledge an imprint of the Taylor & Francis Group

Transferred to Digital Printing 2006

© 2004 selection and editorial matter, Edmund Terence Gomez and
Hsin-Huang Michael Hsiao; individual chapters, the contributors

Typeset in by Keystroke, Jacaranda Lodge, Wolverhampton

British Library Cataloguing in Publication Data
A catalogue record for this book is available from the British Library

Library of Congress Cataloging in Publication Data

ISBN 0–415–32622–2

Publisher's Note
The publisher has gone to great lengths to ensure the quality of this reprint
but points out that some imperfections in the original may be apparent

Contents

List of Tables   vii
Contributors   ix
Preface   xi

Introduction: Chinese Business Research In Southeast Asia   1
    Edmund Terence Gomez and Hsin-Huang Michael Hsiao

1 Singapore   38
    Chan Kwok Bun and Ng Beoy Kui

2 Malaysia   62
    Edmund Terence Gomez, Loh Wei Leng and Lee Kam Hing

3 Thailand   85
    Jamie Mackie

4 The Philippines   101
    Theresa Chong Carino

5 Indonesia   124
    Diao Ai Lien and Mely Tan

6 Taiwanese Business in Southeast Asia   146
    I-Chun Kung

Notes   166
Bibliography   175
Index   202

List of Tables

I.1 Estimated Population Size of Ethnic Chinese in Southeast
Asia in the early 1990s   6
I.2 Four Perspectives on Organization   17
I.3 Chinese-Owned Enterprises Among the 50 Most
Competitive Companies in Asia, 1997   28
I.4 Business Activities of the Largest Ethnic Chinese
Companies in Southeast Asia   29

2.1 Malaysia: Ownership of Share Capital (At Par Value) of
Limited Companies, 1970, 1990, 1995 (percentages)   63

5.1 Control of Economic Sectors by Ethnic Groups in Java, 1930 128

6.1 Taiwanese Investment in Southeast Asian Countries
(1959–96)   147
6.2 Taiwanese FDI in Southeast Asian Countries (in
US$ million)   155
6.3 Distribution of Size of Taiwanese Firms by Number
of Employees in Malaysia (1993)   156
6.4 Distribution of Size of Taiwanese Firms by Number
of Employees in Malacca (1998)   157
6.5 Distribution of Size of Taiwanese Firms by Starting
Capital in Malacca (1998)   157
6.6 Reasons for Choosing to Invest in Malaysia rather than
other Southeast Asian Countries (by Size of Firms)   159
6.7 Role Malaysian Chinese Play in Taiwanese Companies
in Malaysia (Percentages)   159

6.8 Role Different Ethnic Groups Play in Taiwanese Firms in Malacca (1998)   160
6.9 Southeast Asian Chinese Students in Taiwanese Higher Education Institutions (1953–1994)   163

Contributors

Chan Kwok Bun is Associate Professor at the Department of Sociology, Faculty of Arts and Social Science, National University of Singapore, Singapore

Theresa Chong Carino is Honorary Research Fellow at the Centre for Asian Studies,University of Hong Kong, Hong Kong

Diao Ai Lien is Researcher, Centre for Societal Development Studies, Atma Jaya, Catholic University, Jakarta

Edmund Terence Gomez is Lecturer at the Department of Politics and Administration, Faculty of Economics, University of Malaya, Kuala Lumpur

Hsin-Huang Michael Hsiao is Director of the Program for Southeast Asian Area Studies (PROSEA), Academia Sinica and Professor of Sociology, National Taiwan University, Taipei

I-Chun Kung is Research Fellow at the Program for Southeast Asian Area Studies (PROSEA), Academia Sinica and Professor of Sociology, National Taiwan University, Taipei

Lee Kam Hing was formerly Professor at the Department of History, Faculty of Arts and Social Science, University of Malaya, Kuala Lumpur

Loh Wei Leng is Associate Professor at the Department of History, Faculty of Arts and Social Science, University of Malaya, Kuala Lumpur

Contributors

Jamie Mackie is Professor Emeritus at the Department of Economics, Research School of Pacific and Asian Studies, The Australian National University, Canberra

Ng Beoy Kui is Associate Professor at the School of Accountancy & Business, Nanyang Technological University, Singapore

Mely Tan is Chairperson, Research Institute, Atma Jaya Catholic University, Jakarta

Preface

————◆————

Since the early 1990s, a plethora of literature has been published on the dynamics of Chinese enterprise in Asia. We have two major criticisms concerning much of this literature. First, we contest the fashionable thesis that the institutions, norms and practices of ethnic Chinese were the reason for the growth of their enterprises. Second, we question whether Chinese entrepreneurs have depended primarily on business networks based on shared identities to develop their corporate base. Such assumptions, which have also led to the propagation of rather inept generalizations of the operation and influence of Chinese enterprises in Southeast Asia, have been based on inadequate empirical evidence.

We would contend that most of the literature on Chinese business has not really captured – and in some cases understood – the actual the form of development of Chinese capital; nor have they appreciated the quantum change in business style that is transpiring among Chinese enterprises. The form of Chinese capital accumulation is not only dynamic and changing over time, but also varies in different countries in Southeast Asia. We also felt that the essence of Chinese capital has still not been captured, i.e. there is a need to understand what we actually mean by the term 'Chinese business'. Most importantly, in a region fraught with a history of ethnic problems, some of the literature has also unfairly, though probably inadvertently, brought into question the loyalty of ethnic Chinese to the country of their birth.

Recognizing the limited research on Chinese enterprise, and that this has contributed to many misconceptions of how such firms operate, a workshop was organized in November 1997, hosted by the

Program for Southeast Asian Area Studies (PROSEA), at the Academia Sinica in Taipei, to bring together scholars who have been undertaking research on Chinese business in Southeast Asia. The workshop had a modest objective: to identify key areas of research on Chinese business in Southeast Asian countries, as well as to find avenues to encourage research involving empirical work on Chinese enterprise. In order to facilitate the discussion, a review was commissioned of research already published on Chinese business in the five countries in Southeast Asia where the Chinese have established a prominent presence in the economy – Singapore, Malaysia, Thailand, the Philippines and Indonesia. This review involved a brief history of Chinese enterprise in these Southeast Asian countries to understand the circumstances under which such ethnically-owned companies have operated and developed. This approach was also an attempt to determine the main areas that still required research to provide a holistic understanding to the operation of Chinese enterprise in Southeast Asia. Since one key issue in question is whether ethnic Chinese of the diaspora, brought together by common ethnic identity and cultural practices, are cooperating in business, another paper on investment by companies from Taiwan in Southeast Asia, particularly in Malaysia, was also presented at the workshop. We have also provided an extensive bibliography on Chinese business in Southeast Asia in particular and on the concept of ethnic enterprise.

By providing a critique of existing literature, we aim to show why we believe that empirically-based studies would provide nuanced insights into key issues like Chinese networking, entrepreneurship, and organizational and firm development. We have found that this is important, as detailed empirical research has revealed the plurality of business strategies employed by Chinese businessmen. This project is also part of our broader agenda of attempting to bridge theoretical and methodological divides in our understanding of Chinese enterprise.

We believe that there is a special need to develop projects of a comparative nature to help us better ascertain if there are traits particular to ethnic Chinese that determine how they do business and develop their companies. Such comparative research is a means to appreciate the nuances that exist among Chinese enterprises in Asia as well as in other continents. We also hope to use this volume to launch collaborative research projects on ethnic enterprises in comparative perspective, preferably to broaden the field of research to incorporate a larger number of ethnic communities and countries. We believe that our understanding of the operations of such ethnic enterprise could be enhanced by promoting comparative research across a range of other ethnic communities, for example, the Indians, Japanese, Koreans, Jews and Armenians to name a few. Cross-border and cross-ethnic comparisons would help challenge homogenizing assumptions about specific ethnic communities.

In order to promote such research, we are trying to initiate research projects, preferably incorporating a number of institutions, and to create avenues to expedite the publication of the results of such studies. For example, in February 2001, an international conference will be held to assess the impact of the 1997 Asian financial crisis on Chinese enterprises. This conference will also be hosted by PROSEA and partly funded by the Transnational Communities Project under the Economic and Social Research Council (ESRC) in the United Kingdom, which is also undertaking similar research on ethnic enterprise. We are also attempting to use the Chinese Worlds Series under the publishing house, Curzon Press, to promote such research. Curzon Press has undertaken to ensure prompt publication of work emanating from projects of this nature.

We hope that this core group of academics can form the nucleus of a larger group of researchers who are willing to come together to facilitate studies on ethnic enterprise. We also hope that this volume will help make a contribution towards promoting further research on this subject as the realities of ethnic enterprise development continues to unfold. Meanwhile, the need to map out, both empirically and conceptually, our understanding of Chinese enterprise in particular and ethnic enterprise in general in Asia requires further support.

Introduction

Chinese Business Research In Southeast Asia

———◆◆◆———

Edmund Terence Gomez and Hsin-Huang Michael Hsiao

Chinese Business Research

In spite of the extensive contribution of Chinese capital to the development of the Southeast Asian economies, only since the early 1990s has there been growing interest on the operations of such ethnically-owned enterprises. The burgeoning interest in Chinese companies has coincided with increasing focus on the business opportunities available in mainland China. In view of the huge investments flowing into China, ostensibly from ethnic Chinese businessmen in Southeast Asia, as well as those from East Asia, particularly from Taiwan and Hong Kong, it is now widely believed that many Chinese enterprises are collaborating in business ventures. Moreover, given the apparent collective economic strength of Chinese-owned enterprises in East and Southeast Asia, it is now widely presumed that Chinese capital will have an enormous impact of on the global economy in the 21st century. Following the financial crisis that erupted in Asia in mid-1997, a number of analysts have also begun to predict that ethnic Chinese businessmen in this region will emerge potentially stronger, reinforcing their prospects as a global economic force.

Many of these presumptions of the ostensible economic dominance of Chinese capital and of the business networking among members of this diaspora have been fed by a spate of literature (see, for example, Kotkin 1993; Kao 1993; Nasbitt 1995; Rowher 1995; East Asia Analytical Unit 1995; Weidenbaum and Hughes 1996; Hiscock 1997; Backman 1999). Kao (1993), for example, created the term 'Chinese commonwealth,' to argue of the existence of "a network of entrepreneurial relationships" which consists of "many individual enterprises that nonetheless share a common culture." It was, however, the publication of Kotkin's *Tribes* and Weidenbaum and Hughes' *The Bamboo Network*, which popularized the concepts 'global tribe' and 'co-ethnic business networks' respectively, that have contributed most to fueling the notion of extensive interlocking business links between ethnic Chinese of the diaspora which will enable this community to play a significant role in the development of the Asian economy in future.

Several major regional magazines have also been touting the potential economic impact of Chinese capital in Asia. For example, in 1994, the *Far Eastern Economic Review* (14/7/94) estimated that the total volume of Southeast Asian investment in China was US$8 billion, while total investment from Taiwan was US$5.4 billion, and Hong Kong US$40 billion. In 1996, *Asiaweek* (19/7/96) estimated that between 1978 and 1996, of the US$120 billion invested in China, almost 80 per cent of the total investment had originated from 'overseas Chinese'. Apart from this, the World Bank estimated that by 1991 the combined economic output of the businesses of the approximately 50 million ethnic Chinese in Asia outside of China – about 23 million in Southeast Asia, 20 million in Taiwan and the rest in Hong Kong – approached US$400 billion (quoted in Weidenbaum and Hughes 1996: 24–25). Disclosure of such investment patterns in China has fed speculation that members of the Chinese diaspora are channelling funds to the mainland. Apart from this, since the 1980s, it has been conservatively estimated that at least 100 world conventions and conferences have been organized by dialect- and clan-based Chinese organizations. For instance, the Hakka convention was held in 1980 in Tokyo, the Teochew Convention in Paris in 1991, and the International Zhang Clan Association conference in Singapore in 1996 (Liu 1998). The convening of such conferences also suggested that many ethnic Chinese were beginning to consider that their common ethnic identity could be a means to facilitate business ties.[1]

A number of publications have provided some evidence of cross-border business cooperation among a few of Asia's leading Chinese businessmen, particularly between Hong Kong's Li Ka-shing, Malaysia's Robert Kuok, Thailand's Sophanpanich family and Indonesia's Liem Sioe Leong (see for example, Redding 1990; East Asia Analytical Unit 1995; Weidenbaum and Hughes 1996). The business deals among some of these major capitalists have been used to justify the argument that in an increasingly globalized business environment, ethnic Chinese businessmen, particularly those in Southeast Asia, Hong Kong and Taiwan, are creating transnational business networks.

Many of the popular notions about the influence of Chinese capital in the region are fraught with misconceptions, mainly because there is a paucity of empirical evidence to substantiate many of these presumptions. A literature review on Chinese enterprise in Asia would indicate that the research has been limited to a number of key individuals. In Indonesia, for example, most research has centered on Liem Sioe Leong, reputedly the richest ethnic Chinese in Southeast Asia (see, for example, Sato 1993). There has been no in-depth scholarly study of the other major Chinese Indonesian capitalists, including Eka Tjipta Widjaja, Mochtar Riady, Bob Hasan, William Soerjadjaja, Sjamsul Nursalim and Prayogo Pangestu. In the Philippines, most study has focused on Lucio Tan, though no academic research has been undertaken on the development of his corporate base. There has been very little focus on John Gokongwei Jr., Alfonso Yuchengco, Andrew Gotianun, Tan Yu, George Ty and Henry Sy in spite of the enormous presence their companies have in the Filipino economy. In Thailand, there has been important research on some of the country's key capitalists by Suehiro (1989, 1992, 1993) and Krirkkiat and Yoshihara (1989), but there has been little focus on the development of Sino-Thai capital.[2] Although the Bangkok Bank, led by the Sophonpanich family, has apparently played a big role in the development of Chinese capital in Southeast Asia, there has been no in-depth study of the bank's development. Most attention has focused on the Charoen Phokpand (CP) group controlled by the Chearavanont family (see, for example, Brown 1998). In Singapore, most research has been on the Oversea-Chinese Banking Corporation (OCBC) group (see, for example, Wilson 1972) and of the legendary business figure Tan Kah Kee (Yong 1987), while Chan and Chiang (1994) have provided some useful case studies of a number of other important Chinese businessmen that emerged in this country during the colonial period. There has, however, not been any in-depth study on some of the island state's largest Chinese-owned enterprises like the Hong Leong, Overseas Union Bank (OUB), and United Overseas Bank (UOB) Groups, nor of some of the new Chinese businessmen that have emerged in the 1990s. Only in Malaysia has a number of studies been undertaken of the companies owned by leading ethnic Chinese businessmen; these studies, by Heng (1992), Hara Fujio

(1991) and Jesudason (1989, 1997) were, however, not in-depth cases studies, but broad overviews of the state of Chinese capital in Malaysia, while Lee and Chow (1997) published a useful biography of some of the most important Malaysian (and Singaporean) Chinese, which include a number of prominent Chinese businessmen. The most detailed study on the leading Chinese capitalists in Malaysia was published in 1999 (see Gomez 1999), which provides cases studies of the development of the major publicly-listed companies led by Robert Kuok (of the Perlis Plantations Group), Lim Goh Tong (Genting Group), Loh Boon Siew (Oriental Holdings Group), William Cheng (Lion Group), Khoo Kay Peng (MUI Group), and Vincent Tan Chee Yioun (Berjaya Group). In Hong Kong, while Chan (1996) undertook a useful and in-depth study of Li Ka-shing, another leading business-man in East Asia, none of the other three major Chinese companies in the city, Henderson Land, Sun Hung Kai Properties and New World Development, have been researched in any depth. The research on Chinese-owned small and medium-scale enterprises (SMEs) has been even more limited, except possibly in the case of Singapore, though even here the research is quite dated (Chew 1988).

Thus, in spite of the considerable attention Chinese enterprises in Southeast Asia has drawn, there is still very limited research into the formation and development of even many of the largest companies owned by this community. It is now increasingly being questioned whether a few business deals by a handful of Asia's leading Chinese businessmen can be used as the empirical base to support the notions of 'Chinese commonwealth,' 'global tribes' and 'co-ethnic business networks'. A small number of scholars have also begun to challenge popular notions of a dynamic form of 'Chinese capitalism' and of mushrooming intra-ethnic corporate ties by arguing that there is a heterogeneity of styles of business organization and management among members of the Chinese business community (see, for example, Hodder 1996; Brown 1996; Gomez 1999). While much of the popular literature would suggest extensive business cooperation among Chinese capitalists, detailed empirical studies of ethnic Chinese companies have indicated that such ethnic capital is concentrated in the hands of a minority, and that there exists much fragmentation among these Chinese businessmen, both key factors which have not facilitated intra-ethnic business relations (see, for example, Gomez 1999; Hodder 1996).

Recognizing the limited research on Chinese enterprise, this volume has a modest objective: to identify the key areas of research on Chinese business in each Southeast Asian country. In order to do this, these chapters provide a review of research already published on Chinese business in the five countries in Southeast Asia where the Chinese have established a prominent presence in the economy – Malaysia, Singapore, Indonesia, Thailand, and the Philippines. This review involves a brief history of Chinese enterprise in these Southeast Asian countries to understand the circumstances under which such ethnically-owned companies have operated and developed. This approach was also an attempt to identify key areas that still required research to provide a holistic understanding to the operation of Chinese enterprise in Southeast Asia.

Among these five Southeast Asian countries, Malaysia has the second largest ethnic Chinese population, next to Indonesia, though only about 3 per cent of Indonesia's population are ethnic Chinese while in Malaysia they constitute nearly 28 per cent of the country's population (see Table I.1). Moreover, since the economic boom in Southeast Asia, between 1988 and 1997, was generated primarily through foreign direct investment (FDI), much of which came from East Asia, it was interesting to see if common ethnic Chinese identity was a crucial factor in decision-making for Taiwanese investors keen on venturing into Southeast Asia.[3] Although the chapter on Taiwanese investments in Southeast Asia indicates the importance of geographical proximity and economic factors in drawing FDI, more importantly, it reveals the nature of common ties and culture that have a bearing on decision-making by Taiwanese businessmen investing in Southeast Asia. Common culture and ethnic identity have not been useful to Taiwanese businessmen in creating joint business ventures involving shared ownership in Southeast Asia. Instead, the availability of a workforce who share a common language, and the previous experience of Southeast Asian Chinese in Taiwan, especially while pursuing tertiary education, facilitated the development of Taiwanese enterprises in a foreign country.

Chinese Business in Southeast Asia

One problem with much of the literature on Chinese capital in Southeast Asia is that the community is taken as a homogenous unit. Yet, there are a number of cleavages among the Chinese that has impaired unity. These cleavages, which have prevented the Chinese from acting as a collective unit, have been linked to the issues of identity and class.

Table I.1 Estimated Population Size of Ethnic Chinese in Southeast Asia in the early 1990s

Country	Estimated Chinese Population	Proportion of Chinese Population (%)
Indonesia	5.0–6.0 million	2.5–3.5
Malaysia	5.60 million	28.0
Thailand	4.5–5.0 million	10.0
Singapore	2.1 million	77.0
The Philippines	800,000–1.2 million	2.0
Brunei	40,621	15.6
Vietnam	990,000–1.8 million	1.5–2.76
Myanmar	40,956	0.7–0.8
Cambodia	350,000	2.5–5.47
Laos	5,000–6,000	0.19
Total	17.482–23.093 million	3.95–6.04

Sources: Hodder (1996: 2); Pan 1998

The question of identity among ethnic Chinese in Southeast Asia is closely associated with the period when members of this community arrived in the region. Linked through trade, the Chinese have a long history with countries in Southeast Asia, going back at least three centuries. Among the earlier Chinese migrants, there has been a greater degree of assimilation. In Indonesia and Malaysia, the early generation of Chinese settlers and their descendants who have assimilated are known as the *peranakans*, though in Malaysia they are also referred to as the *babas* or 'Straits Chinese' (see Clammer 1980; Tan 1983), while in the Philippines they are referred to as Chinese mestizo (see Wickberg 1965).[4] These hybrid communities emerged as Chinese traders married indigenous women, though later intra-community marriages were more the norm, before subsequently, there were marriages between members of this community and the newer Chinese migrants. The peranakan communities have, however, managed to retain a distinct identity of their own from members of the indigenous community. It is only in Thailand that the level of assimilation and integration by ethnic Chinese has been relatively high.

In the latter part of the 19th century, and particularly during the early part of the 20th century, a new wave of migration began to take place as Chinese from mainland China ventured abroad to participate primarily in the tin boom in Southeast Asia. Significant differences prevail among the Chinese who have been more assimilated and the more recent migrants, who were known as *totok* (in Indonesia) and as *sinkhek* (in the Malayan peninsula). One reason for the differences between the early migrants and the newer generation has been the class factor. In the Philippines, as McVey (1992: 15) has noted, the Chinese mestizo constituted part of the traditional economic elite, having managed to forge, from the 19th century, business links with the indigenous elite. The peranakan heritage can be traced back to Hokkien traders who had emerged as a mercantile and professional class by the time the new generation of Chinese had begun to migrate to the Malay peninsula. Among the peranakans, a number of wealthy businessmen had emerged, the most prosperous of who included the Indonesian Oei Tiong Ham and Tan Cheng Lock, a Malaccan.

Among the more recent migrants, generational differences have emerged, commonly referred to through the terms *huaren* and *huayi*. The term, *huaren*, refers primarily to first generation Chinese migrants who had settled and secured citizenship abroad, though a number of them still probably retain ties with their families in China; it is, however, questionable how many of them still remit money home and consider returning eventually to China.[5] Almost all the second and third generation of Chinese migrants, the *huayi*, view themselves as citizens of the country in which they were born and reside in. Another term used with regard to Chinese migrants is *huaqiao*, which literally translated means 'sojourners'. The term, *huaqiao*, is normally used in reference to Chinese sojourners who had settled abroad, retained their Chinese citizenship, and who probably have the closest ties with China; this generation is now slowly dying out.[6]

Another significant cleavage that exists among the Chinese that has impaired intra-ethnic unity is that the community is divided along sub-ethnic lines. The main sub-ethnic Chinese communities, the Hokkien, Cantonese, Hakka, Teochew and Hainanese, have historically shown little inclination towards overcoming their sub-ethnic identities to act as one community in any country in Southeast Asia. In Malaysia and Singapore, the Hokkiens constitute the largest sub-ethnic Chinese community; in Malaysia, Hokkiens comprise about 32 per cent of the Chinese population and in Singapore about 42 per cent. The second largest sub-ethnic Chinese group in Singapore, constituting half the Hokkien population size, is the Teochew with about 22 per cent, while the Cantonese make up about 15 per cent and the Hakkas and Hiananese 7 per cent each. In Malaysia, the second largest

sub-ethnic community is the Cantonese (about 25 per cent), followed
by the Hakka (17 per cent), Teochew (14 per cent), and Hainanese (6
per cent) (Ratnam 1965: 5; Kwok 1998: 204).[7] There are a large number
of smaller sub-ethnic groups in both Malaysia and Singapore,
including the Kwongsai, Henghwa, Foochow and Hokchia. In
Thailand, the largest sub-ethnic Chinese group is the Teochew, who
make up almost 40 per cent of the Chinese population, while the
Hainanese, the second largest sub-ethnic group constitute just about
18 per cent of the community, the Hakka and Hokkien 16 per cent
each, and the Cantonese 9 per cent (Vatikiotis 1998: 219–20).
Inevitably, a large number of the leading Chinese capitalists in the
Malaysian peninsula and in Singapore are Hokkien, while in Thailand,
most of the leading companies established and run by ethnic Chinese
are under Teochew control.

These cleavages among the Chinese have determined how they
develop their business interests. A number of scholars have already
noted that during the early stages after their migration to Southeast
Asia, common Chinese sub-ethnicity had been a key factor in enabling
them to work together (see Skinner 1957; Purcell 1967). The
establishment and role of clan-based organizations were then
important, and functioned effectively in bringing together sub-ethnic
communities. Many of these sub-ethnic clan-based organizations still
exist, though their importance has been diminishing in Southeast Asia.
Sub-ethnic groups have tended to dominate particular economic
sectors. For example, among these sub-ethnic groups, the Hokkiens in
Malaysia and Singapore were responsible for establishing some major
banks, including the Oversea-Chinese Banking Corporation (OCBC)
and United Overseas Bank (UOB) in Singapore, and Malayan
Banking, Public Bank, and the Hong Leong Bank in Malaysia, though
only the latter two Malaysian banks remain under Hokkien control.
The Teochew, Hainanese, Hakka, Cantonese and Hokchia communities had also managed to create their own niches in the Southeast
Asian economy during the early part of this century. In Thailand, the
Teochews had a long history of domination of the rice trade industry,
which enabled some of them to secure a huge presence in the banking
sector; the best examples of Teochew-developed enterprises which
have emerged through this route are the Bangkok Bank and Wanglee
Chan Bank groups. In Malaysia and Singapore, the Teochews
dominated the pepper and gambier plantations and trade, the
Cantonese played a prominent role as shopkeepers, the Hainanese
were active in the coffee shop catering business and the shipping

industry, while the Hakkas had a good presence in agriculture (Yong 1987: 10). In Indonesia, particularly on the island of Java, the Hokchias had a long history of control over petty trade in rural areas. The control that these sub-ethnic groups had over particular economic sectors has diminished, along with the reduced importance of sub-ethnic clan-based organizations.[8]

By the early 1990s, the population size of ethnic Chinese in Southeast Asia was estimated at between 4 and 6 per cent (see Table I.1). In spite of their small population size collectively in Southeast Asia, as well as in each country – Singapore is the exception here – ethnic Chinese reputedly have extensive ownership of key economic sectors in the region. It is not uncommon to read that Indonesian Chinese "own nine of the top 10 business groups in the country and control more than 80% of the assets in the top 300 groups up from 74% in 1988" (*Far Eastern Economic Review* 28/5/98).[9] In Thailand, it is commonly reported that Sino-Thais own approximately 85 per cent of the economy, while Filipino Chinese reputedly own about 30 per cent of the top 500 corporations in the country (*Far Eastern Economic Review* 15/2/90).[10] The veracity of these reports on ethnic Chinese corporate ownership figures in the Philippines, Thailand and Indonesia has, however, been questioned. Even academics that have referred to such corporate ownership figures have cautioned that these figures have not been verified (see, for example, Lim 1996; Mackie 1992). It is only in Malaysia, where the government has tabulated equity ownership patterns along ethnic lines, has it been easier to quantify the extent of Chinese ownership of corporate equity. In 1995, Malaysian Chinese owned about 41 per cent of corporate stock. This figure, however, has also been disputed, even by leaders of Chinese-based political parties in the ruling coalition government.[11] One reason for the presumption that corporate ownership figures by ethnic communities have been tabulated incorrectly is that it has been a means to justify affirmative action policies favoring the indigenous community.

Those who have undertaken research on Chinese capital in Southeast Asia have argued that such corporate ownership figures are very misleading for a number of reasons. First, a distinction has to be drawn between the concepts of ownership and control. Second, many of these assumptions about ownership are based on the total market capitalization of the companies controlled by ethnic Chinese without taking into consideration the interests of other owners of such stock. Third, such attribution of corporate wealth to all Chinese is problematic as it does not take into account another significant factor, that is much of this wealth is concentrated which has, in turn, contributed to class difference. In the late 1980s, Sino-Thai business groups reputedly controlled 37 of the hundred largest companies in Thailand. Most of this wealth was concentrated in the hands of just a small number of key Teochew families. One Indonesian, Liem Sioe Liong, controls the Salim Group, probably the largest Chinese-controlled firm in Southeast Asia (see Sato 1993), while Bob Hasan, Eka Widjaja and Prajogo Pangestu have extensive ownership of Indonesian corporate equity. In the Philippines, six major Chinese businessmen, particularly Lucio Tan, John Gokongwei, Henry Sy and Alfonso Yechengco, own a major portion of the wealth attributed to all Chinese in the country. Although there appears to be a far more equitable distribution of corporate wealth among ethnic Chinese businessmen in Malaysia, the class distinctions between those who own large, well-diversified business groups and small- and medium-scale enterprises (SMEs) are quite significant. These class differences have been a factor that has hindered business cooperation among the Chinese. In fact, in each Southeast Asian country, what has been noted is not greater intra-ethnic business links between these leading Chinese capitalists but inter-ethnic business cooperation between these businessmen and indigenous capitalists and politicians.

Apart from this, a number of the indigenous elite, particularly in Malaysia and Indonesia, have significant equity ownership of many of the largest companies controlled by ethnic Chinese. For example, although ownership of Indonesia's Bank Central Asia (BCA) was attributed to Liem Sioe Leong before its takeover by the government following a run on the bank, the other BCA shareholders included two children of the former President, Soeharto, who collectively owned 25 per cent of the bank's equity. Soeharto's cousin, Sudwikatmono, has a share in Liem's flour milling, petrochemical, and cement operations, and is also the chairman of the Liem's flagship company, Indocement (*Newsweek* 15/6/98). A number of prominent Indonesians also own an interest in another of Liem's leading companies, Indofood. In the case of Malaysia, individuals aligned to the ruling elite have an interest in some major Chinese companies. For example, Mirzan Mahathir, the eldest son of Prime Minister Mahathir Mohamad, is a major shareholder of Lion Corporation controlled by William Cheng Heng Jem, while some of the shareholders of companies in Quek Leng Chan's Hong Leong Group, Vincent Tan Chee Yioun's Berjaya Group, Francis Yeoh's YTL Corporation and Ting Pek Khiing's Ekran Group include politically well-connected people (see Gomez 1999).

Although such Chinese businessmen may have relinquished some ownership of their company stock, they have still managed to retain control of their enterprises. Thus, the owners of large Chinese enterprises can continue to ascend as this form of accommodation may enable these businessmen to secure more concessions from the state in order to continue to develop their corporate base.

An analysis of the relationship between Chinese capital and the state in Southeast Asia also provides insights into the divisions that exist among ethnic Chinese. A number of studies have noted that the links between the largest Chinese businessmen and indigenous state leaders have been quite close. In Indonesia, for example, the links between Liem Sioe Liong and Soeharto are well recorded (see Robison 1986; Schwarz 1994). In Malaysia, most of the leading Chinese businessmen have direct or indirect links with key Malay leaders or their business associates (see Gomez 1999). While the close links between politics and business reputedly facilitated the rise of a number of the largest Chinese companies in Malaysia and Indonesia, a history of the development of Thailand's largest Chinese-owned enterprises reveals a similar pattern of political patronage (see Suehiro 1989; Laothamatas 1992; Yoshihara 1988). In the Philippines, one of the most prominent Chinese businessman, Lucio Tan, is believed to have been a front man for the former president, Ferdinand Marcos. Since the fall of the Marcos regime, however, Filipino Chinese are emerging as an independent economic force; for example, in the banking sector, ethnic Chinese own approximately 45 per cent of the total assets of private domestic banks, while Chinese dominance of the retail sector is significant (Suryadinata 1995a: 7).

Singapore is the only case where Chinese capitalists have not had close ties with the state or key politicians. In fact, as Chan Kwok Bun and Ng Beoy Kui's chapter in this volume argues, for a long period, the Singapore's People's Action Party (PAP) government had not provided much support for the development of Chinese capital, preferring instead to promote the rise of state enterprises and the involvement of multinational corporations (MNCs) in the local economy. Both state enterprises and MNCs now play a dominant role in the Singaporean economy. When the PAP, led by Lee Kuan Yew, secured power in Singapore, the party was so fearful that the large Chinese capitalists would undermine its influence, that it moved to check the rise of Chinese capital in the country. Thus, during the colonial period, while many of the largest Chinese enterprises in the region were to be found in Singapore, presently, none of the largest and most influential Chinese capitalists in East and Southeast Asia are from the city state.

Such political-business ties provided some Chinese with the opportunity to build up their asset base within a relatively short period. Inevitably, this has meant that in spite of the apparent economic strength of ethnic Chinese in Southeast Asia, Chinese capital is almost totally subservient to the state or to indigenous political hegemony. Moreover, in spite of Chinese majority ownership of some key companies, state leaders can sometimes determine how assets belonging to these companies are deployed; this has occurred in Malaysia, Indonesia and even in the more democratic Philippines. State control over how some assets owned by the largest Chinese enterprises have been deployed has been attributed to the fact that many leading capitalists were linked either directly or indirectly to the ruling elite. In some cases, Chinese businessmen incorporate state enterprises as joint-venture partners in their business endeavors in order to remain on good terms with government leaders as well as to show their loyalty to their country. One well-cited example is the case of President Fidel Ramos getting six major Chinese businessmen to jointly invest US$75 million in a company to help promote infrastructure development in the Philippines (Palanca 1995a: 48–49).

The close links between the large Chinese companies and the indigenous elite in power and in business have contributed to differences between ethnic Chinese who run such enterprises and those who own SMEs. As we have noted, the owners of large enterprises can accommodate the state more, for example, by divesting a portion their corporate equity to state enterprises or to the clients or family members of influential politicians. Such avenues of accommodation are limited among the SMEs. Moreover, there is little evidence that the Chinese who have secured concessions from the state have tried to – or are even willing to – share such concessions with other Chinese, especially owners of SMEs, through sub-contracts or joint ventures. Owners of Chinese SMEs have also complained that a number of Chinese beneficiaries of state concessions have not deployed these privileges productively.

The criticism that Chinese beneficiaries of state concessions have not productively utilized the privileges they have been privy to seems to have been borne out by the well-documented argument that almost all the largest enterprises run by Chinese capitalists in Southeast Asia are merely conglomerates of SMEs in unrelated fields of business (see, for example, Mackie 1992b). Instead of developing horizontal and vertical roots in one primary field of business, the owners of these conglomerates tend to diversify into any area that promises big profits. In contrast to the large Japanese and Korean business groups that have emerged, not one Chinese company in Southeast Asia is identified with a particular brand product. It is only in Taiwan that one businessman, Stanley Shih, has managed to build up a reputation with the internationally known computer product, Acer (Chen 1996).[12] By 1997, Acer had emerged as the seventh-largest maker of personal computers in the world (*Asia, Inc.* June 1997).

These arguments do not mean that Chinese businessmen lack entrepreneurial dynamism. Not all major Chinese capitalists in Southeast Asia have developed because of their close links with state leaders. Moreover, in spite of the long history of discrimination that the community has had to face in Southeast Asia, Chinese enterprise has managed to thrive in the region. In Indonesia, for example, Christianto (1995: 94) quotes a 1980 study of 300 conglomerates which revealed that although 197 of these companies, or 65.7 per cent, were under Chinese majority ownership, only 4.67 per cent of them could be listed as 'crony capitalists,' defined as those companies "formed on the basis of special licensing, or protection provided to friends of officials in an unfair or biased manner." More importantly, Christianto (1995: 94) goes on to add that 87.67 per cent of these 300 conglomerates "gained success through creativity and innovation." Even among the companies that benefited from state patronage, that is those who could be listed as 'crony capitalists,' the top three conglomerates, the Salim, Sinar Mas and Astra Groups, all Chinese-controlled, recorded 77 per cent of the total sales recorded by the 300 conglomerates (Christianto 1995: 98). In Malaysia, Gomez (1999) has shown that some of the leading industrial groups controlled by the Chinese, such as the Loh Boon Siew's Oriental Holdings Group, which assembles Honda model motor vehicles, have never benefited from state patronage. In the Philippines, the rise of Chinese capitalists is a relatively new phenomenon, many of whom managed to benefit from the business avenues made available to them during the Marcos era, particularly during the 1970s. This suggests that the basis for arguing that a dynamic form of 'Chinese capitalism' exists in Southeast Asia should be re-evaluated. In other words, we would argue that the qualities that reveal the entrepreneurial dynamism among the Chinese have not been identified yet.

The popular notion of mushrooming intra-ethnic business networks among the Chinese, including by the owners of SMEs, has also to be questioned. The ostensible significance of business networks has been propagated primarily by Kotkin (1993). Building on the Weberian view that the spirit that drives entrepreneurial behavior in capitalist economies is strongly associated with belief systems, Kotkin (1993: 4) has popularized these views by asserting that "global tribes combine a strong sense of common origin and shared values" and that "the success in the new global economy is determined by the connections which immigrant entrepreneurs carry with them around the world." However, the thesis that a common ethnic identity and culture inspires the creation of intra-ethnic business networks is coming under increasing criticism. If business networks are narrowly defined as the pooling of resources by some Chinese to venture into one particular, short-term project, numerous cases of this can be cited as evidence. If, however, networks are defined as the establishment of interlocking stock ownership ties, a sharing of resources and information, or collective cooperation through the merger of Chinese enterprises that can emerge as a major economic force in terms of asset base and expertise, there is still limited evidence that such networks exist. If we are to argue that the Chinese will emerge as a dynamic force because their combined economic force is significant, this would suggest that Chinese networking should involve long-term, even permanent relationships involving the merging of corporate enter- prises to make an impact in Asia. Insufficient evidence has been provided to support this hypothesis.

We would also question the contention that even the largest Chinese enterprises in Southeast Asia have forged, or are trying to forge, close alliances or business networks based on common ownership (see Redding 1990; Kotkin 1993; East Asia Analytical Unit 1995; Weidenbaum and Hughes 1996). This is not to say that intra- ethnic endeavors to merge their business activities have not been attempted by leading Chinese businessmen. This has occurred in Malaysia, Singapore and Indonesia, both in the colonial period as well as in contemporary times. In Indonesia, as Schwarz (1994) has pointed out, there were equity crossholdings between the two major Chinese capitalists, Liem Sioe Leong and Eka Widjaja, but this appeared to be primarily due to the latter's desire to maintain ties with President Soeharto through Liem. In Malaysia and Singapore, detailed empirical evidence has revealed that almost all cases of co-ethnic endeavors to merge their business activities have not proceeded smoothly. Rather, most Chinese owners of large companies have been very reluctant to merge the companies that they have built with other firms as it would have entailed sharing control of the enlarged enterprise. In fact, biographies of leading ethnic Chinese businessmen have shown that the common trend has been for them to work long enough to gain enough experience and save enough money to venture out on their own (see Chan and Chiang 1994; Lee and Chow 1997). Some scholars have also noted the decline of clan-based organizations, which had served as an important tool for business networking (see, for example, Jesudason 1997). In the case of the Philippines, it has been pointed out by Carino (1998) that five of the six largest Chinese capitalists were not members of Chinese Chambers of Commerce.

In view of the cleavages that exist, and the generational change that has transpired among the Chinese in Southeast Asia, there is a need to re-assess the popular assumption that growing ethnic Chinese investments in mainland China is due to their desire to build up their ancestral 'homeland'. It is also questionable if many ethnic Chinese businessmen from Southeast Asia share a bond based on common ethnic identity with the Chinese in China. There are various other factors that can explain such investments into the mainland. With the opening up of the Chinese economy since 1979, the encouragement and privileges accorded by the government of China to 'Overseas Chinese' – as the Chinese authorities view them – has resulted in increased investments by Chinese businessmen from East and South-east Asia. Government leaders in Singapore and Malaysia have also actively encouraged investments into China. Malaysian Prime Minister Mahathir Mohamad, for example, appears to see much benefit from getting indigenous businessmen to work with Chinese capitalists to encourage domestic economic development as well as enable Malaysian companies to tap into the economic potential that the market in China offers. At the 1996 Second Fujianese World Chinese Entrepreneurs Convention held in Malaysia in 1996, Mahathir said, "Malaysian Fujianese's close connections with their fellow-provincials in different corners of the world will help promote the business and investment opportunities in Malaysia" (quoted in Liu 1998). The influential former Prime Minister of Singapore, Lee Kuan Yew, has been encouraging Chinese businessmen of the diaspora to view ethnic business networking not just as an effective way to move into potentially lucrative markets in China, but also as a means to compete effectively with multinational corporations and to transform the handicap they may feel as ethnic minorities into an advantage, not just in the region, but in the global economy. This would suggest that increased investments in China are not due to tribalism, but to the fact that governments have framed policies to support such investments.

Theoretical Perspectives and Methodological Problems

One of the key issues in the literature on Chinese enterprises is the limited amount of theorizing on the subject. A number of scholars in the field of Chinese business have commented on the problems of theorizing about this subject, or about ethnic enterprise in general, arguing that the theories applied tend to be inadequate to deal with the issues that need to be incorporated in an analysis of such enterprises in Southeast Asia (see Redding 1990; Hodder 1996; Gomez 1999). In some cases, it would appear that the theoretical perspectives brought to the study have determined the direction of the research and have influenced the conclusions (see, for example, Kotkin 1993).

Redding (1990) has argued that "given the complexity in explaining why Chinese companies have managed to develop fast involves a need to incorporate a number of factors – this involves crossing disciplines; theorizing based on a single model is difficult and may not provide a proper tool of analysis." Hodder (1996: 9–12) takes this argument even further, suggesting that since studies of ethnic enterprises deal with how individuals make decisions in business, caution should be applied in using models to determine forms of decision-making in business. Hodder (1996: 11) argues that:

> It is precisely because individuals are spontaneous, unpredictable and multidimensional, and it is because no assumptions can be made about the existence and operation of guiding laws, of chains of cause and effect, of pre-programmed traits and of recursive structures, that there are no set of behavioral, institutional and moral patterns. ... What is of far greater interest and significance is the rotation of multidimensional actions, institutions and values, and the manner in which, and the ends to which, they are directed by individuals, and the motivation and purposes for which individuals create unidimensional presentations.

Redding is quite right to argue that the research on ethnic enterprise would involve the need to adopt an inter-disciplinary approach, while Hodder's cautionary note, that since we are dealing with individuals it is necessary to be wary of adopting very structured frameworks in our analysis, should be heeded. Their views take on added significance when we note that the crux of problem with the literature on Chinese business is the inadequate attention given to securing empirical evidence. However, other scholars, notably Whitley (1992) and

Biggart (1997), who have also voiced similar reservations of the ability of existing theories to explain the functioning of ethnic enterprises, have tried to provide us with suggestions of the primary variables and concepts that need to be identified and used in an analysis of Chinese capital. Biggart (1997), for example, has identified the main variables used in the four main perspectives – the market, cultural, political economy and institutional paradigms – in the study of business organizations in Western countries (see Table I.2).[13]

The important contribution of Table I.2 is that it identifies the most important variables that have a bearing on determining how companies operate and develop. In view of the variety of variables that have to be incorporated in the analysis of ethnic enterprises, this is one reason why there is growing criticism of an over-dependence on a cultural perspective as a means of analysis. The cultural perspective tends to negate a number of key variables, which are important in the context of Asia, though may not be as crucial a factor in the West. For example, as we have already noted, the role of the state in Asian economies has been an important determining factor of the manner of operations and development of Chinese capital, a point also stressed by Biggart (1997).[14]

Table I.2 Four Perspectives on Organization

	Market	*Cultural*	*Political Economy*	*Institutional*
Key Variables	economic	values, symbols	state	ideology, authority
Social action	individual utilitarianism	collective action	class and interest groups	dialectic of structure and individual action
Social order	invisible hand/ self interest	enacted solidarity	stratification (repression, majority rule)	domination
Social change	market forces	continuity	institutional contradictions/ interest politics	historical development
Organization	most efficient structure	symbolic expression of cultural values	expression of bureaucratic and market power	structure of economic domination utilizing cultural understandings

Source: Biggart (1997: 5)

The distinction that Biggart (1997) draws between theoretical models applicable in the West as opposed to Asia bears further consideration. Among the most common models used in the study of the functioning on ethnic enterprises in the West are still the ethnic enclave and minority middlemen theories (see, for example, Bonacich and Modell 1980; Ward and Jenkins 1984). The problem with the ethnic enclave and middlemen perspectives is that both these theories are, at best, applicable in situations where ethnic communities are more recent migrants and where there has been very limited assimilation. The middlemen perspective, for instance, was quite widely used by scholars in an analysis of Chinese capital in Southeast Asia until the late 1970s. For example, in Lim and Gosling's edited volume, *The Chinese in Southeast Asia*, published in 1983, a number of articles used the middlemen perspective to explain the development of Chinese enterprise; scholars however, seldom use this perspective presently.

On the other hand, both the ethnic enclave and middlemen theories are popularly used in the context where large scale migratory movements still exists, particularly in the United States, Canada, Europe and possibly Australia (see for example, Light 1972; Bonacich and Modell 1980; Ward and Jenkins 1984; Light and Bhachu 1993). In all these four regions, migratory movements have persisted even in the modern era, due to political and economic reasons. In contrast to this, in most countries in Southeast Asia, large-scale migratory movements had already begun to cease by the early 1930s. More importantly, most of the non-indigenous communities in Southeast Asia have come to identify themselves with the country of their birth; in some countries, particularly Thailand and to a lesser extent the Philippines, the level of assimilation has been quite significant (see Suryadinata 1997).

Another aspect of studies on the companies run by recent migrants, particularly in North America and Europe, is the argument that these firms have a specific 'ethnic business style' characterized by the use of family firms, trade guilds, rotating credit associations and large intra-ethnic business transactions, locally and with their 'homeland' (Bonacich and Modell 1980; Ward and Jenkins 1984; Light and Bhachu 1993). In the Southeast Asian context, even among the SMEs – in spite of the paucity of research on such enterprises – it appears that inter-ethnic business transactions may be as significant as intra-ethnic transactions, while the importance of trade guilds and rotating credit associations has diminished considerably.

Theoretical perspectives that emphasize culture as the major conceptual tool of analysis have been brought to the study of ethnic enterprises in East Asia, mainly by Redding (1990) and Fukuyama (1995). In the culturalist perspective, one key issue has been the influence of the Confucian ethic on Chinese enterprise. Other issues popularly referred to as the 'cultural' aspects of Chinese business include the 'family firm' model, *guanxi*, trust and, in particular, the forms of networking that exist in their business transactions (see, for example, Wong 1985; Chan 1982, 1992; Redding 1990; King 1994; Hamilton 1996b). Much of this literature concentrates attention on the role of family, kinship and lineage in Chinese companies, as well as the use of cultural institutions such as trade guilds, chambers of commerce and rotating credit associations as a means for capital formation and accumulation. The primary argument in this considerable body of literature is that institutions, norms and practices of ethnic Chinese have facilitated the growth of their enterprises and the emergence of ethnic business networks. These business networks, ostensibly based on trust and kinship, apparently help reduce transaction costs, increase coordination and diminish risks in business ventures (Redding 1990; Kotkin 1993; Fukuyama 1995).

Significant differences, however, exist among those who subscribe to a culturalist perspective. For instance, although both Redding (1990) and Fukuyama (1995) deal with concepts such as trust, kinship, and co-ethnic business networking, and subscribe to the view that a Confucian ethic influences Chinese entrepreneurial behavior, they hold widely differing views on the impact of culture on Chinese business. Fukuyama, in contrast to Redding, argues that there is very little trust among Chinese with members outside the immediate family. For Fukuyama, since Confucian values emphasize the importance of the family and the equal division of family wealth among the sons, this practice tends to undermine the development of Chinese business groups. Such a practice also leads to a dissipation of corporate holdings and competition among family companies, hindering the development of large Chinese corporations.

There has also been criticism of the use of culture as an explanatory tool, since such a value-based approach is open to question on methodological grounds. The most prominent example of such criticism is that by Dirlik (1996), in his article, 'Critical Reflections on "Chinese Capitalism" as a Paradigm'. Dirlik not only challenges the widely-accepted argument that the spirit that drives Chinese entrepreneurial behavior is strongly associated with a Confucian ethic, but even draws attention to "the vagueness of the notion of 'Chineseness.'" For Dirlik, the strategic location of Chinese entrepreneurs in the Asia-Pacific region is the primary structural explanation for their capacity to tap into emerging business opportunities and develop their corporate base. In fact, Dirlik has questioned the very concept of 'Chineseness,' an issue we have already noted above.

There are, however, key issues which have been raised in the cultural perspective that need further discussion, among the most crucial of which are the significance of family firms and of business networking among Chinese businessmen. The theme of family firms remains significant in the Southeast Asian context, even in the present period. The most important study that has attempted to conceptualize the evolution of Chinese family firms, and their limited longevity, is that by Wong (1985), who notes that the companies generally go through four phases: emergent, centralized, segmented and disintegrative. For Wong, the primary factor that contributes to the disintegration of the family firm is the issue of succession. This view, however, is not common just to Chinese firms. Goody (1996: 141–48) has noted similar problems among family firms owned by Indians, while a number of such ethnic enterprises that have grown large have eventually evolved into managerial corporations.

Rose (1993: 131), in her study of western companies, makes a similar point: that a key problem that prevails in family firms is the issue of succession. Rose (1993: 131) quotes the Marshallian view that "when a man has got together a great business, his descendants often fail, in spite of their great advantages, to develop the high abilities and the special turn of mind and temperament required for carrying it on with equal success." This, Rose (1993: 132) argues, also emphasizes the point that generational change brings about profound changes in the way in which companies are run. In her own study of family firms in the 19th century, Rose (1993: 131) quotes a prominent cotton spinner in Manchester as stating: "The only men who make their fortunes are those who began with nothing, who were totally dedicated to business and who practiced an habitual economy. Throughout Lancashire no family survives longer than two generations. Children brought up to habits of luxury and idleness are incapable of salvaging their business when fortunes turn against them."

In the Southeast Asian context, there are already numerous examples of the disintegration of family firms, or of feuds and disagreements among descendants of Chinese businessmen who have built up major companies. It is noteworthy that many of the major Chinese enterprises that emerged in the colonial and immediate post-colonial period no longer function as key companies in the region or even within their own countries. In the case of Malaysia and Singapore, where a large number of prominent businessmen emerged, a number of examples of this can be cited. Aw Boon Hwa, who was famous primarily for producing the 'Tiger Balm' medicinal product, was also involved in the running of thirteen newspapers throughout Southeast Asia, the most prominent of which was probably the Singapore-based *Sin Chew Jit Poh*. Aw was also responsible for setting up the Chung Khiaw Bank in Singapore. The prominence of the Aw family has diminished significantly in Singapore. In the case of Thailand, the corporate empire developed by Khaw family remains the most important example of a family-based enterprise that has failed to sustain itself (see Cushman 1991). In Indonesia, the disintegration of Oei Tiong Ham's large business group stands out, though in his case a number of the companies he owned were nationalized by the government in the early 1960s. The enterprises of a number of prominent tin miners in Malaya and Singapore, who emerged in the early part of this century, including Chung Thye Pin, Lau Pak Khuan and Leong Sin Nam, are no longer major companies. Large enterprises, including Lee Rubber and the OCBC, closely associated with Lee Kong Chian, though still under the ownership of his family, are professionally managed. The situation is similar with the companies owned by the Malacca-based rubber magnate, Tan Cheng Lock, who was associated with the Pacific Bank and United Malacca Rubber Estates (Chan and Chiang 1994; Lee and Chow 1997).

In more recent times, probably the best examples of major Chinese family firms where there are problems among the second generation are Thailand-based Tejaphaibul family's Bangkok Metropolitan Bank and the Singapore-based Kwek family's Hong Leong Group. The late Kwek Hong P'ng, who, with three of his brothers, founded the Hong Leong Group provides a clue to the problem of succession and generational change. The Hong Leong Group is now divided between the branches in Singapore and Malaysia, and there has been competition and differences between the Kwek cousins. When asked about the problems that had emerged among the second generation of Kweks, Kwek Hong P'ng's response was, "... it's not easy to pass down a Chinese-owned business from generation to generation .... The founders were fairer (in distributing benefits). The older generation was more straightforward, and the elders looked after the younger ones. But the new generation mostly look out for themselves" (quoted in *Asiaweek* 15/5/92).

Kwek Hong P'ng, along with three of his brothers established the Hong Leong Group in Singapore in 1941, developing it into a well-diversified enterprise with an involvement in finance, manufacturing, hotels and property development. By the late 1980s, the Group's main holding company in Singapore was Hong Leong Investment Holdings (HLIH) which was owned by 30 members of the Kwek family spanning three generations, and had established ownership and control of more than half a dozen publicly-listed companies and an array of private enterprises in four countries (*Far Eastern Economic Review* 5/12/85). The Hong Leong Group's main interests were in Singapore and Malaysia, with Hong P'ng's son, Leng Beng, and his nephew, Quek Leng Chan, controlling the Singapore and Malaysian operations respectively.[15]

Family feuds can also lead to the loss of control of a company. The most recent example is the case of the Yeo Hiap Seng (YHS) Group which, like the Hong Leong Group, is Singapore-based but had established a separate publicly-listed company in Malaysia. YHS was incorporated in 1955 by the Yeo family who ran a soy sauce production company in the Fujian province in China, a business started at the turn of the century by Yeo Keng Lian. Yeo's son, Thian In, moved to Singapore in 1935, where he established and ran a similar business with his brother, Thian Yew, and his eldest son, Chee Kiat. After World War II, three of Thian In's other brothers, Thian Hwa, Thian Soo and Thian Seng, joined them in Singapore. After its incorporation as a company in Singapore in 1935, YHS grew rapidly, capturing a large section of the soft-drink market by catering to Chinese tastes that its main competitor, the British-based Fraser & Neave Ltd (F&N), had ignored. Later, YHS also secured the franchise to distribute Pepsi and Schweppes products in Singapore, Malaysia[16] and Hong Kong, and the 7-Up franchise for distribution in Hong Kong and Singapore. YHS was quite an innovative company, eventually emerging not just as the largest food and beverage group in Singapore after F&N, but also as a manufacturer and distributor of a diverse range of canned foods, vegetables and sauces. By the early 1990s, although the Yeo family owned about 38.5 per cent of the YHS stock in Singapore, the family retained control of the company by also holding most key executive positions (*Far Eastern Economic Review* 5/10/89).

The problems in the Yeo family emerged when then chairman, Alan Yeo, invited another Chinese company, Wing Tai Holdings, to acquire a stake in YHS in an attempt to use the former's markets, especially in China, to expand YHS' operations. This led to a feud in the Yeo family, which was taken to court in 1994. The 38.5 per cent stake held by the family was split among feuding family factions. This split among the Yeos enabled another Chinese businessman, the Singaporean property magnate Ng Teng Fong of the Far East Group, to emerge as the new largest single shareholder of YHS, giving him control of the company (*Malaysian Business* 1/12/94). Later, YHS was also subject to a takeover by Quek Leng Chan, of the Hong Leong Group in Malaysia, who had acquired about 23 per cent of the company's equity (*The Star* 16/5/95). The most interesting points about the feud in the Yeo family which led to loss of control of the YHS Group was that it emerged during an attempt to develop joint ownership business ties with another Chinese businessman as means to develop its markets. During the family feud, the takeover attempts of this highly innovative firm were by other Chinese companies, including by groups led by Quek Leng Chan and Ng Teng Fong.

The theme of family companies, the issue of succession, and the division, dismantling or even takeover of major Chinese firms remain issues which have drawn little attention in the study of Chinese enterprise in Southeast Asia. In Singapore, a number of major companies have been taken over because of differences among family members over ownership and management of these companies. Among the cases that can be cited as evidence include Malayan Credit, which was controlled by the Teo family, the Cycle & Carriage Group (controlled by the Chua family), the Haw Par Group (controlled by the family of Aw Boon Haw) and the most prominent and recent case, involving the Yeo Hap Seng Group (Ng 1992). In Malaysia, there have been similar takeover attempts of Chinese companies by other Chinese, for example, the attempted takeover of Multi-Purpose Holdings and the Ban Hin Lee Bank by Quek's Hong Leong Group and the attempted takeover of Khoo Kay Peng's Malayan United Industries (MUI) by Vincent Tan's Berjaya Group.[17]

The limited research on the development of family companies would point to the next key issue in the study of Chinese firms. Most ethnic Chinese family firms in Southeast Asia are SMEs. With the possible exception of Singapore, most analysis of Chinese enterprises has been on the largest companies in Southeast Asia. Thus, while we could argue that the evidence we have suggests that there is much heterogeneity in business style among the largest Chinese companies, there seems to be some ambiguity, because of the lack of evidence, as to whether Chinese SMEs subscribe to some aspects of a 'cultural' style of business. For example, whether Chinese SME enterprise is characterized by family-based ownership, significant intra-ethnic cooperation and sharing of resources and information, and mutually beneficial business ventures has not been verified with sufficient evidence, especially in the Southeast Asian context. In Taiwan, however, Lam and Lee (1992), after their study of Taiwanese SMEs, have argued that such companies share these characteristics because, given the size of their enterprises, this facilitates business cooperation for mutual benefit. For Lam and Lee (1992), this is a form of 'guerrilla capitalism' that characterizes the dynamism of Taiwanese SMEs.

The issue of SME dynamism has also been raised by Yoshihara (1988) who has argued that while most large enterprises in Southeast Asia are led primarily by 'comprador capitalists' who have emerged by establishing ties with influential state leaders, the Chinese SMEs in Southeast Asia are more productive and focused in their business. In view of this, Yoshihara (1988) argues that Chinese SMEs could have contributed much more to industrial progress in Southeast Asia if they had received more support from the state. There appears to be some credence to this view, particularly after the financial crisis of mid-1997 that badly affected the economies of a number of countries in East Asia. The factors that triggered off the East Asian financial crisis in 1997 include the impact of currency speculation, unregulated capital flows, particularly portfolio investments, imprudent financial liberalization and weak supervision of the banking sector, as well as the poor quality of state intervention in some countries. Apart from this, there is some evidence that the methods used by enterprises favored by the state, or politically well-connected companies, to deploy government-generated economic concessions in order to build up huge conglomerates within a relatively short period also had a bearing on how the crisis developed (see Gomez and Jomo 1999). In other words, the business style of a company, and the manner of its growth, that is whether a vertical, horizontal or diversified pattern of growth was employed, appears to be a determining factor in the quality of its enterprise.

The much diversified pattern of growth, with an involvement in a number of businesses that are not even remotely related, has been identified as one major characteristic of the largest ethnic Chinese companies in Southeast Asia (see Lim 1996). The history of many of the largest Chinese enterprises has indicated that this tendency to diversify their corporate activities commenced even during the first generation of the family business. This trend towards diversification appears to have been influenced by a number of factors, including state policies, growing intra-ethnic competition, as well as an apparent desire to venture into any field that promises a good profit. In a number of countries in Southeast Asia, the stock market, and a variety of corporate maneuvers, including shares-for-assets swaps, takeovers, reverse takeovers and bonus and rights issues, were employed to pursue a conglomerate style of growth. These methods facilitated the extensive diversification of Southeast Asian Chinese companies.

In Southeast Asia, it appears that most companies which adopted a conglomerate style of growth, provided limited emphasis on developing expertise in a particular industry, gave little attention to research and development, depended much on bank loans to facilitate acquisitions and used various stock market maneuvers to grow, have been most adversely affected by the financial crisis. Most SMEs, on the other hand, do not appear to share such a dependence on bank loans to facilitate corporate development, nor have they adopted a diversified pattern of growth. In view of this, since the crisis, a number of the Southeast Asian governments have become more aware of the need to channel more support to SMEs as a means to check their economies rapid slide towards recession. Moreover, in view of the involvement of the SMEs in productive manufacturing ventures, such companies have emerged as an important source of domestic investment in the post-financial crisis period.

The use of a conglomerate style of growth, with limited focus on developing expertise in a particular industry or with little attention on research and development seems to have come under greater scrutiny by some large enterprises following the 1997 financial crisis. For example, in the post-crisis period, the First Pacific Group, the Hong Kong-based company controlled by Indonesia's Liem Sioe Leong, found itself laden with debts that it managed to reduce by divesting some companies in the Group. First Pacific has since begun adopting a more focused approach, concentrating on a few major industries because, as its management has argued, "We're determined that the conglomerate approach will go out of favor as a result of the Asian crisis. We'll have to invest in fewer, larger businesses ... where we'll be in for the long-term" (quoted in *Far Eastern Economic Review* 17/12/98). In Thailand, the Charoen Phokpand (CP) Group, which also found itself burdened with huge debts following the financial crisis, resorted to divesting its peripheral business activities to raise cash. The CP Group's chairman, Dhanin Chearavanont, is also quoted as stating, "C.P. is resolved to safeguard its core businesses" (quoted in *Far Eastern Economic Review* 28/5/98).

There was, however, growing evidence that some conglomerates, like Indonesia's Salim Group, had begun moving towards becoming more rationally and systematically restructured prior to the eruption of the financial crisis (see Sato 1993). In spite of this, following the financial crisis, the Salim Group had reportedly accumulated around US$1 billion in debts (see *Newsweek* 15/6/98).[18] In Malaysia, a few major companies, both those owned by the Chinese and the Malay corporate elite, had also begun to adopt a more focused approach in business, though many of these companies had just begun to move in this direction before the onset of the financial crisis (see Gomez and Jomo 1999; Gomez 1999). In other words, it appears that a major change in form of corporate development had begun to emerge among some leading companies owned by ethnic Chinese, that is rather than diversify into any field that promised huge profit margins, they had begun to build horizontal and vertical roots in a particular business.

Yoshihara's (1988) contention that most of the largest Chinese business groups in Southeast Asia are led by politically well-connected rent-seekers who have not deployed well the rents they have secured from the state has yet to be adequately tested. A number of studies on the political economies of Southeast Asia have references to Yoshihara's argument that many of the largest capitalists, including ethnic Chinese businessmen, have – or have had – close ties with indigenous members of the political elite which has enabled them to develop their corporate base (see, for example, Robison 1986; Suehiro 1989; Gomez and Jomo 1999). In Thailand, the leading Chinese capitalists had sought out patrons in government to enable them to continue to develop their enterprises, earning them a degree of notoriety, with terms such as 'pariah capitalists' being used to describe their form of capitalism (see Riggs 1966). Yet, more recent research on the business development of some of these Sino-Thai companies has revealed that they possess an entrepreneurial capacity for developing industrial groups (see Suehiro 1989; Brown 1998). In Malaysia, the research undertaken by Heng (1992), Hara (1991) and Gomez (1999) all concur that many Chinese have had no choice but to link up with the Malay political elite to develop their corporate base; however, although this would suggest that many of them would appear to be mere rentiers, there has been a productive element in their enterprise. In Indonesia, Sato (1993) has shown conclusively in her study of Liem's Salim Group that the company had developed a dynamic manufacturing base. That many of these politically well-connected ethnic Chinese businessmen in Southeast Asia have proven to be quite entrepreneurial would, however, not be consistent with Yoshihara's (1988) contention their form of capitalism is 'ersatz,' since their business activities are generally not productive, but speculative in character. Moreover, Yoshihara (1988) believes that because of the protection they receive from the state, many of these companies are hardly competitive. A survey undertaken in 1997 by the regional magazine, *Asia, Inc.* (June 1997), of the 50 most competitive companies in Asia would challenge these arguments made by Yoshihara; as this list indicates, a number of the most competitive companies are owned by ethnic Chinese in Southeast Asia (see Table I.3).

Table I.3 indicates that ethnic Chinese own more than a quarter of the 50 most competitive companies in Asia from Southeast Asia. Among the Chinese businessmen who have made this list include Indonesia's Liem Sioe Leong and Eka Widjaja, Malaysia's Robert Kuok and Thailand's Dhanin Chearavanont and Thaksin Shinawatra, all of who have had access to economic rents from the state. The list in Table I.3 does not include Chinese-owned companies from Hong Kong and Taiwan which, if incorporated, would also include the Taiwan Semiconductor Manufacturing Company (listed at number six and involved in semiconductor manufacturing), Giordano International Ltd of Hong Kong (at number 14 and involved in textile retailing), Taiwan's United Microelectronics Corporation and Mosel Vitelic Inc. (at numbers 18 and 21 respectively and both involved in semiconductor manufacturing), Hong Kong's Gold Peak Industries (Holdings) Ltd (at number 31 and involved in electronics), Evergreen Marine Corporation of Taiwan (at number 32 and involved in shipping), Hong Kong's Sun Hung Kai Properties Ltd (at number 36 and involved in real estate), Li Ka-shing's main holding company Cheung Kong (Holdings) Ltd (at number 44 and involved in real estate) (*Asia, Inc.* June 1997). The combined number of Chinese-owned companies in East Asia would mean that almost half of the most competitive companies in Asia are Chinese-owned.[19]

Another important point regarding the Chinese-owned companies listed in Table I.3 is that, in spite of the very diversified nature of many of these companies, a large number of them are also involved in manufacturing. The attention given by large Chinese enterprises to manufacturing would cast some doubt on Yoshihara's thesis that Southeast Asian Chinese companies are mainly involved in services. Table I.4, which lists some of the largest companies in Southeast Asia owned by ethnic Chinese, reveals a similar characteristic, that is though many of these companies are quite diversified, a number of them are also actively involved in manufacturing.

Table I.3 Chinese-Owned Enterprises Among the 50 Most Competitive Companies in Asia, 1997

Company	Ranking	Country	Owner	Industry	Sales Volume (US$ million)	Profit Margin (%)#
Shangri-La Asia Ltd	12	Hong Kong*	Robert Kuok	Hotel	291	46.6
Jollibee Foods Corp.	15	Philippines	Tony Tan Caktiong	Food	193	13.8
Venture Manufacturing (S) Ltd	17	Singapore	Wong Ngit Leong	Manufacturing	226	9.6
Television Broadcasts Ltd	23	Hong Kong*	Robert Kuok	Broadcasting	353	17.5
Asia Pacific Breweries Ltd	26	Singapore	OCBC Group	Brewing	925	14.2
Indofood	27	Indonesia	Liem Sioe Leong	Food	930	9.8
Keppel Land Ltd	28	Singapore		Real Estate	227	57.7
Genting Bhd	29	Malaysia	Lim Goh Tong	Gaming	997	47.0
Creative Technology Ltd	34	Singapore	Sim Wong Hoo	Electronics	1,185	14.8
Aztech Systems Ltd	39	Singapore	Mun Hong Yew	Electronics	467	3.7
Charoen Phokpand Feedmill	40	Thailand	Dhanin Chearavanont	Agribusiness	609	8.2
Indah Kiat Pulp & Paper Corp	45	Indonesia	Eka Widjaja	Pulp & Paper Manufacturer	923	23.5
Shinawatra Computer & Communications	49	Thailand	Thaksin Shinawatra	Telecommunications	748	26.8

Notes:
Average annual pre-tax profit/sales, 1990–1995
* Owned by Malaysian businessman, Robert Kuok, although the companies are based in Hong Kong
Source: Asia, Inc. June 1997

Table 1.4 Business Activities of the Largest Ethnic Chinese Companies in Southeast Asia

Company	Activities	Controlling Shareholder
Malaysia		
Genting	Gaming, leisure, plantation, power generation	Lim Goh Tong
YTL Corporation	Construction, manufacturing, power generation	Yeoh Tiong Lay
Public Bank	Banking, financial services	Teh Hong Piow
Berjaya Group	Gaming, manufacturing, telecommunications, media, wholesaling	Vincent Tan
Jaya Tiasa Holdings	Manufacturing	Tiong Hiew King
Kamunting Corporation/Multi-Purpose Holdings Group	Construction, gaming, investment holding, property development	T.K. Lim
Hong Leong Group	Finance, banking, manufacturing, property	Quek Leng Chan
Kuala Lumpur Kepong	Plantations, property development, manufacturing	Lee Loy Seng family
Malayan United Industries	Manufacturing, retailing	Khoo Kay Peng
Perlis Plantations	Manufacturing, hotels	Robert Kuok
Ekran	Construction, manufacturing	Ting Pek Khiing
MBf Capital	Finance, property development	Loy Hean Heong family
Tan Chong Motor	Manufacturing	Tan family
Lion Corporation	Manufacturing, retailing	William Cheng
Oriental Holdings	Manufacturing	Loh Boon Siew family
Hap Seng Consolidated	Manufacturing	Lau Gek Poh
Thailand		
Bangkok Bank Group	Financial services	Sophonpanich family
Charoen Pokphand Group	Agribusiness, property development, telecommunications, beer manufacturing	Chearavanont family
Shinawatra Group	Telecommunications, computers, broadcasting	Thaksin Shinawatra
Thai Farmers Bank Group	Financial services, agribusiness, power producer, telecommunications, property development	Lamsam family
Bangkok Metropolitan Bank	Financial services, property development	Tejapaibul family
Saha Pathanapibul Group	Trading, manufacturing	Thiam Chokwatana
Thai Petrochemicals Industries Group	Petrochemicals and cement producer	Leophairatana family
Bank of Ayudhya & Siam City Cement	Financial services, cement and food manufacturing, broadcasting	Ratanarak family
Bangkok Land & Tanayong	Property development, retailing, watch manufacturing, media, transportation	Kanjanapas family

Company	Activities	Controlling Shareholder
Thai Roong Ruang	Sugar	Suree Assadathorn
Metro Group	Agribusiness	Sawang Laohathai
Osothsapha	Pharmaceuticals	Osathanugraph family
Hong Yiah Seng	Textiles, petrochemicals	Liaophairat family
Yip In Tsoi	Textiles, autos, chemicals	Thawat Yip In Soi
Kwang Soon Lee	Sugar	Chawalit Chinthammit
Chawkwanyu	Oil Refinery	Chaw Chawkwanyu
Boonsung	Mining, automobiles	Boonsung family
Sukree Group	Textiles	Phothirattaanangkun family
Mitr-Phol Group	Sugar	Phanitwong family
Sahaviriya Group	Steel	Viriyaphraphaikit family
Indonesia		
Salim Group	Food, beverage, cement, textile, financial services, media, telecommunications, property development, commodity trading	Lim Sioe Leong
Sinar Mas Group	Pulp and paper manufacturing, plantations, financial services, property development, hotels	Eka Tjipta Widjaja
Bob Hasan's Holdings – (Sempati Air, Perta Oil, Nusamba, International Timber Corp)	Timber, pulp and paper, shipping, food processing, financial services, trading	Bob Hasan
Lippo Group	Banking and financial services, property development	Mochtar Riady
Astra Group	Motor vehicle assembler and distributor, telecommunications	Soerjadjaja family+
Barito Pacific Group	Timber and plywood processing, pulp and paper manufacturing, telecommunications, financial services	Prajogo Pangestu
Panin Group	Banking and financial services	Mu'min Ali Gunawan
Gudang Garam	Cigarette manufacturer	Wonowidjojo fsmily
Sampoerna Group	Cigarette manufacturer	Sampoerna family
Gajah Tunggal Group	Rubber tyre manufacturer, petrochemical and cable manufacturing, financial services, textile, eletronics, telecommunications	Sjamsul Nursalim
Singapore		
Oversea-Chinese Banking Corporation (OCBC)	Banking, finance, insurance, securities, information technology, manufacturing, construction, property development, food and beverages, retailing, publishing and printing	Lee Kong Chian family
Overseas Union Bank (OUB)	Banking, finance, securities, hotels	Lien Ying Chow

Company	Activities	Controlling Shareholder
United Overseas Bank (UOB)	Banking, finance, insurance, securities, property development, manufacturing	Wee family
Tat Lee Bank	Banking, finance	Goh family
Hong Leong Group~	Banking, finance, property development, hotels, construction, manufacturing	Kwek family
Lee Kim Tah Holdings	Construction	Lee family
Lim Kah Ngam	Construction, property development, hotels, restaurants	Lim family
General Corporation	Construction	Low Keng Huat
Far East Organization	Property development, hotels, foods and beverages	Ng Teng Fong
Goodwood Park Hotel@	Hotels, property development, investment holdings	Khoo Teck Puat
Hwa Hong Corporation	Investment holding, trading, construction, property development	Ong family
C.K. Tang	Retailing	Tang Wee Kit
Kuok (S) Ltd~	Hotels, shipping	Robert Kuok
Creative Technologies	Electronics and Information technologies	Sim Wong Hoo,

The Philippines

Company	Activities	Controlling Shareholder
Lucio Tan's Holdings – (Asia Brewery, Allied Bank, Philippine Airlines, Fortune Tobacco)	Beer and tobacco manufacturing, airlines, financial services	Lucio Tan
House of Investments	Financial services, construction, power generation, agribusiness, property development	Alfonso T. Yuchengco
Fuga Internationale	Copra trading, textiles, banking, hotels, property development	Tan Yu
Metropolitan Bank	Financial services	George Ty
SM Prime Holdings Group	Retailing, financial services, property development	Henry Sy
JG Summit	Retailing, property development, telecommunications, food, power generation	John Gokongwei
Filinvest Group	Property development, financial services	Gotianun family

Sources: Gomez 1999; Hiscock 1997; Suehiro 1992: 51, 54; Singapore Corporate Handbook 1997
@ apart from hotels, Khoo has interests in property development and control of an investment holding company
~ *holding companies*
+ *Although the Soerjadjaja family lost control of the Astra Group in the early 1990s, the family has been rebuilding their interests in the company. Prajogo Pangestu had emerged as one of the largest shareholders of the company.*

The empirical evidence from Tables I.3 and I.4 would suggest that although a number of the largest Chinese-owned enterprises in Southeast Asia have had – or still have – close ties with the indigenous political elite (with the exception of Singaporean companies), many of them have managed to develop a strong manufacturing base. A growing number of these companies have also begun to venture abroad where they have to compete with other international companies. The most competitive companies in Asia, all of which have also shown a capacity to venture into productive activities, include Robert Kuok's Shangri-La Hotel chain, the Charoen Pokhphand (CP) Group which is involved in the agribusiness industry, and Indonesia's Indofood and Indah Kiat Paper & Pulp, owned by the two largest Chinese enterprises, Liem's Salim Group and Eka Widjaja's Sinar Mas Group respectively. Indofood is the world's largest noodle manufacturer (*Far Eastern Economic Review* 26/12/96). Thailand's CP Group manufactures, apart from animal feed, a diverse range of products including motorcycles and cosmetics. In 1996, the CP Group was also the largest individual foreign investor in China, having established 130 joint-ventures in all but two of the country's provinces. Robert Kuok has created an international hotel chain, while also establishing himself as international trader in commodities, particularly sugar, and has growing interests in the media and property development industries in East Asia, as well as a burgeoning manufacturing base in China (Gomez 1999). In the Philippines, the fast-food operator, Jobilee Foods, has outstripped even the multi-national fast-food corporations McDonald's and Kentucky Fried Chicken in terms of sales. In 1996, while Jobilee Foods had 190 outlets in the Philippines, McDonald's had 87 and Kentucky Fried Chicken only 47. Apart from this, Jobilee Foods had also gone international, establishing outlets in Malaysia, Indonesia, Guam, Hong Kong and the Middle East (*Far Eastern Economic Review* 26/12/96). Henry Sy and John Gokongwei, who have established major department chain stores in the Philippines, also have interests in banking, property development and food manufacturing. In Singapore, a number of new Chinese-owned companies, involved in the electronics industry, are developing rapidly; for example, Creative Technology is known for developing Sound Blaster, a multi-media card for personal computers. Among the more established companies, the banking groups OCBC, OUB and UOB have established branches in a number of countries while the Hong Leong Group has an international and diversified interest in financial services, manufacturing and property development.

Since there is evidence that Chinese companies are venturing abroad, this raises the next issue which has preoccupied many analysts of Chinese enterprise: the extent of networking among these businessmen. As we have noted above, in order to test the hypothesis that the Chinese are emerging as a major economic force because of the business linkages they have created, the most useful concepts that can be used for determining the creation of long-standing business links would be interlocking stock ownership as this would suggest joint commitment to a long-term business endeavor. Another concept, though less useful, would be the use of interlocking directorships; though such interlocking may not necessarily mean that there is joint ownership of a company, this concept would help indicate cooperative ties that have emerged. There is limited evidence that any of the companies listed in Table I.4 have established interlocking stock ownership and directorate links, either domestically or across borders, with other Chinese-owned companies.

There have been, however, numerous accounts of disputes between Chinese businessmen that have tried to cooperate in ventures involving joint ownership; such disputes have prevented them from cooperating to promote their individual business interests. In the Philippines, Carino (1998) has shown how the disputes between the older generation, or 'traditionalists,' and a new breed of businessmen led to the formation of two Chinese Chambers of Commerce. The division between these Filipino Chinese businessmen facilitated the promulgation and implementation of the Retail Act that badly hindered the development of all Chinese capital. In Singapore, three banks owned by a group of Hokkien Chinese merged their activities to form OCBC, but the new bank's board of directors was soon fraught with divisions. Such divisions led to a break away by some of OCBC's senior managers who went on to found other banks, including Malayan Banking and Public Bank, which emerged as serious competitors. In Malaysia, the Chinese did try to work together when the government began implementing the New Economic Policy (NEP) that entailed state intervention in the economy as a means to accumulate corporate equity on behalf of the indigenous Malays. However, the intra-ethnic collaborative efforts to check state intrusion in the economy through the NEP did not include most of the older, well-established Chinese capitalists. This attempt to get Chinese capitalists to work together, known as the 'corporatization move-ment,' was led by a new emerging breed of businessmen who eventually abused the movement for vested interests, much to the detriment of Chinese unity in Malaysia (see Gomez 1999; Heng 1992).

The joint business networks that have been created have primarily been between Chinese businessmen and MNCs, particularly those from Japan. In Indonesia, Robison (1986: 272–73) points out, the economic environment that emerged under Suharto's New Order "offered Chinese capitalists a much more favorable environment. Economic growth and rehabilitation became a priority and the government turned to those best equipped to invest capital and expand corporate activity. The re-entry of foreign capital into Indonesia was especially favorable to Chinese capitalists, who were best able to take advantage of various joint-venture arrangements to expand the capital and corporate bases." In Thailand, Suehiro (1992) has shown that many of the leading ethnic Chinese capitalists had forged joint-ventures with the Japanese as a means to learn new technology and develop their enterprises. More recently, among the most well-known joint-ventures in China are those between the Charoen Phokpand (CP) Group and the Dutch retailing company, Makro, and with the US-based construction and property management corporation Bush and Koll (Brown 1998). In the Philippines, Palanca (1995a: 51), while noting that the partners of most Japanese investors are ethnic Chinese, cites the example of Toyota Motor Corporation, in which the Chinese holds 60 per cent of the company's equity. In Malaysia, case studies on some of the largest Chinese companies have revealed similar evidence. Loh Boon Siew established close links with the Japanese to develop his interests in car assembly and component manufacturing, while YTL Corporation, controlled by the Yeoh family, established joint-ventures with European companies, from England and Germany, to develop its expertise in construction and in power generation. Building on the expertise gained from such joint-ventures, YTL Corp has begun expanding its power generation business abroad, securing contracts in Singapore, Thailand, China and Zimbabwe (see Gomez 1999).

Major Research Themes

Based on the discussion here, it could be argued that to provide a holistic understanding of the operation of ethnic Chinese companies in Southeast Asia, three broad themes need to be brought into the analysis – state, society and capital. Under the theme of state, a number of issues are important, that is the impact of state policies, including ethnic redistribution endeavors, deregulation initiatives, industrialization drives and market control legislation and regulations.

State policies have shaped ownership and control patterns, determined access to financial capital and government projects and influenced the involvement of ethnic communities, MNCs and state enterprises in economic sectors. Policy changes affecting ethnic minorities have determined forms of business practices and corporate and political alliances, and have also influenced decision-making in business ventures, including whether to diversify or to expand business operations abroad. State-business linkages, in various forms, are common in Southeast Asia, and include business ties between Chinese enterprises and local and foreign state-owned corporations. For example, investment patterns in China by Singaporean state-owned companies and their business linkages with Chinese public enterprises are expanding, while in Malaysia, Chinese companies which have established links with government-owned enterprises have found it easier to gain access to state rents. The prevalence of patron-client linkages, which have determined how economic rents could be deployed, is common and widespread in a number of Southeast Asian countries, particularly until the onset of the financial crisis in 1997. Such issues, broadly linked to Yoshihara's thesis on 'rentier capitalism,' have had an impact on the development of the corporate sector in particular and on economic development in general in Southeast Asia. The ties between businessmen and politicians have been, and remain, significant in Southeast Asia, including in more democratized countries like Thailand and the Philippines. The growing concentration of power in the office of the executive arm of the state, particularly in Malaysia and in Indonesia, had a bearing of how inter- and intra-ethnic business ties were forged and on how economic policies evolved and were implemented; it has also determined how companies have fared in the post-financial crisis.

The theme of capital incorporates issues such as the way in which markets were created, the importance of family firms, the role of MNCs in the domestic market and their links with Chinese capital, the impact of state-owned corporations on the sectors dominated by Chinese companies, and the business links among Chinese-owned large enterprises and among SMEs, as well as those between large enterprises and SMEs. One key issue is the role and significance of family business. With rapid modernization, important changes have been transpiring within family-run companies, with more bureaucratization of its management through the induction of professionals, while gender changes are increasingly obvious with women family members playing a more prominent role in management. Related issues include impact of inheritance arrangements and generational change on companies. Generational change appears to have significantly affected business linkages, in that the new generation views inter-ethnic ties very differently, seeing it as an important avenue to develop their corporate base. Although most research on Chinese enterprises has focused on the largest companies, almost all these studies have provided little data on ownership and control patterns, form of growth and changes in business strategies, sources of financing and organizational structure and management style. There is almost no focus on how Chinese enterprises have been affected by market concentration, barriers to market entry, labor costs and competition. In view of the extensive investment by MNCs in Southeast Asia, particularly by companies from Taiwan, Japan and South Korea, there have been linkages between these MNCs and ethnic Chinese companies. It appears that many of such tie-ups between MNCs and Chinese companies are an attempt by Chinese companies to acquire 'know how,' while MNCs have used the Chinese companies as a means to gain entry into domestic markets. It is widely believed that Western MNCs also hope that such tie-ups will enable them to gain entry into the market in mainland China. There has, however, been little attempt to trace how much transfer of technology has occurred and whether there has been an attempt by Chinese companies to build on the know-how that they have had access to. In some Southeast Asian countries, East Asian MNCs have been used by governments to bypass Chinese companies, that is to prevent the latter from gaining access to, or developing their interests in particular economic sectors. There have been limited studies analyzing why control over particular economic sectors, historically dominated by particular sub-ethnic Chinese communities, for example, rice trade, food processing, textiles and banking, has diminished. Given the ostensible Chinese business networking, including the supposed networking among sub-ethnic groups, this would have suggested further concentration of ownership of these sectors.

On the theme of society, there is a need to contest essentialist arguments that culture, shared identities and value systems determine ethnic business activity and typify a universal form of 'Chinese capital'. There is, however, little dispute that culture and ethnicity are social phenomena that can be manipulated by governments, businessmen and community organizations in the pursuit of their own goals. This would suggest that concept of 'ethnicity,' and the ways in which 'ethnic identity' has been manipulated by individuals, groups and the state to promote their own interests requires further analysis. For example, just as the government in mainland China has developed policies to attract investment from Chinese of the diaspora, Chinese businessmen have also recognized the potential gain from using their ethnic identity to open doors in China as well as facilitate business deals with other members of the diaspora.

Since there are obviously a number of factors that impinge upon the decision-making process of individuals, there is a need for determining new forms of appraising Chinese business performance. A historically-based, micro-oriented level of analysis is necessary to better understand Chinese entrepreneurship, while the research into the dynamics of these enterprises should preferably be undertaken through an inter-disciplinary approach. This data could help provide insights into new theoretical perspectives or models that could be developed to explain more cogently the operations of Chinese capital. In other words, what is required, apart from the need for in-depth analysis of business records, is the need to focus greater attention on forms of entrepreneurship and technological innovation within the firm. Among Chinese companies, there are also significant variations in corporate behavior and structuring of ownership, patterns of capital formation and accumulation, areas of investment, forms of business linkages, marketing strategies, technology development and labor relations. This combination of empirical work and more innovative theorizing would help develop a more nuanced understanding of Chinese enterprise.

1

Singapore

—◆◆◆—

Chan Kwok Bun and Ng Beoy Kui

Chinese Business in Singapore

In Southeast Asia, the ethnic Chinese are alleged to play a significant role in the regional economy as well as respective local economies, in spite of their minority status as an ethnic/racial group. Naisbitt (1997), among many others, even attributed the so-called 'Asian miracle' (prior to the Asian economic crisis beginning in July 1997) to the successes of ethnic Chinese business. This characterization, we maintain, is not applicable to the ethnic Chinese enterprises in Singapore. In Singapore, ethnic Chinese as a group constitute about 75 per cent of the population, but their enterprises play only a minor role in the national economy, taking only third place after multinational corporations (MNCs) and government-linked corporations (GLCs).[1] Moreover, a majority of these Chinese enterprises are small and medium enterprises (SMEs), which are mostly labor-intensive in their operations and are oriented primarily towards the small domestic market. Only a minority of – and only until recently – these business enterprises are involved in large-scale operations, though still confining themselves mainly to banking, light manufacturing and real estate and property development.[2] Of the ten largest ethnic Chinese enterprises in Singapore, three are in banking, another three in real estate and property, and the rest in light manufacturing and hotel. Only one Chinese corporation is in the high technology and computer industry (*Yazhou Zhoukan* 1998). In this essay, we attempt to argue that amidst all the generalizations and claims made about ethnic Chinese business in Southeast Asia, the Singapore case presents itself as a bit of an anomaly. An important part of our analysis and interpretation of such a state of affairs in Singapore is a historical one. The history of ethnic Chinese business in Singapore can be divided into four periods. In the first period, from 1819 to 1958, when entrepot trade boomed in Singapore, ethnic Chinese played important roles as merchants, middlemen, compradors as well as bankers. During this period, the British colonial government adopted a non-interventionist policy in economic affairs, especially the free trade policy with hardly any exchange restrictions. Ethnic Chinese, through their hard work and business acumen, were able to exploit the potentials in regional trade.

In the second period, between 1959 and 1975, the government emphasized its 'two-legged' policy, which involved MNCs and GLCs directly in its industrialization effort and the restructuring of the national economy. As it happened, ethnic Chinese business was left alone, with little attempt to pull it into the mainstream of the national economy. After 1975, the beginning of the third period, the government's attitude towards Chinese capital began to change slightly. The government realized that if its efforts at economic restructuring were to succeed, it would be necessary to secure the cooperation of Chinese capital in replacing labor-intensive with capital-intensive methods of production in the economy. For the subsequent ten years, the government did engage the ethnic Chinese business by providing them, on an ad hoc basis, with technical and financial assistance. But the response from the Chinese business community was lukewarm, as the application procedures for such assistance were seen as cumbersome and bureaucratic. Following the severe recession in 1985, the government felt a need for the SMEs, in particular Chinese capital, to be integrated back into the economic mainstream both for political and economic reasons. The government eventually abandoned its 'two-legged' policy in 1989. The fourth period, starting from 1989, consolidated the policy change begun in the third period. With the publication of the SME Master Plan, the government instituted various schemes to assist the small and medium enterprises, a majority of which were owned by ethnic Chinese, to upgrade and help build the 'external wing' of Singapore through regionalization.[3] The period also saw the active promotion of 'technopreneurs' in Singapore.

Merchants, Middlemen, Compradors and Bankers

In the first period from pre-colonial days till the eve of self-government in 1959, ethnic Chinese played the roles of merchants and middlemen in the entrepot trade of the region. As Singapore is strategically situated in the middle of the Malay archipelago, it quickly developed from a humble fishing village into an international port on the eve of Independence in 1963. In the pre-colonial days, Singapore served mainly as a transhipment trade centre, transferring cargoes from one ship to another within the region. Most of the goods in this trade were Straits-produced which were imported by Bugis traders from the east and southwest coasts of Borneo, the Celebes and Bali. There was also the Chinese junk trade, which brought along with it the new Chinese immigrants, the *sinkhek*. These newcomers constituted a system of indentured labor that smacked of slavery but significantly helped populate Singapore with hard-working and enterprising Chinese (Wong 1991: 44; Chan and Chiang 1994).

In this connection, ethnic Chinese enterprises played a major role in three branches of trade. In the transhipment trade, the Chinese community played the role of a middleman – between Bugis traders and other traders such as Arab and Indian merchants. Eventually, the transhipment trade was extended to imports for local consumption and the export of new local produce. It was mainly during the British rule that Singapore further developed as an entrepot trade centre, especially after the opening of Suez Canal in 1869 which enabled Chinese businessmen to import from the West manufactured goods, and then export them to other parts of Southeast Asia. Similarly, the new canal also facilitated the export to the West by ethnic Chinese businessmen of primary commodities such as copra, sago, gambier, species, coffee and rattan imported from the region. Such entrepot trade in Singapore continued into the 1950s and 1960s.

Apart from trading, some Chinese in Singapore ventured into gambier and pineapple production for export. They were also involved in the processing of agricultural produce, including pineapple canning for which some Chinese gained a reputation, and minerals, particularly tin smelting. The Chinese were also involved in light manufacturing of soap, edible oils, saw milling, rubber products, beverages, biscuits, soya source and food cannery.

Among the wide range of economic activities engaged in by Chinese businessmen, the roles of merchants, middlemen and compradors were significant. As merchants, they traded with the natives for primary produce; they engaged Indian and Arab traders for their spices, and Europeans for their manufactured goods. In view of their extensive engagement with many parties in their trade and commerce activities, the Chinese over time became middlemen mediating amongst various parties, notably between the natives and the Europeans. Those who were more successful in their business endeavors also became compradors to the European business corporations. Some of these rich businessmen later assembled among themselves to set up banks to provide finance to their fellow merchants and to help send remittances to China (Tan 1961; Lee 1974). Throughout the 19th century and during the first half of the 20th century, Chinese merchants had an interdependent relationship with Western agency houses. As Wong (1991: 62) observed, "at the apex were Western banks, agency and managing agency houses; in the middle the Chinese dealers, and at the base the producers of the Straits produce, who were also the principal consumers of imported manufactured goods." This relationship of interdependence contributed to the flourishing of an entrepot trade and the evolution of Singapore into an international port.

Political Alienation by the Government

By the eve of self-government in 1959, the Chinese business community had established itself as a political force to be reckoned with. Ethnic Chinese for the first time would be given citizenship and electoral suffrage by the colonial government to prepare for self-government. While the Chinese were somewhat divided along dialect lines, they were relatively united under an encompassing institution – the Chinese Chamber of Industry and Commerce – when they were confronted with issues such as language and culture. The Chinese business community indeed wielded considerable financial and economic resources, which could be deployed during election campaigns. With these advantages, the Chinese business community attempted to exert influence on local politics, especially on issues regarding culture and language. This desire by Chinese businessmen to be assertive possibly had less to do with protecting their vested commercial interests than as a social obligation to serve the Chinese community. These efforts culminated in the establishment of the Nanyang University in 1955, which used Chinese as the main medium of instruction. After self-government rule was attained in 1959 with the People's Action Party (PAP) in power, the Chinese community, under the leadership of Tan Lark Sye, had become critical about the government's educational and cultural policies. These policies attempted to de-emphasize the 'Chineseness' of Singapore by forging a multi-racial and multi-cultural society – a response to "the internal ethnic imperatives as well as the regional geographical compulsions" (Vasil 1995: 34). This conflict between the PAP and the Chinese business community led to the latter's open backing for the opposition Socialist Front which was sympathetic to the promotion of Chinese culture and education (Rodan 1989: 98; Leong 1998).

Following the separation of Singapore from Malaysia in 1963, the PAP government alienated the Chinese business community further by pursuing its 'two-legged' policy. Under this policy, MNCs were encouraged, particularly through favorable tax incentives, to come to Singapore to realize the government's industrialization initiative. At the same time, GLCs such as INTRACO, the Development Bank of Singapore (DBS) and the Jurong Town Corporation (JTC) were set up to participate in a series of wide-ranging economic activities. The purpose of these GLCs was to "obviate any need for the PAP government to look to the Chinese-educated and China-oriented Chinese, who had traditionally made up Singapore entrepreneurs, to drive its industrialization initiative" (Huff 1994: 320). In this respect, MNCs and GLCs emerged as the two types of 'entrepreneurial substitutes' for economic development – to bypass the need to depend on the dominant Chinese business community. Inevitably, this meant that Chinese business enterprises were left on their own, securing little assistance from the government. In many cases, the GLCs even encroached on the traditional economic activities of the Chinese business community, thus exerting a 'crowding-out effect' on Chinese enterprises.

Apart from the 'two-legged' policy, the government also tried to reduce the influence of Chinese clan associations by setting up rival organizations such as People's Association and a multitude of community centres to provide better substitutes in social and cultural activities (Chong 1992). In the longer run, the government also tried to forge a multi-racial outlook among the younger generation through an educational policy that attached special importance to the English language (Vasil 1995).

Economic Restructuring and Engagement

The political alienation of Chinese enterprises by the government could not, however, last for long for two reasons. First, Chinese businessmen wielded significant influence on constituents in the Housing and Development Board (HDB) heartland; any further political alienation by the government would have provided opposition parties with an opportunity to gain political ground. Second, and more importantly, given the economic success of the government's industrialization drive in the 1960s and the first half of 1970s, there emerged a growing shortage of labor in Singapore. Concurrently, since Chinese businesses still operated labor-intensive enterprises, which had low productivity outputs, the government felt an urgent need to upgrade these local enterprises as part of the strategy of economic restructuring.

With this in mind, the PAP government promulgated the Small Industries Finance Scheme in 1976 to provide financial support for the expansion, modernization and diversification of small firms engaged in manufacturing and related industries, as well as to assist the setting up of viable small enterprises. In June 1980, a small industry advisory committee was set up to advise the Economic Development Board (EDB) on measures to develop and upgrade local small industries. To further promote the development of small industries, the Material Application Centre under the then Singapore Industrial Standard and Industrial Research (SISIR) and the Small Industries Technical Assistance Scheme under EDB were also instituted. However, the assistance extended by the government was limited to companies involved in the manufacturing industry. SMEs in other sectors were still not given much attention. Two other government initiatives in 1979 led to sharp increases in labor cost, affecting the SMEs badly. In the same year, the government introduced a corrective wage policy' – sometimes referred to as the 'Second Industrial Revolution' – through the National Wages Council (NWC). Subsequently, the mandatory contribution by employers to the Central Provident Fund Board (CPF)[4] was also increased to 25 percent of an employee's monthly wage. Many Chinese enterprises had failed to restructure from labor-intensive to capital-intensive methods of production because they lacked the capital required and their operations were too small to enjoy any scale economies. With the sharp appreciation of the Singapore dollar in the first half of 1980s, Singapore lost its competitiveness and, by 1985, the economy went into a recession.

Full Partnership in Economic Development

During the recession in 1985, the government realized the crucial contribution of SMEs, which were owned mainly by ethnic Chinese, to the economic development of Singapore. However, as Toh and Low (1993: 212–213) pointed out, SMEs, because of their sheer physical presence (constituting 90 per cent of total establishments and 44 per cent of total employment), could be deemed as wasting scarce resources, since their labor-intensive companies were also low-productivity enterprises. A successful restructuring of these local enterprises would release scarce labor for other uses. Secondly, the SMEs could be positioned as suppliers and subcontractors to MNCs, thus facilitating technology transfer from MNCs to local enterprises. The existence of these SMEs as suppliers and subcontractors, which could serve as an integral part of the industrial structure, could be a pulling factor to attract more foreign investment to Singapore. Thirdly, the dearth of entrepreneurial spirit among the younger generation has been a concern to the government. Thus, any policy to strengthen SMEs would send a signal to the Singapore community that entrepreneurship and innovations were much valued by the government. This was especially so when the government intended to develop an 'external wing' of the Singapore economy by encouraging local enterprises to venture abroad.

In view of the importance of the SMEs, the government set up an Economic Committee to study, among other matters, measures to assist the SMEs. The recommendations culminated in the SME Plan in 1989. In December 1989, the Singapore government also introduced the 'growth triangle' concept[5] as part of the strategy to re-allocate labor-intensive SMEs to neighbouring Johor in Malaysia and Batam in Indonesia. To further develop the SMEs, a venture capital fund was established to provide critical seed money for these firms to innovate and grow. To complement such assistance, a second board called the Stock Exchange of Singapore Dealing and Automated Quotation (SESDAQ) was set up to provide an avenue for SMEs to be listed and to raise the necessary capital for expansion. The EDB also provided a wide range of assistance to SMEs; by 1998, there were 60 government schemes to help the SMEs (*The Straits Times* April 1998). Presently, SMEs are considered as a full partner in the economic development of Singapore.

Identity, Ethnicity and Investment in China

Chinese identity and ethnicity has been a key issue widely discussed in both the academic and journalistic literature on the ethnic Chinese residing in Southeast Asia (Suryadinata 1997). One problem with the literature is the classification of ethnic Chinese in Southeast Asia as a homogeneous group. This implies that the ethnic Chinese in one sense or another owe their political allegiance to their motherland, China. The failure to distinguish different types of ethnic Chinese in the region has caused controversy and sometimes distress to the local Chinese residents. The racial riot that occurred in May 1998 in Indonesia is a manifestation of such distress.

Over the decades, governments of Southeast Asian countries have attempted through various measures to get their respective Chinese communities to view themselves as less 'Chinese'. Ethnic Chinese of Southeast Asia have since shifted their political allegiance to their respective country of residence, especially after the takeover of mainland China by Chinese communists in 1949. In spite of this change in political allegiance, many authors still continue to label ethnic Chinese in Southeast Asia as 'overseas Chinese' (see Seagrave 1996; Hodder 1996; Kotkin 1992; Tanaka, Minako and Yoko 1992; Weidenbaum and Hughes 1996). Such labelling not only suggests a lack of loyalty among ethnic Chinese to their respective country of residence but also reinforces mistrust between the indigenous and ethnic Chinese communities. This distrust of ethnic Chinese has sometimes been translated into an unwritten policy to disallow ethnic Chinese from holding important military posts.

Authors of much of the journalistic literature on Southeast Asian Chinese do not differentiate, for instance, between ethnic Chinese in Singapore and those in the Philippines. Ethnic Chinese in the region may appear to share superficially a sense of common identity. Nevertheless, in terms of mindset and behavioral orientation, they are not of the same kind (Suryadinata 1997; Tan 1997). This is basically the result of assimilation or integration policies adopted by Southeast Asian governments involving ethnic Chinese over the past decades. Countries like Indonesia, Thailand and the Philippines adhere closely to an assimilationist policy, which attempts to reduce visible manifestations of Chinese identity to a minimum. In these countries, Chinese names, Chinese culture and Chinese education are prohibited to varying extent. Other countries, like Malaysia and Brunei, adopt an accommodationist policy that restricts manifestations of Chinese identity during official functions. Singapore, on the other hand, follows a more pluralistic approach to forge a collective sense of nationhood among the country's multiple ethnic communities. Even then, Singapore's model of pluralism is not simply an attempt to create a multi-racial society, with the Chinese as its majority race. Singapore's model of cultural pluralism requires a balance, which often leads to a paradox. As Clammer (1985: 100) observed, "on the one hand the logic of the multiracial model points towards the production of a synthesis – a uniquely Singaporean culture – but on the other hand forces individuals to identify ever more closely with their own ethnic group and its culture. But if one is too much for synthesis one is rootless; but if one is too much for one's own source culture then one is a chauvinist."

In Singapore, the Chinese community has evolved, over three and a half decades, from being 'overseas Chinese' (before 1950s) to becoming Chinese Singaporean (Chiew 1997). Presently, while hardly anyone would consider themselves 'overseas Chinese,' or *huaqiao*, they would probably see themselves as Singaporean first and *huaren*, or ethnic Chinese, second; this is the case particularly among the younger Singaporeans. Equally important, their loyalty is to Singapore, while China is just another foreign country. However, while in the company of other ethnic Chinese groups, a Chinese would feel he belongs to one of the dialect groups: Hokkien, Teochew or Hakka. There is also an observed difference in the degree of 'Chineseness' among Singaporean Chinese of different generations. The older the generation, the higher the degree of 'Chineseness'. Even the language spoken is different among the different generations. The first generation tends to speak one of the Chinese dialects as a primary means of communication. The middle generation would be either English-speaking or Chinese-speaking, while the youngest generation is usually bi-lingual, fluent in English and Mandarin, and also tends to have a strong sense of national identity.

As Chan and Ng (1999) have observed, there are also significant differences among Chinese businessmen. Broadly speaking, they can be classified into two groups: one is culturally more Chinese than the other. The culturally more Chinese group is the dominant group and belongs mainly to the first generation. However, this group is not homogenous in terms of company size or style of management. Generally, the smaller the size of the business, the more Chinese and traditional the outlook of its owners. In contrast, the larger the size of the company, the more westernized is its management style and corporate culture. The more culturally Chinese group tends to operate family-owned companies and is typically involved in banking, retail trade, hotel and restaurants, light manufacturing and property and real estate. The members of this group tend to be actively involved in the Singapore Chinese Chamber of Commerce and Industry (SCCCI). They also participate actively in clan associations and alumni bodies of local Chinese schools. The second group of Chinese businessmen is more westernized in outlook and is still relatively small in number. Companies in this group are not based on traditional family lineage, many of whom have been incorporated relatively recently. More importantly, they are heavily involved in electronics, computer, and telecommunication products and usually adopt a western management style. The owners of these companies are younger and better educated. They may have worked in MNCs previously and therefore have the capacity to benefit from technology transfer. Hence, they will be important partners to MNCs in developing the high-technology industry in Singapore. Moreover, they have the potential to set up joint ventures with MNCs and GLCs abroad.

One often-discussed issue in the literature on Chinese business is the motive behind the rush by ethnic Chinese businessmen from Southeast Asia, including Chinese Singaporeans, to invest in mainland China since 1979. One widely held view (especially among Indonesian newspapers) is that the 'overseas Chinese,' including Chinese Singaporeans, invest in China for emotive reasons, particularly to participate in the development of their ancestral homeland. Such a perception may have been true before the 1950s. Wang (1995) suggested two models of this perception. The first is the Tan Kah Kee model. Tan Kah Kee, a Chinese businessman who was loyal to his motherland, China, mobilized financial resources in Malaya and Singapore and channelled funds to China to fight the Japanese during World War II. After the War, Tan donated a large sum of money to help build China, before eventually returning to his homeland for good. Under this model, Wang (1995: 21) argued, "philanthropy was extended to cover investments in local industry, but mainly to support the philanthropic projects that had been started" in a person's hometown. This type of philanthropy is almost extinct among present-day Chinese Singaporean businessmen, especially the younger entrepreneurs.

The other model suggested by Wang is the Sincere-Wing On model according to which Chinese businessmen invested in China on the basis of rational business decisions but "did so as a prelude to or as preparation for their eventual return to China" (Wang 1995: 21). Such a perception is equally not applicable to the present-day Singaporean businessmen who have invested in China. Chinese Singaporean businessmen invest in China to exploit opportunities for their own business gains, but not to return to the mainland eventually.

Investments in China by Chinese Singaporean are perhaps no different from investments by other national groups such as

Europeans or Americans. While the older, Chinese-educated seem to be more adept at exploiting their ethnic identity when they enter the China market, this in itself does not guarantee business success. A comparative ethnic advantage does not always culminate in the building up of strong *guanxi* in one's business dealings in China. Like others, the cultivation of *guanxi* by Chinese Singaporean businessmen often involves high transaction costs (Chan and Tong 1999). This is contrary to the widely held view that ethnic Chinese enjoy a 'cultural sameness' with their counterparts in mainland China that awaits to be exploited for business gains.

Structural Weaknesses of Chinese Capital

Yoshihara observed in his book, *The Rise of Ersatz Capitalism in South-East Asia*, that a majority of the Chinese entrepreneurs in Southeast Asia are weak in terms of technological expertise; he called them 'ersatz capitalists,' not industrial capitalists. These 'ersatz capitalists' are basically monopolists, rent seekers and speculators – all with the support of the ruling elites in the region. Coupled with other factors, this kind of capitalism has not brought about genuine industrialization in Southeast Asia. For Yoshihara, the industrialization in Southeast Asia over the past decades is a form of 'industrialization without development,' or 'technologyless industrialization'. While Yoshihara did provide anecdotal evidence to prove his hypothesis in other parts of Southeast Asia, he could not provide evidence to show that Chinese Singaporean businessmen, like their Southeast Asian counterparts, also belonged to this category of monopolists, rent seekers and speculators (Yoshihara 1988: 68–86). Yoshihara did, however, argue that Chinese Singaporean businessmen were not heavily involved in heavy manufacturing, which promotes industrial capitalism. Yoshihara attributed this to the small size of the Singaporean economy, which does not allow for "cross-fertilisation and industry cooperation that are essential for technological innovation." The other factor inhibiting the development of industrial capitalism is the severe competition for limited manpower resources from multinational corporations and the services sector, such as banking and tourism (Yoshihara 1988: 115–117).

Yoshihara's thesis of 'technologyless industrialization' among Chinese entrepreneurs in Singapore still requires further study. According to a survey by *Yazhou Zhoukan* in 1997, out of the 500 largest Chinese companies worldwide, 8.9 per cent, or 44 companies, were based in Singapore. However, only ten of these 44 companies were involved in light manufacturing, and another five in manufacturing electronics and computer products; one of these companies was a subsidiary of a Taiwanese electronic firm. Of the ten largest Chinese companies in Singapore, only one was involved in manufacturing personal computers and multimedia products, two in light manufacturing, three in banking, and the rest largely in property and real estate, hotels and investment. In comparison, Taiwan had 183 companies in the 500 group; one third of these Taiwanese companies were involved in electronics and telecommunications technology.

The other important factor contributing to such low concentration in high-technology industry in Singapore is that the Chinese enterprises are still dominated by business firms owned by the first or second generation, who generally have relatively little formal education compared to the younger Chinese businessmen. A number of the first generation of immigrant Chinese who have established a significant corporate base belong to the category of 'rags-to-riches' entrepreneurs (Chan and Chiang 1994).

According to Tan (1996), the technological backwardness of Chinese enterprises was due to their 'short-term' and 'opportunistic' outlook. In the 1940s and 1950s, many Chinese businessmen considered their business ventures as only a temporary endeavor, in view of the social-political unrest then prevailing in the country, the confrontation between Malaya and Indonesia, and the eventual separation from Malaysia. Accordingly, they avoided venturing into the manufacturing sector, particularly the high-technology industries, which normally required much capital investment and took a longer period to secure returns on investment. In subsequent years, Chinese businesses were left far behind in all economic sectors except in banking, playing second fiddle to the MNCs and GLCs. Chinese businessmen continued to concentrate on the traditional sectors, such as wholesale and retail trade, light manufacturing and hotels and restaurants.

Another structural weakness often cited as a key factor limiting the growth of Chinese businesses pertains to the social organization of Chinese firms, which is often centred on the family. Fukuyama (1995: 64) noted that "a single family, no matter how large, capable or well educated, can only have so many competent sons, daughters, spouses and siblings to oversee the different parts of a rapidly ramifying enterprise." This is especially so for small and medium Chinese firms that are, according to Redding (1990), generally characterized by paternalism, nepotism, personalism and fragmentation. There are, however, also exceptions: a number of Singapore family-owned Chinese businesses have indeed grown into MNCs. One way to remove such limits to growth is through internationalization. The Hong Leong group, for example, ventured into Malaysia and Hong Kong and became a conglomerate with centripetal control (Tong 1996). The second way is through 'family-ization,' by coopting professional managers into the family through marriage (Chan and Chiang 1994), which has become less prevalent in modern Singapore than in the 1920s. The third way is to hire professional managers as trustees to manage the family firm on the owners' behalf. Trusteeship and professionalism are the two key elements in this kind of arrangement. In Singapore, a case in point is the Overseas Union Bank (OUB). Following the retirement of Lien Ying Chow at the age of 89, none of his direct heirs replaced him as chairman of the banking group. Rather, Lee Hee Seng, not a member of the Lien family and a former chairman of the Housing and Development Board (HDB) and a managing director of a finance company, was appointed to take charge of the OUB group (Zheng 1996: 58–63).

The other popular means for business consolidation and growth used by Chinese businessmen is to improve the business acumen of their successors by sending their children overseas for tertiary education and subsequently training them personally to take over the management of their companies. Some examples of companies that have used this method are the Wah Chang and Yeo Hiap Seng (YHS) groups. In the case of the Wah Chang group, Ho Rih Hwa passed on his management control to Ho Kwon Ping, who has a graduate degree; under his leadership, the Wah Chang group has adopted a modern management style. Yeo Thian In handed over management of the YHS group in 1985 to the younger Yeos, who hold various degrees in economics, accountancy and physics (Chuang 1987). The new chairman, Alan Yeo, a chemistry graduate, introduced modern management into the company, continuing to enhance YHS' reputation as a drinks manufacturer; YHS is the second largest soft drink manufacturer in Singapore. Unfortunately, a family feud among the Yeos led to the takeover of the YHS group's Singapore operations by Ng Teng Fong of the Far East Organisation, another family business specializing in property and real estates in Singapore.[6] Finally, expansion of family business is made possible through mergers and acquisitions. The United Overseas Bank (UOB) group, under the chairmanship of Wee Cho Yaw, is a typical example. Since 1970, the

UOB group has been expanding its banking operations by acquiring a number of banks, including Chung Khiaw Bank (in 1971), Lee Wah Bank (in 1972), Far Eastern Bank (in 1984), and Industrial and Commerce Bank (in 1987) (Chew 1993).

The structural weaknesses of Chinese family business arise from the non-separation between ownership and management control. Chinese family businesses, including those in Singapore, tend to be preoccupied with the family identity in business. To them, family ownership and control is of prime importance, while professional management and expertise is of secondary importance. The Singapore government has viewed such preoccupation as a stumbling block for family businesses to be professionally managed. The banking liberalization in 1999, especially on ownership and controls in the sector, was deliberately designed, among others, to break such family lineage through market forces.

Against this background, the Chinese enterprises in Singapore could not withstand severe competition posed by MNCs and GLCs. Competitive pressure in the form of the 'crowding-out effect' had contributed to the eclipse of traditional Chinese business in Singapore (Tan 1996). The 'crowding-out effect' was especially felt in the services sector, in particular in wholesale and retail trade, and in the banking sector, through competition with well-established foreign banks from developed countries. With the liberalization of ownership and control in the banking sector announced in 1999, the 'crowding-out effect' is expected to be more severe than before. The 'crowding-out effect' also arose from compulsory employer contributions to the Central Provident Fund (CPF) – sometimes to the extent of preventing businessmen from accumulating enough start-up money for business capital formation. Similarly, the then Post Office Savings Bank (now merged under the Development Bank of Singapore) competes directly for savings deposits with local banks which are mainly owned by ethnic Chinese – such as Oversea-Chinese Banking Corporation (OCBC), UOB, OUB and the former Tat Lee Bank (Tan 1996: 359–361).

Tan (1996), Lee and Low (1990) and Krause et. al (1987) all agreed that the 'crowding-out effect' felt by the SMEs was mostly in the labor market. The effect arose from the stiff competition for young talents among the civil service, GLCs, MNCs, as well as ethnic Chinese firms. The GLCs and the civil service, as part of their strategy to attract talents, offer attractive scholarships and subsequently bind the scholars to the public sector through six- to eight-year bonds. To retain good staff, the MNCs also offered their employees similarly attractive scholarships and good career prospects. In contrast, Chinese SMEs normally could not afford to offer their employees such benefits, nor did many people view employment in SMEs favorably. Only the big Chinese banks such as OCBC, OUB and UOB were able to compete with the GLCs and MNCs for scarce human resources. The Chinese SMEs thus had no alternative but to contend with poorer quality of human resource. Tan (1996: 165) also observed that Chinese SMEs suffered from considerable outward mobility of skilled manpower resource to the GLCs and MNCs with every round of wage increase.

Koh (1987), however, viewed the 'crowding-out effect' by MNCs and GLCs not as a threat to the mostly Chinese-owned SMEs, but as an inducement to the latter to upgrade, move into areas where they have a greater comparative advantage, and to invest abroad. Also, the MNCs can serve as a medium through which technology transfer can be secured and are thus a training ground for future entrepreneurs. Toh and Low (1993), in a study undertaken later, argued many new SMEs were established by former employees of MNCs, who were better educated and were trained to develop further the technological skills they had acquired.

Guanxi, Corruption and Crony Capitalism

Guanxi has been used liberally in the literature as an analytical concept to refer to interpersonal connections for social and economic exchanges with undefined social obligations. There are basically two types of *guanxi*. The first type is horizontal and equalitarian in terms of its relationship structure. It entails social obligations based on social values such as trust, dependability, reciprocity and preservation of 'face'. The second type evolves out of social relationships between businessmen and government officials while both parties engage in exchanges of rights and privileges for own gains. Redding (1990) asserted that such vertical networks originally emerged in Chinese agrarian society as a strategy for peasants to deal with the insecurity arising from their encounter with state officials whose behavior was authoritarian and often unpredictable. As China entered into a modern age in the early part of the 20th century, such relations had been transformed somewhat but with its social aspects such as patronage and, sometimes, 'protection' to facilitate the procuring of business opportunities. This was still necessary as formal institutions of law and bureaucracy were still not well developed, and *guanxi* remained instrumental in exploiting economic rents, sourcing business opportunities, and dealing with failures to fulfil contractual obligations. The power relations of this type of *guanxi* are vertical and asymmetric in nature. Both the journalistic and the scholarly literature fail to differentiate the two types of *guanxi*. The distinction is important in that the first type of relations often cuts down transaction costs and increases informational efficiency and business opportunities while the second results in cronyism, corruption and nepotism in Southeast Asian countries except Singapore.

The web of the first type of relations among ethnic Chinese outside mainland China has been popularly termed 'overseas Chinese network' or 'bamboo network' (Tanzer 1994: 139; Weidenbaum and Hughes 1996) in both the scholarly and journalistic literature. This same literature often cites such web of relationships, as well as its cultural components such as trust, dependability, and reciprocity, as factors to explain the rapid development of ethnic Chinese business in Southeast Asia.

Ethnic business networks emerge and develop because of an asymmetric information problem (Akerlof 1970), which often entails considerable increase in transaction costs and loss of business opportunities. The business network serves as a conduit through which business information and connections are institutionalized to reduce transaction costs. Business networks increase informational efficiency, enabling mutually beneficial trade and exchange to be conducted. In the context of a Chinese business community outside mainland China, a network may exist in the form of *huiguan*, or a network of clan associations, based on family surnames, kinship, province, district, dialect, etc. Such networks also extend to alumni associations of local Chinese schools. During the colonial period of Southeast Asia, such associations acted as financial intermediaries through which Chinese business groups could borrow money, exchange business information, recruit workers and forge new *guanxi*. In such a network, there was an unwritten rule that if a businessman failed to comply with a contractual obligation or a verbal agreement, the entire business community would refrain from doing business with the guilty party because of his loss of *xingyong* or trustworthiness. Such sanctions could be very severe, as the trust violator might have to close shop.

In Singapore, the development of immigrant entrepreneurship in the first half of the 20th century was attributed to, among other factors, *guanxi* and *xingyong* (Chan and Chiang 1994). During this period of limited legislation and regulation of business activities, clan associations such as the Hokkien Huay Kuan, or the Hokkien Association, functioned as para-legal institutions regulating the business conduct of a 'moral community'. Of particular significance was the founding of the Singapore Chinese Chamber of Commerce and Industry (SCCCI) in 1906. Through such social networks, Chinese merchants, compradors and middlemen conducted their business transactions. Cultural factors embedded in the networks also acted as an anchor for self-discipline, for example, to guard against the ruin of a businessman's reputation (Chan and Chiang 1994). In those days, *guanxi* were not merely business connections. Cheng (1995) wrote that in the 19th and early 20th centuries, new Chinese immigrants, or *sinkhek*, sought and secured an assortment of assistance through contacts with such networks in Singapore.

In the 1960s and 1970s, these Chinese associations constituted a potent political force and were vocal about government policies on Chinese education and culture. To reduce the influence of such associations, the government set up an extensive network of community centres – and established the People's Association to serve as a substitute for the clan associations. With the creation of an ever-increasing English-speaking class through education, the influence of these Chinese associations began to decline. However, during the 1980s, when the government began to promote its 'Asianising Singapore' programme (Vasil 1995), these Chinese associations were encouraged to revive their activities, though with a difference. To form an association, a clear demarcation between business and politics, and between cultural activities and politics, had to be drawn. In this context, the Singapore Federation of Chinese Clan Associations (SFCCA) was formed in 1986 to focus on cultural activities, leaving SCCCI to concentrate on business and economic matters. Consequently, these traditional associations are now less of a Chinese business network. Entering into the new millennium and with the emergence of the computer and telecommunication technology in the 1990s, these associations, with a continuously declining membership, are quickly facing the threat of redundancy and irrelevance.

To this date, the older generation of businessmen, especially those who run SMEs, still appear to use – albeit to a lesser degree – family ties, *guanxi* and *xingyong* to conduct their businesses (Yao 1987; Menkhoff 1993). However, the use of *guanxi* and *xingyong* by ethnic Chinese to develop business relations has its limit in a modern, sophisticated business environment. Once the conditions for exploiting ethnic resources and cultural practices through *guanxi* and *xingyong* disappear, the Chinese business enterprises no longer enjoy a comparative advantage in obtaining information and developing business relations for business expansion. In fact, in Singapore, such conditions are fast disappearing with a firmly entrenched legal system. Together with a widespread of English education and growing western influence, Chinese clans and associations have failed to serve as useful networks for business transactions.

Even if one were to invoke business networks, *xingyong* and Confucian values to explain the growth of traditional Chinese business, there is still insufficient empirical evidence to test this hypothesis. Much of the literature using this cultural approach has not incorporated other important factors at work at the same time, such as the business environment, government policy, regional economic issues, macroeconomic stability, and so on. It is equally difficult to isolate the contribution of such cultural factors from that of structural factors – in quantitative terms. Even if one can do so, there is no certainty that these factors are peculiar to the ethnic Chinese (Dirlik 1997; Hodder 1996). As Hiscock (1997: 11–12) noted, *guanxi* are also practised among Japanese, Koreans and other Asian groups.

Another variant of *guanxi* involves exchange of rights and privileges for own gains between at least two parties. Typically, government officials enjoy considerable powers given to them by an authoritarian state. These same officials are also poorly paid by the state. On the other hand, the capitalists are generally well off. There thus exists an opportunity for mutually beneficial trade between the two parties – the exchange of power for money, and vice versa. When officials abuse their administrative or political powers for their own personal gains (including their families'), nepotism arises. When the officials and the capitalists join forces and the latter become cronies of the former, the resultant economic structure is one of crony capitalism. This type of relationship or *guanxi* often results in corrupt practices, nepotism, paternalism and cronyism. It thrives when the state is authoritarian, and the legal system as well as other institutions, especially those pertaining to prevention of corrupt practices and good corporate governance, are not well developed or poorly enforced. Under these circumstances, some ethnic Chinese entrepreneurs tend to perceive corruption as part of business cost (Yan 1997). To expand their enterprise, ethnic Chinese join forces with the ruling class and become their cronies so that they can circumscribe rules and regulations for their own gains. Backman (1999) cited several examples of such cronies (usually rich Chinese businessmen) in Indonesia and Thailand. Yet others try to evade or circumscribe government's affirmative action by colluding with the ruling elite (Ng 1998a; Ng 1998b).

Several authors (Yoshihara 1988; Backman 1999) have blamed ethnic Chinese businessmen for the rampant corruption and cronyism in Southeast Asian countries. Yoshihara (1988) noted that majority of ethnic Chinese entrepreneurs in Southeast Asia are "monopolists, rent seekers and speculators". Through their close connections with the ruling elite, they act as cronies. Their style of business also involves "high turnover and quick returns" (Clad 1989: 146–147). Backman (1999: 28) went as far as arguing that paternalism and reciprocity embedded in Confucianism incubate nepotism and corruption that seems to prevail in the ethnic Chinese business community. He argued that in Confucianism, reciprocity obliges a recipient of a favor to return his favor in the form of a 'gift', a bribe.

Whatever the accusation, the blame makes little sense in the Singapore context. Chan and Ng (1999) observed that the conditions for breeding nepotism and cronyism were fast disappearing in Singapore since 1960 when the PAP government built a legal system with more transparent corporate governance. As a consequence, tight rules and regulations, and their strict enforcement, have prevented a widespread of corrupt practices, misappropriation of funds, and evasion of taxes within the business community. Over the past four decades, the Singapore government has also institutionalized a number of safeguards against corruption among civil servants. Among them are transparency in rules and regulations, severe punishment including jail terms, and confiscation of accumulated wealth through illegal means. Moreover, any Singaporean involved in corruption overseas can be brought back to Singapore courts for legal prosecution. The most effective deterrents against corruption are high salaries and respected jobs in the civil service, which represent a high opportunity cost for government servants if they are found to be corrupt. In addition, all business transactions have to be formalized in Singapore to provide redress to aggrieved parties as well as to prevent corruption and evasion of taxes. Crony capitalism and corruption of a scale like Indonesia and Thailand do not exist in Singapore.

Emergence of Technopreneurs Amidst Weak Entrepreneurship

Tan (1996) emphasized the 'crowding-out effect' as a major factor that had weakened entrepreneurship in Singapore. Lee and Low (1990), however, attributed such weak entrepreneurship to a number of other factors. Among these factors are, first, better salary, benefits and career opportunities offered by MNCs and GLCs. Second, there are less credential barriers and 'blocked opportunities' for young graduates working in the MNCs and GLCs. Third is a 'kia-su'[7] mentality, that is a desire to avoid failure by not taking risks. Fourth, a generally negative attitude by government officials towards Chinese business-men, who are perceived as 'Chinamen,' who practice a non-progressive, traditional and nepotistic business style, maintaining two sets of accounts – one for themselves and the other for tax purposes. Lastly, through the scholarship bonding system and because of financial resources (such as the high CPF contribution rate), there has been a diversion of manpower towards the public sector.

The first two factors suggest high opportunity costs in becoming an entrepreneur in Singapore. The third factor reflects the intensity of risk-averse behavior among Singaporeans who are now more well off and affluent than before. The fourth factor is possibly a misperception on the part of English-educated civil servants who are less conversant with Chinese business culture. This reflects a culture gap between the civil servants and traditional ethnic Chinese businessmen who usually have low educational background or are graduates of Nanyang University where the medium of instruction is Chinese. The last factor is a typical 'crowding-out effect'.

Despite the unfavorable environment for entrepreneurship, a new breed of ethnic Chinese entrepreneurs has emerged since the 1980s (Chan and Ng 1999). Unlike their predecessors, these newcomers to the business world do not typically conduct their transactions within a traditional network embedded with *guanxi*, family ties and *xingyong*. More importantly, they are no ordinary entrepreneurs in the usual sense but are technopreneurs who use technological innovations and translate such technology into commercial products and services (Lee, Chan and Tang 1999).

Chew (1996) attributed the emergence of this new crop of entrepreneurs to five factors. First, there is greater competition among graduates for jobs. Second, there has been an appreciable increase in the number of graduates. Third, technological advancement in Singapore has reduced technical constraints encountered by business-men. Fourth, a conducive business environment for local private businessmen has began to emerge in Singapore; and, finally, the increased affluence of Singaporeans and the rapid economic develop-ment in the Southeast Asian region. These factors can be analysed in terms of, first, reduced opportunity cost of becoming an entrepreneur; second, increased reward potentials for entrepreneurs; and third, a culture bestowing high esteem and respect on entrepreneurs. The increase in the number of graduates and growing competition among them for jobs in the MNCs and GLCs serve as a 'blocked opportunity' of a different kind. This increase in graduate supply and competition for limited executive positions lowers opportunity costs and acts as a stimulant to becoming an entrepreneur. The third factor, the level of technological advancement in Singapore, has prepared new entrepreneurs for the high-technology and knowledge-based sector which has high reward potentials for those who have innovative ideas; this is especially so for those who have previously worked in MNCs. The fourth factor, a conducive business environ-ment, may not be in itself an important factor in cultivating entrepreneurship but it does serve to reduce uncertainty in business. It is, however, also true that the safety net or moral hazard[8] implicit in the conducive business environment of the domestic market may inhibit these entrepreneurs from going abroad. The last factors, especially that of increased affluence among Singaporeans, may encourage high rewards in business; however, the cultural obstacle, in the form of the 'kia-su' mentality, would need to be overcome first.

To encourage technopreneurship, the Singapore government signalled in April 1999 a strong support for high-techonolgy firms with an introduction of the Singapore's Technopreneurship 21 Concept Plan, which has four initiatives covering education, facilities, financing, and regulations. A Technopreneurship 21 Executive Committee was also set up in the same year to make recommendations to promote technopreneurship in Singapore. Following the recom-mendations of the executive committee, the government announced in July 1999 a number of specific policy changes which include higher tolerance for failure by increasing higher debt level for bankruptcy, and allowing earlier discharge for bankrupt. The government also allows investors' losses in start-up to be tax-deductible. To lower start-up costs, HDB flats and private estates are now allowed to be registered as home offices. In addition, foreigners who set up high-technology ventures in Singapore will be allowed to stay longer on social passes (*The Straits Times* 3/7/99).

One notable example of this new breed of technopreneurs in Singapore is Sim Wong Hoo who, without family lineage resources, founded Creative Technology Ltd in 1981 with two co-founders, Ng Kai Wa and Chay Kwong Soon (Tang 1996). Presently one of the ten largest private Chinese firms in Singapore, Creative Technology specializes in multimedia and computer products. Sim is also the Chairman of Private Sector Sub-Committee of the Technopreneurship 21 Executive Committee. He has twice received the Businessman of the Year in Singapore award, in 1992 and in 1998, and has quickly become the role model for the new breed of technopreneurs

Conclusion

An economic sociology must also be a historical sociology. We have chosen, in this essay, to take a long historical eyepiece in examining the role of ethnic Chinese business in Singapore, especially its relationship with the state in the course of time. During the colonial days, the middleman role played by Chinese businessmen – in between the Western agency houses and the indigenous communities in Southeast Asia – enabled their rise in the region's economies. This mediating role continued into the 1950s and 1960s, as Singapore's reputation as an international port involved entrepot trade between the West and the East. Their subsequent alienation by the PAP government diminished their importance in the then rapidly growing national economy. It was only in the mid-1980s, after a recession, that the Singapore government began to realize the need to support Chinese business as one of the necessary means to promote regionalization and globalization.

The issue of national identity of Singaporeans conjoins itself with the larger issues of loyalty of the 'overseas Chinese' to their 'motherland,' China, and of the prospect of resinification in view of the rising economic as well as political significance of China on the world stage. In spite of growing investments in China by Chinese Singaporean companies, there is little evidence that the underlying motive is emotive or ethnic/racial in nature. We have also noted in our essay that Chinese enterprises in Singapore, unlike their counterparts in Southeast Asia, are structurally weak when compared with MNCs and GLCs, due primarily to state policies. Other weaknesses of ethnic Chinese businesses include lagging behind in technological innova-tions as well as the many intrinsic limits to growth of family firms, according to which the bulk of Chinese businesses in Singapore are organized. Although cultural factors have been identified in much of the literature on Chinese businesses to account for their growth – networks, *xingyong* and the ability of ethnic Chinese to bypass bureaucratic red-tape through intra-ethnic co-operation – in Singapore, however, such cultural factors are quickly disappearing. The Singapore case thus throws up a lot of research opportunities to deconstruct the many myths and generalizations about the so-called 'Chinese business conduct'. Not all Chinese businesses are successful. Not all successful businesses are Chinese. That the ethnic Chinese dominate the Southeast Asian economies is perhaps exaggerated (Mackie 1999). In Singapore, most Chinese operate SMEs, often as family firms – until recently, they remain unprotected by state policies, a condition labelled as the 'crowding out effect'. Though a majority group, the Chinese in Singapore, ironically, like other Chinese minorities in the Southeast Asian region, must also contend with the political and economic policies of the state. In that sense, a comprehensive economic sociology must incorporate the state and politics in its analysis. An economic sociology must also be a political sociology.

There are a number of methodological problems in much of the scholarly literature on Chinese business in Singapore. One common problem, which often leads to erroneous conclusions, is that no effort has been made to distinguish between the many Chinese SMEs and the few large Chinese business conglomerates. To illustrate, when the research is on limits to growth of Chinese business, small and medium enterprises are used as examples; however, when the research is about business networks, typically, Chinese conglomerates are examined. Most of the literature has also tended to ignore the heterogeneous character of ethnic Chinese and their businesses in Southeast Asia – the Chinese variety or differential Chineseness thesis we have put forward in greater detail elsewhere (Chan and Ng 1999; Chan and Tong 1995). Even within the Chinese business group in a particular country, Singapore being a case in point, one observes vast variations in terms of outlook, management style and product focus.

Several research themes and directions can be identified for future study. While the tendency has been to emphasise solidarity and cooperation among the ethnic Chinese, the study of conflicts and disharmony has been neglected. Conflicts and tensions such as family feuds, rivalries between family and non-family members, forcing out minority partners, intra-family competition for authority, nepotistic retention of key positions for family members, succession problems, fragmentation of business, hostile takeovers, and so on, have not been well researched. This is partly due to difficulties in obtaining information on these aspects as Chinese are generally disinclined to reveal the internal workings of the family in public. The privacy, or if you like, secrecy, of Chinese family business can be understood (but not easily overcome) at several levels. First, culturally, Chinese are prone to maintain and defend, when necessary, a private/public divide. Second, sociologically speaking, the family is a total institution off limits to its outsiders. Third, business enterprise is an organization, like many other organizations, sociologically intent on safeguarding its autonomy and maintaining its outer boundaries. Both family and business have their own secrets, a lot more so for family businesses. Researchers in the field of ethnic Chinese business may want to heed the methodological advice of criminologists who have long realized the private and secretive character of crimes. In a profound sense, both business and crime are stubbornly resisting the gaze of the analyst.

Another possible research area is in the study of joint-ventures between different ethnic groups. The logic and rationality of commerce necessarily obliges the Chinese to do business with the non-Chinese, in spite of the many myths surrounding the popular 'bamboo network' idea. Indeed, there has been growing evidence of inter-ethnic business ventures; attempts by Chinese SMEs to enter into joint-ventures with MNCs seem to continue to play an important role in the development of technology transfer and access to markets abroad. The future sociological gaze must then not be on how the Chinese businessmen work between and among 'their own kind' – itself a myth – but on how they negotiate and work with the non-Chinese (Liu 1999). The analytical focus must no longer be internal, but external.

Our last observation has to do with a return to the alleged uniqueness and, by extension, 'internal' sameness of the Chinese, as set apart from the non-Chinese, and their business conduct – a sort of Chinese exceptionalism and essentialism as a result of considerable myth-making. Our vexation with the literature on Chinese capitalism is: why are the Chinese often drawn so sharply from others? Does it have anything to do with the Chinese being seen as racial types or categories, not as persons or individuals? To the outsiders, the Chinese and their social conduct appear more similar than they actually are: a social psychology of inter-group perceptions when racial sameness and differentness are artificial and subject to social construction. The appropriate cure for such distorted perceptions is good comparative ethnographies, constantly juxtaposing and contrasting Chinese and non-Chinese business enterprises. The sociologist is well advised to wear their comparative lenses.

2

Malaysia

———◆◆◆———

Edmund Terence Gomez, Loh Wei Leng
and Lee Kam Hing

Chinese Business in Malaysia

In 1998, ethnic Chinese constituted about 28 per cent of Malaysia's almost 20 million multi-ethnic population. Indigenous *Bumiputera* (or 'sons of the soil'), particularly the Malays, account for 61 per cent of the population, Indians 8 per cent, and other minor ethnic groups the remaining one per cent. In 1995, ethnic Chinese owned approximately 40.9 per cent of the total share capital of Malaysian companies, down from 45.5 per cent in 1990 (see Table 2.1). In spite of this fall of almost 5 percentage points in terms of their share of corporate equity between 1990 and 1995, the Chinese still own the largest amount of corporate assets among the major ethnic communities in Malaysia, almost double the volume of equity held by Bumiputeras and state institutions which totalled 20.6 per cent in 1995.

In an independent study of corporate ownership patterns undertaken in 1991, it was estimated that ethnic Chinese owned 50 per cent equity of the construction sector, 82 per cent of wholesale trade, 58 per cent of retail trade and about 40 per cent of the manufacturing sector; apart from this, almost 70 per cent of small scale enterprises were Chinese-owned (see *Malaysian Business* 16/1/91). These figures, which provide an indication of the enormous presence of Chinese capital in the Malaysian economy, take on added significance when it is noted that Chinese enterprises have had to operate in a political environment that has not been conducive to its growth since the colonial period.

Under British colonial rule, which commenced in 1786, mass migration of Chinese into the country had been encouraged from the

Table 2.1 Malaysia: Ownership of Share Capital (At Par Value) of Limited
Companies, 1970, 1990, 1995 (percentages)

Ownership Group	1970	1990	1995
Bumiputera	2.4	19.3	20.6
Bumiputera Individuals & Institutions	1.6	14.2	18.6
Trust Agencies	0.8	5.1	2.0
Non-Bumiputera	28.3	46.8	43.4
Chinese	27.2	45.5	40.9
Indians	1.1	1.0	1.5
Others		0.3	1.0
Nominee Companies	6.0	8.5	8.3
Foreigners	63.4	25.4	27.7

Sources: Third Malaysia Plan 1976–80; Seventh Malaysia Plan 1996–2000

second half of the 19th century, primarily to feed labor for the tin
mining industry. The Chinese had, however, established trade links
with local communities in major ports in the Malay archipelago since
at least the 15th century. Chinese traders had also settled around the
Malayan peninsula, particularly in the port cities of Malacca,
Singapore and Penang, inter-marrying with the local community.
Their descendants, the 'Peranakan Chinese' or 'Babas,' adopted local
language and customs, emerging eventually as a distinct, but small,
community in the country.[1] Apart from the Chinese, other Asian
communities had also established major trading networks in the
region, long before the arrival of European traders. These Asian-based
trading networks included those operated by the Arabs, Indians,
Javanese and Bugis.

The intrusion by European traders into regional trade networks did
not initially disrupt the activities of the major Asian trading
communities, who retained their autonomy and distinctiveness.
Indeed, some of these Asian trading communities benefited from the
enhanced business environment created by European traders. However, as the countries in Southeast Asia, with the exception of
Thailand, came under colonial rule, by the Portugese, Dutch,
Spaniards, British and Americans, this had an enormous impact on
the development of these Asian trading networks.

In the Malay peninsula, the Portugese conquered Malacca in 1511.
In 1641, the Dutch took control of Malacca. The British first
established themselves in Penang in 1786 and then Malacca in 1795.

Among these western colonizers, it was the British who managed to consolidate territorial expansion in the Malay peninsula, particularly after 1874 when they secured control of the tin-rich state of Perak. Through the establishment of elaborate legal and administration systems in Malaya, the British supported the development of Western enterprises that came to dominate the tin mining and rubber plantation sectors. Malaya eventually became the major world producer of rubber and tin, emerging also as one of Britain's most profitable colony.

It was, however, the Chinese who had dominated the tin industry in the Malay peninsula before the British eventually secured control over this sector. The Chinese had managed to maintain control over the tin mining sector as they were able to mobilize labor from China to work the mines, until the British introduced more sophisticated mining techniques that were less labor intensive. Nevertheless, potential economic opportunities, in terms of jobs, petty trade and small-scale business, continued to attract migrants from China. A number of Chinese migrated to Penang and Singapore as these two cities emerged as major trading centres, while increased tin mining in the western states of the peninsula augmented demand for labor. Most of these Chinese migrants were from southern China, and comprised members of various dialect groups, particularly the Hokkiens, Cantonese, Hakkas, Hainanese and Teochew.[2] In this new and unfamiliar environment, common dialect and district background bonded members of the Chinese immigrant community.

In some areas of the economy, Chinese migrants managed to create an important and exclusive niche for themselves. For example, colonial reliance on revenue farms created opportunities for capital accumulation by the Chinese.[3] The revenue farm was a monopoly, leased out by the ruler of a state, and later the colonial government, to Chinese middlemen. The 'farm' pertained to an area of business or involved the collection of taxes for a particular activity. Such activities included monopoly rights over the sale of goods, the most important of which was opium, or the collection of taxes, duties or levies on services such as gambling and trade. Revenue farming brought Chinese from different parts of Southeast Asia into joint economic activities. They ventured into tin mining, rubber production and subsequently banking. Among the most prominent Chinese capitalists who emerged from revenue farming were the Khaw family, who ran such activities in Malaya and Thailand (see Cushman 1991).

During the late 19th century to the early 20th century, even though the revenue farming system was phased out, there was significant expansion of Chinese capital. Almost within one generation, a number of businessmen developed large business enterprises, most of which were involved in a diverse range of activities. Among the most prominent Chinese businessmen who emerged during this period were Eu Tong Sen, Lau Pak Kuan, Chung Thye Phin, Loke Yew and Tan Kah Kee and his son-in-law Lee Kong Chian.[4]

Some of these businessmen showed a capacity to develop the technological base of their enterprise. One important technological adjustment made by the Chinese in the 1880s in the trading and shipping sector was the replacement of the old junks with modern steamships. This led to the incorporation of some major Chinese shipping companies in the major ports of Southeast Asia.

The modernization of the shipping industry in the Malay peninsula supported an expanding Chinese commercial role in Southeast Asia. Modern shipping facilitated intra-regional trade conducted by local Chinese and transported commodities like rice, sugar, rubber and tin around the major ports such as Singapore, Saigon, Surabaya, Batavia, Bangkok, Manila and Rangoon. Members of these trading groups then moved into financial services, such as insurance and banking, primarily as a means to secure easier access to funds to expand their business. The expansion of Chinese capital was also possible in this period because of their association with non-Chinese enterprises, particularly Western companies and the Indian chettiar financial network (see Brown 1994; Dobbin 1996). Chinese business links with Western companies and individuals provided the former with access to new technological advances in the steamship, rubber plantation and tin mining sectors. Such access to technology was also facilitated by Chinese employment experience in Western firms, recruitment of European managers by Chinese companies and acquisition by Chinese of equity in Western firms, an avenue through which they also gained experience in the insurance and banking sectors. Most Chinese businessmen, however, relied heavily on the Indian chettiars for financing, until they began establishing their own banks.

During the British colonial period, Chinese capital, whether large- or small-scale enterprises, was predominantly family-controlled. This was one reason why, as colonial rule was coming to an end after World War II, the leading Chinese capitalists cooperated in forming a new institution, the political party, Malayan Chinese Association (MCA), to protect their economic interests in the post-colonial period.[5] The MCA forged a coalition with the United Malays' National Organization (UMNO) to form the Alliance, ostensibly as a means to promote inter-ethnic cooperation. This Alliance was, however, mutually beneficial as UMNO had wide grassroots base that was crucial in enabling the MCA to secure seats for itself in a federal election, while UMNO relied heavily on the cash-rich MCA to fund the coalition's electoral campaigns. Another ethnically-based party, the Malayan Indian Congress (MIC), also joined the Alliance in 1955. In the first federal election held in 1955, the Alliance secured a major electoral victory, and when the first post-colonial government was formed, ethnic Chinese had control over cabinet portfolios dealing with Finance and Trade & Industry. The MCA's control over these ministries helped ensure that Chinese capital interests were protected, while some Chinese businessmen also had access to government economic concessions to further develop their corporate base. However, the Malayan government, under Malay hegemony, ensured that foreign capital continued to dominate the major economic sectors in the country in the post-Independence period, mainly as a means to check Chinese ascendancy in the economy.

During the general election held in 1969, the Alliance barely secured a majority in parliament, while the opposition also wrested control of two state governments. In order to strengthen its position in the federal government, in 1973, UMNO expanded this tripartite Alliance by incorporating the leading opposition parties into an even larger multi-party coalition, the *Barisan Nasional* (National Front). The induction of additional Chinese-based parties in the Barisan Nasional reduced the MCA's influence in government. With its position in government weakened considerably, the MCA eventually lost control of the Finance and Trade & Industry ministries, and has since held only relatively minor cabinet portfolios.

The May 1969 general election results were also significant as it led to the end of an era of a relatively *laissez-faire* economic system, favored by Chinese enterprises. This change to the economic system was justified as a response to the factors that contributed to the race riots that erupted soon after this general election. Since the racial turmoil was partly ascribed to the inequitable distribution of wealth among the Malays and the Chinese, the government introduced the New Economic Policy (NEP) in 1970, an ambitious twenty-year social engineering plan to achieve national unity. The NEP aspired to achieve this goal by 'eradicating poverty,' irrespective of race, and by 'restructuring society' so as to achieve inter-ethnic economic parity between the predominantly Malay Bumiputeras and the Chinese. The NEP's second objective, the restructuring of society, was evidently the main emphasis of the policy. In 1969, the Bumiputera share of corporate wealth (by individuals and government trust agencies) amounted to a meager 2.4 per cent. Chinese equity ownership stood at 27.2 per cent, while a bulk of the remaining equity was under foreign ownership (see Table 2.1). One major goal of the NEP was to increase Bumiputera corporate equity ownership to 30 per cent by 1990.

The NEP entailed greater state intervention in the economy, primarily for ethnic affirmative action, including the accelerated expansion of the Bumiputera middle class, capital accumulation on behalf of the Bumiputeras, and the creation of Bumiputera capitalists. To fulfill the NEP objectives, the government increased public sector expenditure, particularly to fund the growing number of government-owned enterprises participating in business activities. In contrast to the ten public enterprises in 1957, there were 841 by 1986.

Controversial legislation, such as the Industrial Coordination Act (ICA), were introduced to ensure effective implementation of the NEP. The ICA, promulgated in 1975 to help implement the government's industrialization policies by ensuring the orderly development of manufacturing, alarmed Chinese investors who perceived it as an attempt to advance Malay interests in this sector. The ICA gave the government increased authority over the establishment and growth of manufacturing enterprises, and provided the bureaucracy with the means to ensure that development of the manufacturing sector would be in line with the ethnic redistributive objectives of the NEP. Following the introduction of the ICA, there was a marked slump in foreign and domestic investments in almost all key sectors of the economy.

The Chinese tried unsuccessfully to protect their economic niches by getting public enterprises to concentrate their acquisition of equity in business sectors controlled by foreigners. There were also repeated appeals by the Chinese to the government for the ICA to be revised. Chinese concerns over new government legislation, which increased state controls over the private sector, and of growing corporate equity ownership by public agencies, resulted in their support of the MCA's call for Chinese companies to overlook narrow clan divisions and participate in a 'corporatization movement'.

The corporatization movement involved structural reforms to Chinese businesses, to allow them to cope with the implications of growing state intervention in the economy. The most significant of these reforms entailed increased cooperation between small-scale and family-based Chinese businesses and a revamp of their management techniques (see Yeoh 1987). When the MCA incorporated a major holding company, Multi-Purpose Holdings Bhd (MPHB), to pool Chinese resources, ostensibly to venture into business to protect and advance Chinese capitalism, the party project was, initially, a phenomenal success. Through MPHB, the MCA obtained for the first time the support of working class Chinese who were convinced that the party had found a means to help the community maintain a strong presence in the Malaysian economy (see Gale 1985; Yeoh 1987; Gomez 1994: 175–239).

In the mid-1980s, however, leading Chinese politicians, including the MCA president Tan Koon Swan, who had led MPHB (and other entities developed under the auspices of the corporatization movement), were convicted for criminal breach of trust, involving the abuse of the company's funds. The scandal brought MPHB precipitously close to bankruptcy and contributed to the failure of the corporatization movement. With the MCA racked by scandal and loss of support, the new party president, Ling Liong Sik, promised to stop mixing politics with business.

Exacerbating the plight of Chinese capital during the 1980s was growing concentration of power in the hands of the UMNO-dominated executive, particularly after 1981 when Mahathir Mohamad was appointed Prime Minister. Under Mahathir, important political and economic developments have occurred in Malaysia, which have had a bearing on the expansion of Chinese capital. For example, the Prime Minister's desire to achieve 'fully developed nation' status for Malaysia by 2020 has had a significant bearing on the form of concession distribution by the government and the development of ethnically-based capital in the country. UMNO's control over the bureaucracy helped advance the development of a 'new rich,' i.e. politically well-connected businessmen who had managed to gain control and ownership of a significant amount of corporate stock (see Gomez and Jomo 1999: 117–65). The promotion of this 'new rich,' justified by government leaders as one of the goals sanctioned by the NEP, is attributable primarily to the Prime Minister's desire to help create a new class of internationally recognized Bumiputera capitalists.

Consequently, one major outcome of the NEP has been the emergence of businessmen linked to senior UMNO leaders who have come to own a substantial portion of local corporate stock through political patronage. Wealth concentration, in turn, helped centralize power in the hands of the executive and diminished further the influence of the MCA among Chinese businessmen. By the late 1980s, most prominent Chinese businessmen were beginning to directly fund prominent Malay politicians in order to benefit from state patronage. From the early 1990s, even the most established Chinese businessmen who had previously been independent of Malay patronage were beginning to cultivate influential Malay politicians or incorporated well-connected businessmen in joint business activities. By the early 1990s, even medium-scale Chinese companies were starting to appoint influential Bumiputeras as directors of their enterprises (see Hara 1991; Heng 1992; Gomez 1999). This encouraged greater inter-ethnic business cooperation, particularly between those Chinese capable of implementing the contract and those Malays who have benefited from state patronage.

While owners of major Chinese enterprises are establishing inter-ethnic ties in a quest for Malay patronage, it appears that small-sized Chinese companies probably still adhere to the notion of intra-ethnic business cooperation as a means to counter the growing influence of well-connected Malays over the corporate sector. There is, however, little evidence of significant mobilization of intra-ethnic resources for mutual economic benefit among Chinese-owned small-scale enterprises. This is the case even though thousands of small- and medium-scale Chinese enterprises (SMEs) that comprise the largest segment of domestically-owned businesses have, for the most part, been excluded by ethnic preferences from enjoying the benefits that accrue from such political patronage. These Chinese SMEs have, for example, shared only to a limited extent the benefits of government incentives, like those provided under its export-oriented industrialization drive in the 1970s. The attempts by Chinese SME owners to establish partnerships with foreign manufacturers have not been very successful as the latter prefer Malay partners to secure investment approvals and access to a sympathetic regulatory ear in high places.

This suggests that with growing Malay dominance over politics and business, intra-ethnic business networking is now seen as the most viable option open to Chinese businessmen to ensure the expansion of their corporate base. Chinese entrepreneurs appear to have decided that in order to develop their enterprise, it is important also to establish inter-ethnic business ties, preferably with well-connected Bumiputera businessmen. This seems necessary as Chinese-based socio-economic and political institutions no longer serve as important avenues for protecting and developing the corporate base of Chinese businessmen. Some analysts, like Heng Pek Koon (1992), argue that leading Chinese business groups appear to have chosen a two-pronged strategy in developing their enterprise: working closely with Bumiputera political patrons to achieve business success in Malaysia, while at the same time building relations with non-Malaysian capital, preferably other so-called 'Overseas Chinese' capital, that can serve as a potential source of wealth.

On the other hand, the UMNO-dominated government has found it necessary to accommodate Chinese capital. Following a severe recession in the mid-1980s, the government recognized the importance of Chinese – and foreign – capital for sustaining growth and promoting industrialization. The recession also highlighted the need for the government to check the activities of rentier capitalists. From the early 1990s, the Prime Minister saw the opening up of China's economy as offering potentially lucrative business ventures for Malaysian capital. This appears to have encouraged Mahathir's call for greater business cooperation between Chinese and Malays.

The Prime Minister also believes that there is a need to encourage greater inter-ethnic business cooperation if he is to achieve his developmentalist goals for Malaysia. In view of this, the executive seems to have become somewhat more restrained in continuing to blatantly favor the Malay business elite. Mahathir also indicated that he would no longer tolerate rentiers who wasted the concessions they secured from the government. For Mahathir, the dynamic, entrepreneurial Bumiputera class he wished to create had to develop the capacity to compete and perform in an international business environment. Thus, Mahathir argued that those who productively and profitably utilized concessions received from the government would stand to benefit from more state patronage. Mahathir also used this reason to legitimize the award of government concessions to favorite non-Malay businessmen, in spite of some protests from within his own party, UMNO. Among those Chinese businessmen who have developed their companies with concessions from the state include YTL Corporation Bhd (controlled by the Yeoh family), Ekran Bhd (controlled by Ting Pik Khiing) and the Berjaya Group Bhd (controlled by Vincent Tan Chee Yioun).[6] This was one reason a new breed of Chinese businessmen emerged as major corporate players during the NEP period, which came to an end in 1990.

In 1991, the Barisan Nasional government outlined its long-term goals for Malaysia through its Vision 2020 statement and the National Development Policy (NDP). The government's primary objective was for Malaysia to achieve 'fully developed country' status by the year 2020, mainly by accelerating industrialization, growth and modernization. In view of Vision 2020's explicit commitment to forging a Malaysian nation that transcends existing ethnic identities and loyalties and its emphasis on the private sector, rather than the public sector, to encourage growth, there had been some enthusiasm, especially on the part of non-Bumiputeras, for the policy's goals. This was one factor that helped the Barisan Nasional secure significant support from the Chinese after 1990; this was reflected in the impressive Barisan Nasional victory in the 1995 general election (see Gomez 1996).

Foreign investors, however, were still courted as their investments, especially in export-oriented manufacturing, continued to be the most productive in the local economy. Although domestic manufacturing was still dominated by Chinese capital, local enterprise was not as dynamic as foreign firms, partly due to limited government support. This was another indication that government policies had hindered the potential growth of productive local enterprise. To encourage Chinese capital, various reforms, including easier access to listing on the stock exchange and greater official encouragement of small- and medium-sized industries were introduced.

The limited dynamism among local manufacturing enterprises, the inadequate attention to research and development, and the repercussions of creating huge conglomerates primarily through acquisitions financed by bank loans were some of the important lessons learnt from the 1997 financial crisis. One outcome of the financial crisis was that there was growing awareness of the need to re-assess the pattern of growth of companies, with the government also acknowledging the importance of providing greater support for SMEs, in spite of their dominance by ethnic Chinese (see *The Star* 14/4/99).

As the financial crisis deepened, the government hinted that ethnic Chinese would be allowed to take over companies owned by Malays to prevent the latter from going bankrupt. Most of the Chinese identified as possible candidates for the takeover of Malay-owned companies were those who had benefited from state patronage.[7] Since the Chinese businessmen called in to save near-bankrupt Malay businessmen have also benefited from government patronage, they may not be allowed to hold on to these corporate assets in the long term. Finance Minister Daim Zainuddin touched on this when he said: "I'd allow them [the Chinese] to rescue ailing companies. After they recover, they can talk about ownership" (quoted in *Far Eastern Economic Review* 19/2/98). This selective use of Chinese businessmen to help bailout some well-connected Malay businessmen reflects Chinese capital's subordination to Malay political patronage.

Research Themes and Literature Review

This brief historical profile of Chinese business in Malaysia highlights a number of important research themes. First, Chinese migration and the early development of their enterprises. Second, the structure and organization of Chinese businesses, in particular the role of the family, lineage, kinship and community. Third, the differences in the form of accumulation and development of Chinese enterprise, especially between large-scale enterprises and SMEs. Fourth, the impact of government policies on Chinese enterprises. Fifth, the importance of ethnic Chinese networks, the forms they took, and how such networks have evolved with time. Sixth, the relationship between Chinese enterprises and the state, politicians in power or well-connected businessmen. Seventh, the impact of growing inter-ethnic business ties on strengthening or eroding ethnic differences. Eighth, the relationship between Chinese capital and foreign companies in the colonial period and in recent decades. Ninth, the form and impact of regional and international intra-ethnic business networking on the development of Malaysian Chinese capital. Finally, the impact of growing calls by government leaders in East and Southeast Asia for increased networking among Chinese businessmen on Malaysian Chinese enterprise.

Despite this abundance of themes that require research, a review of the literature on Chinese business in Malaysia would indicate a dearth of in-depth study on the subject. Some of these themes have, however, been discussed in a number of essays, notably by historian Wang Gungwu in his sixteen-essay volume, *China and the Chinese Overseas*. This collection of essays is especially insightful on the themes of migration and the trading and entrepreneurial skills of the Chinese. With regard to migration, Wang stresses the value of a historical perspective because, he argues, "Chinese migration has meant different things at different periods and to different peoples" (Wang 1991: 3). More importantly, the outlook of Chinese business-men during specific periods would depend on their general orientation towards their society – as a merchant, having no intention of permanently settling in the country where the trade is being conducted; as a laborer or sojourner (relevant especially during the periods 1850–1920 and 1900–1950s respectively) only temporarily in the country to earn a living and to make a fortune before returning to the homeland; or as a person of Chinese descent who has opted for citizenship in the adopted country.

In other words, Wang suggests that we can only begin to understand the modus operandus of a particular businessman if we view his business operations within the broader context of his world-view and sense of identity. If viewed from the perspective of the authorities in the receiving countries, whether native or colonial, Wang finds that throughout history, both native rulers and Western colonial governments in Southeast Asia welcomed the *huasheng* (trader/merchant) and found the reason for their presence in the country quite acceptable. What was unacceptable for most governments was the *huaqiao* (sojourner) mentality, certainly the aggressively nationalistic and revolutionary features of it.[8] The entrepreneurial, hardworking and law-abiding Chinese, who had previously been valued and admired, were often quickly transformed in the eyes of these foreign and colonial governments into chauvinists who might be agents of the Chinese government (Wang 1991: 17). From this point of view, local policy response to Chinese migrants was predictable; depending on the type of migrants and their behavior, relations between ethnic Chinese and power holders were either conflictual or close and mutually beneficial.

On the second main theme in Wang's articles, the business skills of the Chinese, the essay 'The Culture of Chinese Merchants,' specifically the sub-section, 'The Chinese Merchant Outside China,' which draws on the literature by western scholars on the competitors of Chinese merchants in key trading ports in Asia, provides some useful insights for further research. For Wang, Chinese merchants "emerge as ingenious and adventurous traders who had remarkable flair for profit-seeking and risk-taking under conditions that were often dangerous if not actually hostile" (Wang 1991: 189). In 'Merchants Without Empires: The Hokkien Sojourning Communities,' which examined two cases of merchant communities, in Manila from the 1570s and Nagasaki after 1600, a comparison of their experiences with that of European merchants revealed the main difference between the two groups – official backing from their governments. The Hokkiens who formed the majority of the overseas traders between the 13th and 18th centuries enjoyed official support until 1368, which accounted for their success in trading. After that, however, the Hokkiens were so hard-pressed to compete with the Portuguese, that eventually they had to be content with becoming merely participants, "even supporting agents, in the merchant empires that their counterparts from smaller states with state-backed organizations were able to build" (Wang 1991: 97–99).

The picture we can delineate from these essays is the ability of Chinese merchants to adapt, and to adapt well in difficult conditions abroad. This theme, adaptability, has also been developed by Edgar Wickberg (1994: 68–84) who states that "[a]daptation . . . is not just what an immigrant does; it is an ongoing process for residents past the immigrant stage." In this adaptation process, Wickberg identified how Chinese sojourners formed organizations and established connections that helped them to adapt in a foreign environment; the role and importance of these organizations differed as Chinese communities adjusted to their new environment. This theme of adaptation is developed further in Wang's essay 'Political Chinese: Their Contributions to Modern Southeast Asian History'. Wang's main point here is that political connections facilitate business endeavors, a theme well developed in much of the literature on Chinese business in Malaysia (see, for example, Yoshihara 1988; Heng 1992; Gomez 1999). The analytical framework presented in this essay presents us with an opportunity to explore how the political orientations of major Chinese groups (identified by their political interests and activities) influenced business strategies and decision-making in different political conditions at different periods in history.

In the essay, 'Little Dragons on the Confucian Periphery,' Wang discusses another theme that has become common in contemporary literature on Chinese business, i.e. the impact of Confucianism in determining business behavior (see, for example, Redding 1991; Fukuyama 1995). Wang (1991: 271) argues that Confucian values had not been a factor that influenced decision-making in business. In spite of the growing volume of literature stressing on the importance of the Confucian ethic in determining Chinese business behavior, this is one hypothesis that has yet to be tested with detailed empirical research.

Another area of research on Chinese business that has been covered in some depth is that of the corporate ventures of Tan Kah Kee, probably the most prominent Chinese businessman who emerged during the early 20th century. The most authoritative historical account on Tan Kah Kee (1874–1961) is provided by C.F. Yong, in his volume *Tan Kah Kee: The Making of an Overseas Chinese Legend*. The historical approach used by Yong is interesting because it helps to contextualize the development of Tan's business within the political economic situation in both Malaya and China.

Yong's business biography of Tan Kah Kee is an excellent example of a sound research methodology incorporating exhaustive use of available source material, from official documents, contemporary newspapers, interviews with Tan's acquaintances, as well as his memoirs; this has enabled Yong to present a comprehensive study of Tan's life and business ventures. Placing Tan's life in the context of historical developments in China and Southeast Asia, we are better able to understand the rise and fall of Tan's economic fortunes, how his social standing was achieved and the extent and impact of his political contributions. Venturing out in business on his own in 1904, after the collapse of his father's firm, Tan first endeavor was in pineapple production and canning, before diversifying into rubber planting and rice milling. Tan's entry into the rubber plantation sector was timely as he was able to reap huge profits during the rubber boom of 1910. Subsequently, where others faltered, Tan availed himself of the opportunities arising during World War I, moving into shipping (in the days of great shipping shortages) and converting one of his pineapple mills into a rubber mill which helped him make a huge profit. Although the war had badly affected his distribution of pineapples in the European market, demand for rubber increased appreciably during this period.

By investigating all facets of Tan's life, from his business involvement to his role in the Chinese community and larger society, Yong helps us to see the connections between wealth and social status. For instance, by putting his wealth to good use, through his educational, charitable, social and political endeavors, Tan was able to build up by the 1920s an important social position in the Chinese community. As a consequence of British recognition of Tan's socio-economic standing, his application for naturalization as a British subject was approved, paving the way for him to become the owner of two ships, during a period when only British subjects could be shipowners.

Half of Yong's research on Tan explores the links between politics and business, a key theme in contemporary Chinese business research (see Gale 1985; Yeoh 1987; Heng 1992; Gomez 1994). Yong's study on Tan presents us with an opportunity to assess the form and outcome of the relationship of one prominent Chinese businessman with the colonial authorities.

In addition, the theme of the links between immigrants and their country of origin at different historical periods recurs in the Yong's biography of Tan. Tan is a prime example of the sojourner pattern of migration, common especially in the first half of the 20th century. By the 1950s, however, as Yong (1987: 355) points out, "the majority of the Chinese in Southeast Asia had chosen the region as their first homeland." The Tan Kah Kee model reflects the attitude of migrants of his time, whose contributions to their homeland and adopted country were in equal proportions. The different themes covered in Tan's biography has ably demonstrated how a careful study of selected key personalities can be important in elucidating the factors that influence decision-making in business by ethnic Chinese.

Two essays in Leo Suryadinata's edited volume, *Southeast Asian Chinese and China: The Politico-Economic Dimension*, provide a useful perspective for research on Chinese business in Southeast Asia. Jamie Mackie's 'Economic Systems of Southeast Asian Chinese' and Yoshihara Kunio's 'The Ethnic Chinese and Ersatz Capitalism in Southeast Asia,' though addressing issues on a regional level, raise some relevant points for consideration in an analysis of Chinese business in Malaysia. Mackie explores broadly features common to all Southeast Asian Chinese business, as well as their differences. Mackie stresses the need to be wary of attributing the ability to develop a large corporate base to essential values and characteristics derived from Chinese culture; instead, he argues for the need to examine the interaction between culture and structure. By concentrating on the latter, Mackie argues that we would be able to recognize that Chinese enterprise in each Southeast Asian nation has its own peculiar features, distinguishing one from the other.

For Mackie, research on Chinese enterprise in each Southeast Asian country would involve the need to ascertain the key factors that determine the growth of the Chinese firm, conglomerate or network. Mackie's own survey demonstrates that the Chinese in the five ASEAN countries "have become quite distinctive communities with diverse economic and political interests, linguistic codes and capabilities, education system and folkways", and that "the activities of Chinese enterprises in all countries of the region are becoming more intertwined with the activities of the indigenous sectors and increasingly indistinguishable from them" (Mackie 1995: 34–5). In other words, a focus on context and environment, rather than a reference to Chinese culture, may provide more informed insights into the operations, practices and success or failure of Chinese enterprises.

Yoshihara's main theme is that capitalism in Southeast Asia is 'ersatz' because it is confined to the tertiary sector and most major capitalists are merely rent-seekers and speculators, not involved in industrial production. Leading ethnic Chinese businessmen are also ersatz capitalists rather than genuine entrepreneurs as they rely heavily on political connections to develop their business ventures. Most of these Chinese capitalists are mainly involved in light industry where the technology incorporated in their business is imported, hence a dependence on foreign technology if they wish to move into high technology and heavy industries. Yoshihara points out the limited stress on technological development among Southeast Asian businessmen, comparing South Korea with Thailand, where the former was able to leapfrog over the latter to become technologically independent due to its larger base of engineers and skilled workers. This then is Yoshihara's main contribution, i.e. he identifies the direction in which countries like Malaysia should move towards: local businessmen should pay more attention to science and technology and to research and development in order to strengthen local technological capabilities and reduce dependence on foreign technology.

Yoshihara's thesis on rent-seeking among Chinese capitalists has been subject to much criticism, including by Mackie, who points out that businessmen in other parts of the world have also made use of political links to develop their enterprises. That factor alone cannot account for the numerous success stories among Chinese businessmen, nor for the exceptional growth rates experienced by Southeast Asian economies, especially during the past two decades. Multi-national corporations (MNCs) and state enterprises cannot take all the credit for the region's rapid growth and development. There is much evidence that Chinese enterprises, including the SMEs, which constitute a majority of enterprises in the domestic private sector in Southeast Asia, are involved in manufacturing and have steadily increased their contribution to growth in the region.

James Jesudason has also highlighted the theme of SME dynamism in the Malaysian economy in his volume, *Ethnicity and the Economy: The State, Chinese Business and Multinationals in Malaysia*. Jesudason argues that following the implementation of the NEP and the growing attempts by the state to promote Bumiputera participation in the manufacturing sector, the dynamism and potential contribution of Chinese SMEs to this sector was curbed. This, according to Jesudason, also undermined the quality of industrial development in Malaysia. However, the problem with Jesudason's analysis is that there is insufficient empirical evidence to substantiate this argument. This highlights one key area of research in Chinese business that has been badly neglected. Undoubtedly, the Malaysian government, until very recently, has provided Chinese capital with minimal support, and this has been particularly felt by the SMEs. Yet, in spite of having to operate under such circumstances, these SMEs have managed to sustain themselves, with some even showing the capacity to develop appreciably the scale of their operations. Such dynamism among Chinese SME manufacturers has been noted in other countries, particularly in Singapore, Taiwan and Hong Kong.[9] In Malaysia, there has been no study on SMEs that provides insights into the operations of Chinese enterprise.

The overriding concern of most contemporary research on Chinese-owned enterprises in Malaysia has been on the links between politics and business, primarily involving the largest firms in the country; another closely related subject of study is the corporatization movement, initiated by the MCA. Apart from Jesudason's volume, which touches on this link between politics and business, the articles by Heng Pek Koon – 'The Chinese Business Elite of Malaysia' – and Hara Fujio – 'Malaysia's New Economic Policy and the Chinese Business Community' – also deal with this theme. Heng and Fujio contend that Chinese businessmen have had to establish ties with the Malay political elite to quantitatively increase their corporate base, but that there has been much productive deployment of the economic rents secured through such collusion. In this regard, Heng and Fujio challenge the contention made by Yoshihara (1988) that most big Chinese capitalists are primarily 'comprador capitalists' who are merely rent-seekers who have emerged by colluding with the Bumiputera political elite. The problem with the articles by Heng and Fujio is that neither provides in-depth case studies to conclusively prove their argument. In Yoshihara's case, even though his volume, *The Rise of Ersatz Capitalism in Southeast Asia*, has an impressive database providing information on most of the key capitalists in Malaysia (as well as in Southeast Asia), there is no detailed historical study of the growth of their companies to justify the contention he makes. As mentioned, his hypothesis has been disputed by a number of other researchers.

There has, however, been much in-depth research on the corporatization movement and Multi-Purpose Holdings Bhd (MPHB), the most prominent holding company developed under the auspices of this movement. Bruce Gale's pioneering study, *Politics and Business: A Study of Multi-Purpose Holdings*, provides the first in-depth research of the events that led to the incorporation and early growth of this company. Gale took a rather sympathetic – and one could add uncritical – view of the mix between politics and business and of the need for a company like MPHB to act as a vanguard of

Chinese capital. However, just a year after the publication of Gale's volume in 1985, many MCA leaders, including those who led the corporatization movement, were implicated in a fraudulent scandal involving MPHB. Some of these leaders eventually served jail sentences in Malaysia and Singapore. The near demise of MPHB and the failure of the corporatization movement are the main areas of research of Yeoh Kok Kheng's (unpublished) masters dissertation, 'A Study of the Malaysian Chinese Economic Self-Strengthening (Corporatization) Movement – With Special Reference to MPHB, Other Communal Investment Companies and Cooperatives'. Unlike Gale, Yeoh traced the rise of Chinese enterprise from the colonial period, in the process indicating the rather clannish and individualistic nature of Chinese businessmen. It was only when these businessmen began to feel that their economic interests and prospects for business development were being increasingly threatened by the NEP that they began to consider the appeal by the MCA to pool their resources for the purpose of economic self-strengthening through the corporatization movement. E.T. Gomez's chapter on the MCA in his volume, *Political Business: Corporate Involvement of Malaysian Political Parties*, also deals with the corporatization movement, specifically the repercussions of the mix between politics and business. The studies by Yeoh and Gomez take further the study by Gale, but provide a more critical overview of the implications of the mix between politics and business, analyzing also the issues that affected Chinese enterprises enough to allow the MCA to act as their vanguard in the development of Chinese capital in Malaysia. Despite their concentration on the corporatization movement, and of the business activities of cooperatives and companies like MPHB that emerged under this movement, these three studies do not provide an analysis of how Chinese companies operate.

Heng (1992) is the only researcher who has done some comparative study of both Chinese firms owned by leading Chinese businessmen and of companies that emerged during the corporatization movement. As mentioned, the problem with Heng's article was its limited empirical work. One of her conclusions, however, was interesting. Heng contends that the reason for the failure of companies that emerged under the corporatization movement, despite the backing of the MCA, was that they had no support from the Malay political elite. While providing a historical overview of the development of the corporatization movement, Gomez (1994) and Yeoh (1987) also draw reference to another interesting development, i.e. that the movement had also begun to pose a threat to established Chinese businessmen, which appeared to precipitate distrust between them and the MCA. Inevitably, the large Chinese enterprises gave little support to the corporatization movement which hindered its emergence as a countervailing force to state enterprises during the NEP period.

One volume that provides detailed case studies on the development of the largest Chinese-owned public-listed companies is E.T. Gomez' *Chinese Business in Malaysia: Accumulation, Ascendance, Accommodation.* This study had two primary objectives: First, to trace the factors that have enabled the owners of Malaysia's largest Chinese companies to develop their enterprise despite working in an environment that had provided little support for their interests. Second, to ascertain if intra-ethnic business linkages had been a crucial factor in enabling Chinese businessmen to develop their corporate holdings in Malaysia. The empirical evidence provided by Gomez dispels the notion that the owners of these large enterprises had to depend heavily on intra-Chinese business cooperation to develop their corporate base in Malaysia. In most cases, there was also little or no business cooperation between these entrepreneurs and ethnic Chinese businessmen outside Malaysia.[10] Gomez' detailed profile of a number of Chinese-owned companies, their growth contextualized within the economic development of Malaysia, revealed a heterogeneity of business styles. These differences in business style among leading Chinese entrepreneurs were due to a number of factors, including the impact of state policies, resources available to these businessmen, the entrepreneurial endowment of individual businessmen and their access to state patronage through links with influential government leaders. In most cases, a combination of factors had contributed to the growth of major Chinese-owned firms. These factors included a productive use of experience gained in an industry before venturing into business, entrepreneurial deployment of resources generated from an initial investment in a company, and a rather focused approach to one trade rather than diversifying into any area of business that appeared potentially profitable. In some cases, educational qualifications, access to funds and inherited wealth had been important in enabling some Chinese to develop their enterprises.

The overriding issue that comes across from this review is that there is a paucity of in-depth empirical research on Chinese SMEs. There has been no research on the extent of interlocking stock ownership and interlocking directorates among Chinese SMEs. Most Malaysian Chinese SMEs have remained largely family-owned companies, and it has not been conclusively proven that much intra-ethnic business cooperation may have occurred among such firms as they struggled to cope with state policies. Since it has also been suggested that what constitutes 'Chinese capital' is more prevalent amongst the business practices of such SMEs (Lam and Lee 1992), this is an area of research that requires much concentration.

The need for more in-depth work on Chinese enterprise has become imperative as increasing attention worldwide is being focused on capital accumulation and intra-ethnic business networking by ethnic Chinese outside China. A new debate has emerged, especially since the early 1990s, regarding the potential impact of transnational Chinese capital, during a period when cross-border business investments and capital flows have grown appreciably. Such investment and capital flows have contributed to the assumption that ethnically-based transactions are being conducted through business networks created by the Chinese in Asia. In view of this, it is widely believed that the Chinese business community will spearhead Asia's economic growth in the new millennium (see Kotkin 1993; Nasbitt 1995; Rowher 1995; East Asia Analytical Unit 1995; Weidenbaum and Hughes 1996; Hiscock 1997).

There are two major problems with much of the literature on the networking among ethnic Chinese businessmen. First, the presumption that the values and socio-economic institutions characteristic of the Chinese are universal has to be contested. Chinese of the diaspora are not the same everywhere and can no longer be regarded as identical as those living in China or even in the rest of Southeast Asia. The homogenizing assumptions of much of this literature do not take into account the specificities and particularities of the experience of the diasporic business communities which have reconfigured their sense of identity and belonging to a nation-state.

The second major problem is that most of the recent literature treats all Chinese as a monolithic group. This community, as pointed out earlier, comprises various sub-ethnic groups that have not managed to transcend these divisions to act as a unified ethnic force. A careful reading of the history the Chinese in Malaysia indicates that sub-ethnic ties had only been crucial in helping migrant communities develop their business. For example, as Heng (1988) notes, during the colonial period, Chinese Chambers of Commerce, trade associations and sub-ethnic associations, like the Hokkien, Hakka and Cantonese Associations, were important avenues through which the sub-ethnic Chinese communities could act collectively for mutual benefit.

However, even among sub-ethnic Chinese groups, collaborative business ties are diminishing (see, for example, Jesudason 1997).

The best example of sub-ethnic Chinese business cooperation in the colonial period was the establishment in 1932 of the Singapore-based Oversea-Chinese Banking Corporation (OCBC), a product of the merger of three Hokkien-owned banks. The Hokkiens had emerged as among the largest Chinese entrepreneurs in Malaya and Singapore. OCBC was formed during the Great Depression when these Hokkien banks, badly affected by the economic crisis, merged their banking activities to form an enlarged institution that remains one of the leading Chinese-owned banks in Asia.

Yet, OCBC was also the nucleus of three other major banks in Malaysia. Three men formerly in the employ of OCBC would break away to establish Malayan Banking Bhd (Maybank), MUI Bank Bhd (now renamed the Hong Leong Bank) and Public Bank Bhd. Maybank, Malaysia's largest bank in terms of deposits and capitalization and founded by Khoo Teck Puat, is now under the control of the Malaysian government, while the founder of MUI Bank, Khoo Kay Peng, lost control of the bank to another Hokkien, Quek Leng Chan. Teh Hong Piow, who founded Public Bank, is the only former OCBC employee who remains in control of a bank in Malaysia. Following the financial crisis in East Asia in 1997, the Malaysian government intensified its drive to get the country's numerous banks to merge to form larger enterprises with a bigger asset base which could make a greater impact in the local and global financial market. While a number of banks have begun to implement mergers, none of the Chinese-owned banks have entered into negotiations to achieve this goal. Among the Chinese-owned banks in Malaysia, apart from the Hong Leong Bank and Public Bank, are the Ban Hin Lee Bank Bhd, Southern Bank Bhd and Pacific Bank Bhd, all controlled by Hokkiens.[11]

It has also been argued that the most effective and long-term intra-ethnic business cooperation can be found among the Foochows (seen by most non-Chinese as part of the Hokkien community) (see *Asian Wall Street Journal* 21/12/94). There is some evidence that suggests that the Foochows had cooperated to corner the timber industry in the state of Sarawak, particularly during the early half of the 20th century.[12] In the present period, however, there is growing evidence of keen competition in the timber sector among the Foochows in Sarawak.

It appears that trade organizations and sub-ethnic associations no longer serve as important 'interest groups' to Chinese businessmen through which representations can be made to the government concerning their problems. Diminishing Chinese support for these organizations reflect, among other things, this community's heterogeneity, divided by place of origin, sub-ethnicity, and social and class background. Generational change also helps account for the diminishing support for these organizations, as local-born Chinese are less inclined to participate in them. One qualification has to be made here. Some businessmen have realized that ethnically-based organizations can serve as an important avenue to establish links with other Chinese businessmen of the diaspora that could facilitate business deals. This has contributed to renewed interests in Chinese organizations by businessmen seeking to exploit common ethnicity as a means to forge business deals.

However, the corporate deals that have been established between ethnic Chinese in East and Southeast Asia do not suggest any joint, long-term business collaboration. In many cases, Chinese entrepreneurs prefer to establish joint-ventures with MNCs, usually Japanese and European-owned companies, as a means to acquire technology and know how to develop their enterprise (see Gomez 1999; Gomez and Jomo 1999). Such joint-ventures have enabled the more innovative of these Chinese businessmen to develop expertise and some repute in a particular industry. One example is the case of the public-listed construction firm YTL Corporation which, after securing a licence from the government to produce electricity, a field in which it had no experience, went into a join-venture with the German firm, Siemens, to implement this project. YTL Corporation, after having learnt the technology in producing electricity, has begun to venture abroad, developing an international reputation in power generation (see Gomez 1999: 163–71).

The case of YTL Corporation reflects a phenomenon common among most of the largest Chinese-owned companies in Malaysia. A majority of such companies are involved in a range of activities, though they probably have some expertise in one particular industry that also serves as the major cash cow for the group. Inevitably, this also means that a majority of the companies in large Chinese business groups have not built horizontal or vertical roots in a particular business. There is, however, growing evidence that with the rise of a new generation of businessmen, many of whom are professionally qualified, and with government encouragement to develop expertise in a particular field of industry, there may be a significant change among Chinese enterprises in their style of doing business.

The growing literature on the development of transnational links among Chinese of the diaspora leads us to the next important research theme – nationalism. In the context of growing belief among government leaders and indigenous groups of the existence of business networks, involving complex triadic-relations between the Chinese of the diaspora, the host countries and their 'homeland,' China, what are the implications of this on nation building? Ill-defined and under-researched arguments regarding the functioning of ethnically-based transnational networks tend to embed in the minds of government leaders and indigenous groups the idea that ethnic minority groups have a sense of belonging to another 'homeland,' that of their ancestors, not that of the country of their birth. In the process, the arguments regarding the ostensible triadic relations involving the Chinese diaspora in Southeast Asia has led, albeit unintentionally, to problems among ethnic Chinese communities struggling for the creation of a new understanding of national identity and the need for the emergence of a more inclusive state.

Conclusion

Our literature review on Chinese enterprise in Malaysia has indicated that in order to provide a holistic understanding of capital development by this community, there is a need to incorporate in the analysis a range of issues. One major methodological problem with much of the literature on Chinese business in Malaysia is that most of this research still provides very little information on ownership patterns, company structures, business strategies, forms of diversification, sources of funding, and the extent of intra-ethnic business cooperation. From a theoretical perspective, since a study of Chinese enterprise involves research into the decision-making by individuals, to understand the factors that have influenced the development of such companies, the research into the dynamics of Chinese business would necessitate the adoption of an inter-disciplinary perspective. This is important as we have noted that detailed profiles of a number of Chinese-owned companies have revealed heterogeneity of business styles. Only a rich collection of empirical material will allow us to develop new theoretical insights into the actual constitution and dynamics of 'Chinese capital'.

3

Thailand

———◆◆◆———

Jamie Mackie

Chinese Business in Thailand

The business world of the ethnic Chinese in Thailand resembles that of the other Southeast Asian countries in several basic features. Nearly all Chinese small-, medium- and large-scale enterprises (SMEs and LSEs) are still essentially family-owned firms, and they tend to rely on traditional networks of kinship, clan and common place of origin for all kinds of ancillary services. As in all Southeast Asian countries, a small number of very large business groups, or conglomerates, has come to dominate the modern sector of the economy since the 1960s. However, the socio-economic position of the Sino-Thai, as they are now frequently and most appropriately called, since it emphasizes that they *are* primarily Thai nationals, not Chinese, differs from that of their counterparts elsewhere in the region in several important respects, especially in regard of its big business groups.[1] Some of these business groups have greatly facilitated the growth of the Sino-Thai business class over the last 40 years and largely contributed to its remarkable economic and even political strength (to some extent) in the 1990s.

The most important of those differences is that the Chinese who have immigrated to Thailand and then settled there over the last two hundred years have been more readily absorbed into the broader Thai society (and partly 'assimilated,' although that is such a question-begging term that it is best avoided) than their counterparts in other parts of Southeast Asia, to a point where it is now almost impossible to draw a clear line of distinction between the indigenous Thai and modern Sino-Thai.

Intermarriage and a high degree of social, political and cultural identification with the host society have had the effect of so blurring any such line that it is becoming almost useless and meaningless to try to draw it in most cases. It is difficult even to estimate at all precisely the size of the Sino-Thai minority for that reason, although it is generally accepted that about 10 per cent of the country's population is Sino-Thai, or around 5 to 6 million people in 1997.[2]

Second, the Teochew (originating from around Shantou/Swatow in southern Fujian) are by far the largest Chinese speech group (*bang*) in Thailand, estimated to number around 40 per cent of all Chinese in the early 20th century, more than double the Hakka, Hainanese or Hokkien groups, or the even smaller Cantonese group. The Teochew tended to dominate the rice trade and much of the lucrative remittance business back to China in the years before World War II. The Teochew also provided the most eminent Chinese community leaders in Bangkok, in much the same way as the Hokkien have tended to dominate in Singapore or Manila, at a time when speech-group differences mattered to businessmen there far more than they do today.

The third major difference is that the ethnic Chinese have been playing economic roles of great importance throughout Thailand for well over two hundred years. The Chinese now dominate the economic life of the country to a far greater extent than other Southeast Asian Chinese do elsewhere in the region. Among the thirty or forty largest business groups in Thailand in the mid-1990s, prior to the economic crisis of 1997, none are controlled by ethnic Thai families, apart from a small handful of state-connected enterprises.[3] Nearly all are owned predominantly by Sino-Thai families. While the situation is not so one-sided among SMEs in the smaller towns, the prominence of Sino-Thai enterprises at the level of companies of this size too is very striking.[4] Yet, this has not often given rise to serious social or political conflicts with the indigenous Thais since the 1950s, as in neighboring countries, largely because of the strong self-identification of the Sino-Thai with Thailand and its culture. Sino-Thai economic dominance has rarely grown into a major political issue in recent years, despite occasional attempts by maverick politicians to muster indigenous votes through anti-Chinese rhetoric.

Fourth, the capital invested by ethnic Chinese businessmen who settled in Thailand in the late colonial era exceeded in volume that of the European capitalists who came there, unlike the situation in the British, Dutch, French and American colonies. Inevitably, ethnic

Chinese made a far more significant contribution than European capital to the country's overall economic growth. They have therefore played a very prominent part in the country's development for well over a century. The amount of capital invested by the Sino-Thai since 1945 has also far exceeded foreign capital in Thailand in both volume and developmental impact.[5]

These features of the Sino-Thai position in the country's socio-economic life are so intimately intertwined with and so strongly shaped by the local context in which they are embedded that it is almost pointless to argue about which of them, if any, can be regarded as the most basic causal factors behind the various processes involved. Skinner (1960) has given the best explanation of their successful integration in Thai society, through his comparison of the reasons why they were so much more successful than the Chinese in Java in adapting to local conditions. Skinner attributed the different levels of integration by ethnic Chinese in Thailand and Java mainly to the religious differences between the two countries. Chinese immigrants had little difficulty in adopting Thailand's Theravada Buddhism whereas they were much more reluctant to embrace Islam in Indonesia – or were rarely encouraged to convert to Islam, even though a few have done so. But while religion has clearly been an important factor in all this, it has by no means been the only one. Perhaps equally crucial was the fact brought out by Skinner that the leaders of the Chinese communities in Thailand had strong motivations to merge into the Thai elite, and relatively easy opportunities to do so – initially with the ruling aristocracy, later the military-bureaucratic elite – through close identification with them in the provision of commercial and financial services, as well as through marriage alliances and appointments to official positions, ranks and titles. By contrast, the Chinese in the Dutch colony that became Indonesia were drawn much more towards Dutch society, language, education and culture rather than Javanese (or other 'native' societies) during the last century of colonial rule. Hence, the Chinese came to be regarded by local nationalists as mere lackeys of the Dutch, with economic and political interests very different from those of the indigenous peoples, and often in conflict with them.

Not many case studies of the careers of Sino-Thai businessmen or women (few of the latter have yet emerged into prominence, although there are some) have yet been published in English, despite their great economic importance over many decades. But for earlier periods, we have four of the best books on the business activities of Southeast

Asian Chinese in any part of the region – Skinner's (1957,1958) two great classics, now rather dated, Suehiro's (1989) admirably comprehensive historical account of *Capital Accumulation in Thailand* up to the early 1980s and Jennifer Cushman's (1991) fine account of the Khaw family enterprises of the late 19th century. Some suggestions about the types of field research that would be most useful to fill out our knowledge of the business activities and methods of the Sino-Thai over the last decade or so will be put forward at the conclusion of this chapter.

Development of Sino-Thai Business Enterprises

The big business groups that now dominate the modern sector of the Thai economy have nearly all come into being since the 1950s, under the stimulus of the rapid growth that has occurred there over that time, averaging more than 8 per cent between 1960 to 1995. For a fuller understanding of the socio-economic background to that recent phase of development, however, it is necessary to look back briefly at the form of merchant capitalism that began to emerge in the late 19th century, which has been described excellently by Suehiro (1989) in the most comprehensive survey yet made of the contributions of Southeast Asian Chinese businessmen to the development of any country in the region up to the mid-1980s.

That form of merchant capitalism did not radically change, according to another survey by Suehiro (1992: 40–42), until the overthrow of the authoritarian military regime in 1973. In that connection, it is worth noting that the rate of economic growth in Thailand during the half-century before World War II, although steady, had been sluggish, insufficient to generate any increase in per capita incomes and hence aggregate domestic purchasing power, which might have led to the kind of economic diversification that occurred after 1960, or in prewar Malaya. Thus, the economic environment in which those early Chinese businessmen were operating was very different from that confronting their successors, or even their contemporaries in the other countries of Southeast Asia. However, even in those early years, significant changes were occurring among the leading Sino-Thai businessmen (there were no women of any importance among them at that time) and there were frequent cases of a rise-and-fall among them.

Suehiro (1989) notes that there were basically three paths into modern business activities for the Chinese in the late 19th century.

The first was to make a start as a tax farmer in opium, gambling, etc. to Thai officials, local or central, accumulate some wealth, and then invest in junk trading to China (which had been going on for several centuries or more) or in the newly expanding rice export trade. Two of the most famous of the Chinese who followed this pattern of development were Khaw Soo Cheang (1797–1882) and Kim Seng Lee (1842–1919). Khaw Soo Cheang rose from rags to riches as a tax farmer and promoter of tin mining in the southern province of Ranong, was appointed governor of the province for his services to the Thai monarchy and founded a family commercial empire which flourished in the south until the early 20th century on the basis of tin-mining and shipping industries there (Cushman 1991). Kim Seng Lee got his start in teak logging and tax farming in Chiangmai, then moved into rice milling, sawmills, a bank and a shipping company; by 1910, he controlled the largest enterprise in Thailand, but ran into financial difficulties soon after and collapsed entirely.

A second path was to become a comprador to a European trading house or bank, which usually required a knowledge of English and some education, and in due course move out into one's own business, utilizing the savings and contacts achieved in that role. A third path was taken by a new wave of Swatow-based merchants who became dominant in rice milling and rice export trade after World War I.[6] These merchants relied less on political patrons or government appointments to help them as they were able to utilize their own trading and financial networks in the intra-Asian rice trade at a time when it was expanding vigorously. All these traders were confined by circumstances almost solely to commercial activities, since Thailand's treaty obligations precluded any possibility of moving upstream into manufacturing to any extent.

After the 1932 overthrow of the monarchy and the establishment of a more bureaucratic military-civilian regime, a new set of leading groups of Chinese merchants emerged, with new patrons but faced with a more intensely nationalist (and partly anti-Chinese) batch of economic policies. A new array of Big Five family groups came to the fore, with their roots still in the rice trade, but increasingly inclined to diversify into banking and other commercial activities. The most prominent and enduring of these five families were the Wanglee group, the wealthiest and most influential group between the 1940s and 1950s, although gradually declining in power as others adapted more successfully to changing political and economic conditions, the Bulakun group and the Lamsam family group, which is still prominent today.[7] About a dozen Thai commercial banks emerged in the 1930s, alongside several European ones and branches of Hong Kong or Singapore Chinese banks, but they had difficulty in challenging the superior capital resources of the latter in the post-Depression years and only one of them, the Wanglee Bank, survived into the postwar era. The disturbed conditions of the Pacific war and Japanese dominance of Southeast Asia were damaging to the rice trade, although advantageous to the Chinese traders as their European rivals were hurt much more seriously. Yet, it was in the disrupted conditions of 1945 to 1960 that new patterns of business and political relationships developed which set the scene for the 'economic miracle' of rapid growth that has occurred in Thailand since then.

The growth of the banking sector in the postwar years was one of the first big changes to occur. New banking legislation resulted in the formation of eight new Chinese banks and 25 insurance companies in the years 1944 to 1951, out of which emerged five large bank-based business groups which played a major part in Thailand's development trajectory over the next twenty years. Among the largest of these groups in the 1950s was the Asia Trust group, based around the Bangkok Bank, which grew under the leadership of Chin Sophonpa-nich to be the country's most successful business group by far. Another was the Thai-Hua group, based on the Bangkok Mercantile Bank and an assortment of importing and trading companies, which outranked even the Asia Trust group in size in the late 1950s although it later fell far behind it. Two other big banking groups were the Bank of Ayudhya group, today headed by the Ratanarak family, and the Thai Farmers Bank group, headed by the Lamsam and Wanglee families, which had earlier been one of the largest business groups in the country and has persisted since then to be second only to the Bangkok Bank group in the 1990s. All these groups have since been prominent as the main financial backers of Thailand's new industrial, commercial and financial enterprises which brought about the post-1960 'economic miracle,' although the rank order among them had changed radically by the 1980s, with the Bangkok Bank and Thai Farmers groups outstripping the others dramatically.[8]

The Chinese commercial class was described by Fred Riggs (1966) in the early 1960s as a bunch of 'pariah entrepreneurs' in his influential book, *Thailand: The Modernization of a Bureaucratic Polity*, since they seemed to wield no organized political power, and were basically dependent on the patronage of the Thai ruling class of generals and bureaucratic officials. Riggs (1966) painted a very pessimistic picture of the country's prospects of making progress towards a more vigorous capitalist society and economy, since he believed the ruling class had no interest in changing the country's socio-economic structure, while the Chinese had no chance of bringing about the institutional reforms necessary to create real capitalism there. Important changes were, however, taking place in Thailand just at the time when Riggs was formulating this analysis. These changes soon gave rise to an economic transformation that led in due course to the crumbling of the bureaucratic polity, along with the emergence of a vigorous and increasingly autonomous Sino-Thai business class controlling nearly all the commanding heights of the country's economy. Ruth McVey, in her 'Materialization of the Southeast Asian Entrepreneur' (in McVey 1992: 18–30), showed how and why a new class of Southeast Asian capitalists, predominantly ethnic Chinese, were able to develop even within the bureaucratic polities of Thailand and elsewhere as the indigenous elites gradually changed from being 'parasites' to 'promoters' of Chinese businessmen as they realized it was more lucrative for them to not kill the goose that laid the golden eggs.

What has been called 'pillow and mat capitalism (Phongpaichit and Baker 1996) began to blossom dramatically in Thailand from the 1960s, largely as a result of the business activities of about thirty Sino-Thai 'shophouse tycoons' who nearly all rose from being penniless immigrants with little more in their possession than a mat and pillow to become Thailand's major commercial dynasties after 1960. They all relied heavily at first on the close relationships they established with local Thai powerholders, much as their predecessors had done, but many of them grew to be increasingly independent of patrons in later years. They were able to accumulate new capital from the profits of various kinds of privileges and monopolies they were granted, or from the import or manufacture of consumer goods for the growing domestic market, thereby expanding the scale of their operations gradually to a point where they achieved dominance of particular markets. However, what initially propelled Thailand forward towards the rapid growth rates of the 1980s to 1990s was not so much the contributions to development in the manufacturing and services sectors as the rapid expansion of the agricultural sector. Farm area doubled over the next 30 years as new lands were opened up, while agricultural exports increased in value by about 20 per cent per annum, diversifying far beyond the country's former reliance on four main commodities, rice, teak, rubber and tin. Several of the big Sino-Thai tycoons played important parts in that process, especially in the sugar industry where dramatic growth occurred, although they were not in the front rank of the big business groups by the 1990s when manufacturing and financial services were the leading growth areas (Krirkiat and Yoshihara 1983; Yoshihara 1988).

The pattern of socio-economic development began to change in the 1970s after the overthrow of the Thanom-Praphat military-backed regime in 1973, which opened up the path towards a more pluralistic political system over the next 20 years, and ultimately a more democratic one. That period coincided with an increase in the annual GDP growth rate from around 4 per cent to 6 to 7 per cent in the 1970s, and then to 9 to 10 per cent (and even more, occasionally) during the 'boom' decade after the devaluation of the baht and the world currency realignments of 1985, which brought a vastly increased stream of foreign capital into Southeast Asia. More than any other ASEAN country, Thailand seemed at that time to fit with the general proposition that economic development leads to demands for progress towards democratization from the growing middle class (Crouch and Morley 1998). With the sudden expansion of Thailand's exports and the dramatic diversification of her economy during the boom years, the country turned 'first into a typical cheap-labor sweatshop and then into a platform for high- technology industries' (Phongpaichit and Baker 1966: 34), while a host of new Sino-Thai tycoons emerged to seize the lucrative opportunities that were opening up. The flood of foreign investment fortunately did not swamp local enterprises but helped to spur them ahead, with the volume of domestic investment far exceeding the sum total of foreign direct investment and portfolio investment.

In Thailand's boom years between 1986 to 1997, yet another phase of development in the pattern of big business enterprise unfolded which marked a shift from that of the previous period as an enormous expansion of new investment occurred in new and diverse modern-sector activities (Phongpaichit and Baker 1996: 56–90). A massive volume of foreign capital flooded in, some in the form of loans, joint ventures or portfolio investment, some as foreign direct investment, which gave a big boost to the economy, but was only a small part of total domestic capital formation. It made it much easier for rising firms to raise capital and new technology on a highly competitive market, thereby reducing their dependence on the Big Four banks and opening up new opportunities for entrepreneurial firms of all sizes to grow as the domestic market expanded. Hence, the world of Sino-Thai big business expanded and diversified to an unprecedented extent during that decade. While some of the largest of the old-established Sino-Thai business groups also continued to grow fast throughout this period, playing important roles in opening up new industries (for example, a huge petrochemical complex was pioneered by the Bangkok Bank, Siam Cement and TPI groups), they were no longer as dominant in the total picture as they had been in earlier decades, for they could not maintain monopoly strength in export markets as easily as formerly in domestic ones. Moreover, the spectacular rise of the Charoen Phokpand group to become Thailand's largest conglomerate by the mid-1990s, and the emergence of new, highly entrepreneurial enterprises like the Shinawatra telecommunications group, and other telecoms groups like Jasmine, Ucom and Samar in the 1990s, almost overshadowed the continued but now less dramatic expansion and diversification of the two biggest banking groups based around the Bangkok Bank and Thai Farmers Bank. Some of the less adaptable of the older groups fell behind in the race and several collapsed entirely, while others, like the Sahavirya steel group and Saha Union, grew vigorously. Many of these firms borrowed recklessly in the mid-1990s or undertook excessive investments in the booming real estate market or the stock exchange, with the result that they were severely burned when the baht was devalued in mid-1997 and the stock market collapsed; but the exact extent of that disaster is still not clear.

Case Study: Charoen Phokpand (CP) and Bangkok Bank Groups

The rise of the Charoen Phokpand (CP) group from its modest beginnings as a small seed, fertilizer and (later) stock-feed firm in the 1920s, a classic Chinese family firm, to become Thailand's largest non-bank conglomerate by the early 1990s is one of the most fascinating stories of all Southeast Asian Chinese business enterprises. Under its founder, Chia Ek-chor, the firm experienced solid but not spectacular growth through its first 40 years, then expanded rapidly from the 1960s into chicken and egg production as well as slaughtering, processing, wholesaling and exporting of chickens, and later fast food outlets and other vertically integrated activities. After the founder's son, Dhanin Chearavanand, took control of the group in the 1980s, CP entered a new phase of astonishingly rapid expansion and diversification, now horizontal as well as vertical, and international as well as domestic. CP had already formed joint-ventures with some of the world's foremost multinationals, such as Arbor Acres of USA for its seed and grain business, with which it engaged in operations in China,

Indonesia, Turkey and elsewhere. CP floated part of its stock as a public company on several regional stock markets as these bourses became an easily accessible source of capital, thereby freeing itself of its earlier financial dependence on the Bangkok Bank. CP became a major player in the burgeoning telecommunications industry in Thailand through Telecoms Asia, in conjunction with British Telecom.

CP was one of the first foreign companies to start operations in China, after Deng Xiao-peng began to liberalize the economy there in 1979, initially in feed-mills, seeds ands fertilizers, across many provinces, later in a wide range of manufacturing and services ventures also, most notably the large Ek-chor motorcycle factory in Shanghai. It was rewarded for putting its trust in China so early by the success Dhanin achieved in building up good political connections in Beijing as well as in the provinces. By the 1990s, CP was said to have invested over US$1 billion in China and to be the largest overseas enterprise there. Its investments in China were thought to exceed its outlays in Thailand by then. Handley (1998: 113) suggests that Dhanin looked on his expansion into China as a means of turning CP into a world-class conglomerate, comparable with the South Korean chaebols, the Thailand market being too small to permit growth on that scale.

The 1997 crisis hit CP hard, forcing it to refocus on its core agricultural activities. CP has since tried to sell off many of its other activities, both in China and Thailand, where it did not have the same expertise. CP is probably in a better position to ride out the crisis than many Sino-Thai enterprises because its export agro-industries are still very profitable, but its debt burden remains a problem.

The Sophonpanich family founded in 1944 the Bangkok Bank. Under the legendary Chin Sophonpanich, Bangkok Bank grew steadily to become the largest bank and bank-based conglomerate in both Thailand and all Southeast Asia by the late 1960s, with the largest network of international branches and personal contacts (initially very lucrative, later much less so) throughout the region. Chin had established the Bangkok Bank's offshore branches during a period of exile in Hong Kong, after the overthrow of his patron, Police General Phao, by General Sarit, in 1957. It was, however, Bangkok Bank's dominant role in financing the post-1960 growth of the Thai economy that mainly brought about its primacy. After Chin's return to Bangkok in 1964, he took care to spread his political risks across a broader spectrum and to maintain a lower-profile political role. Chin's great success as a banker had been due initially to his remarkable skills in foreign exchange dealings, honed in the difficult post-1945 years of fluctuating exchange rates, later to his political connections to some very shady generals in the 1950s, and above all to his astute commercial judgment as the principal financier of the companies whose rapid expansion in the 1960s to 1970s laid the foundations for Thailand's economic miracle, the textile industry in particular.

After Chin's retirement in 1984, his son Chartri headed the Bangkok Bank group, pushing further the modernization of its operations while expanding its market share domestically and reducing its international operations. By the 1990s, the group had extensive interests in various types of non-bank enterprises, notably petrochemicals. Bangkok Bank and the Thai Farmers Bank group had become far bigger than all rival private sector banks even though competition for market share in new banking services was intensifying. Bangkok Bank is said to have suffered big losses during the 1997 to 1998 economic crisis although it appears to be in no danger of collapse.

Features of Sino-Thai Business Enterprises

At the SME level, the myriad Sino-Thai shop-houses and larger family firms in the small towns, villages and Chinatown areas of the few larger towns of Thailand, including Bangkok, do not differ greatly in basic structure from those that can be found in most other Southeast Asian Chinese communities, although little has been written about them anywhere. At the LSE level, however, some striking differences can be observed between the thirty or forty largest Sino-Thai business groups and the big conglomerates in Indonesia, Malaysia, the Philippines or Singapore. Many of the largest Sino-Thai companies are older than all but a handful in those ASEAN countries, most originating in the 1960s or even earlier, whereas relatively few are of recent origin. The reasons for that are to be found in the socio-economic history of Thailand (and the other countries) over the last half-century rather than in any intrinsic characteristics of Sino-Thai business enterprises, but they are for that reason more deeply rooted in the country's economy and society than many of their counterparts elsewhere. There has also been a high degree of continuity among these Sino-Thai enterprises since the 1960s, with relatively few failures (prior to the 1997 crisis), not many newcomers into the higher ranks and not much change in the rank-order among the top thirty or so business groups, at least until the early 1990s. Nearly all of the top thirty business groups have been prominent for three decades or more, some even longer. On the other hand, none of the old Big Five rice-trading enterprises of the 1930s is still as dominant as it was then, apart from the Lamsam-TFB group.[9] There has also been a tendency towards a high degree of concentration of ownership in many fields, apart from financial services, due to various forms of semi-monopolistic market dominance. However, some loosening of the earlier patterns of market dominance has been occurring since the early 1980s in the more open and competitive economic and political climates that have been developing. The firms and business groups which were able to establish a strong position of market dominance in the 1950s to 1960s have found themselves subject to a far more competitive environment in the 1990s than previously, with the result that some of the less adaptable or efficient companies have lost ground considerably.

Another distinctive feature of the Sino-Thai business groups has been the sharp division between financial capital and industrial capital in the decades prior to about 1980, with most commercial and manufacturing enterprises heavily dependent in their early years on one or more of the Big Four private banks, which later came to be mainly two powerful and highly diversified groups, the Bangkok Bank and TFB groups in particular. Nothing comparable with this situation is observable elsewhere in Southeast Asia. State banks played a far less significant part in financing economic development in Thailand than in the other countries, while neither the stock exchange nor other capital market institutions were at all well developed until the 1990s, lagging far behind Malaysia and Singapore. So the Sino-Thai private banks were initially the main source of capital, except to the extent that foreign joint-venture partners could be tapped for funds, or foreign loans obtained in the later years of Thailand's 'economic miracle'. That situation has changed over the last fifteen years or so, as the commercial and manufacturing sectors have been able to gain access to other sources of capital, from the stock market and the foreign capital flooding into Southeast Asia in the 1990s. Hence, the basic structural features of the corporate ownership patterns in Thailand were slowly changing in the years before the 1997 crisis, although not yet to any dramatic extent. Continuity has always been the striking keynote to modern Thailand's development. What effect the financial crisis will prove to have had on the big business groups cannot yet be foreseen with any clarity, although it appears that nearly all the big banks and many other large enterprises are in trouble, having suffered huge losses from bad loans and given their overexposure to unhedged foreign borrowings in the mid-1990s.

Several other features of the political and socio-economic context within which the Sino-Thai business groups have been operating over the last half-century are also noteworthy. Sino-Thai business groups, unlike their counterparts in Malaysia, Singapore, Indonesia and the Philippines, have had to face almost no significant competition from either local indigenous capitalists or from entrenched colonial-era foreign enterprises or from large state banks. Discriminatory measures against them, 'decree indignization' as it has been called (Golay et al. 1969), has not been a major problem for them since the brief anti-Chinese phase of Phibul Songkram's dictatorship in the 1940s to 1950s. Most of the larger Sino-Thai business groups have been able to assure themselves against any repetition of that kind of harassment by incorporating many of the country's leading indigenous political leaders and military officers into directorships of a largely honorary kind. Recruitment of able young Thais into managerial positions has also helped to blur the lines of ethnic discrimination considerably. No one can be in any doubt that these firms are owned and controlled by Sino-Thai families (or in a few cases clusters of families), yet there seems to be surprisingly little indigenous resentment at the fact.[10]

State intervention in economic life has been considerably less in Thailand than in Indonesia, Malaysia or Singapore since 1958, when Marshal Sarit reversed the strongly etatist (and deliberately anti-Chinese) policies of his predecessors in favor of an openly pro-private enterprise, free market economy. The policies which were put in place in the years following have been broadly maintained and even extended since then by a group of technocratic economic planners and senior bureaucrats who have been able to keep control of the main lines of state policy despite numerous changes of government. State-owned enterprises no longer extend much beyond the main public utilities like electricity, telecommunications, railways, airlines and a couple of medium-sized banks. In general, the Sino-Thais have been the main beneficiaries from these policies and the boom they generated.

Finally, it is noteworthy that the political changes that have occurred in Thailand since heyday of the monolithic 'bureaucratic polity' in the 1950s have proved to be advantageous to the Sino-Thai in general and to the powerful business groups in particular, by opening up new opportunities for them to exert influence on economic policy-making within an increasingly pluralistic political system, both at the macro level and in more specific cases of the allocation of licenses and government contracts. During the years of the Sarit and Thanom-Phaphat military governments (1958–1973) in which patron-client relations were still vital, many Sino-Thais were able to use their money to ensure good relations with the highest authorities. Sarit's coup in 1958 had disrupted many of the older vested interests and cosy business-government relationships of the previous epoch, and created a new set, but essentially it ushered in a period when new Sino-Thai business enterprises flourished which laid the foundations of Thailand's later 'economic miracle'.

The overthrow of the military regime in 1973 and the brief 'democratic experiment' of 1973 to 1976 were followed by a brief return to authoritarian rule from 1976 to 1979, then a gradually liberalizing semi-authoritarian regime under General Prem between 1980 and 1988, and an essentially parliamentary system thereafter. Businessmen found it necessary to diversify their patronage links as the authority of particular generals waned and the need to build up political connections with the emergent political parties increased. In the 1980s, a number of Sino-Thai business leaders like Boonchu Rojanasathien and Chartichai Choonhavan were able to play active roles at the head of political parties and in government coalitions, while the links between the parties and their financial backers now became a major theme of Thai politics. Since 1988, the leaders of the main political parties and all but one of Thailand's five prime ministers have been Sino-Thai in part or whole (Chartchai, Chuan Leekpai, Barnharn and Chavalit). Many of the wealthy provincial political leaders funding the various parties who are in some cases elected to parliament, commonly known as *jao pho* ('godfathers' or 'dark forces'), are Sino-Thai. Curiously, while the big metropolitan business groups with their own distinct political interests are also engaged in funding the various parties to some extent (many of them spreading their risks by making contributions to several of them) – *jao sua*, as they are known – there is no clear pattern of 'money politics' or political alignments of great significance among them. While vote-buying is a major problem everywhere, it seems to be more prevalent, or more crucial to election outcomes in the countryside than the cities.

Conclusion

There are still many aspects of the commercial life and business practices of the Sino-Thai about which little has yet been published (in

English), compared with the other Southeast Asian Chinese communities of the region. Further research on Sino-Thai enterprise could prove extremely valuable, since we can currently draw only the most tentative general inferences about them from highly incomplete and impressionistic data. The most obvious, of course, is the impact of the 1997 financial crisis afflicting the whole of Southeast and East Asia, which has already caused bankruptcy or collapse for some of the corporations and business groups of the mid-1990s and is likely to create huge difficulties and restructuring problems for many more over the next few years (reliable details of which are still very hard to obtain). Hence any list of Thailand's largest business groups at the beginning of the 21st century will probably differ quite considerably from a mid-1990s list, and the socio-political implications of the changes will be very important, just as were those changes that occurred during the period of the 1950s to 1960s. Several other issues, however, also deserve closer investigation than they have yet had.

One of these issues is the extent to which the major business groups are now becoming more focused on the core activities where their basic strengths are concentrated and abandoning the sort of fringe investments in (momentarily) high-yielding fields like real-estate development or financial services, the proliferation of which gave rise to the bubble economy of the mid-1990s. We have noticed that Charoen Phokpand has already started to move in that direction, and many others are almost certainly doing likewise, although detailed accounts of the process are scarce. Further, what effects will that sort of change have on the balance between LSEs and the medium or smaller enterprises that survive the crisis? We might expect, prima facie, that the SMEs, being less likely to have been as highly indebted and overleveraged as the larger firms, will emerge from the crisis in a relatively stronger position; but until empirical research into that question has been done, we are just guessing.

Second, the impact of the crisis on the capital structures and patterns of ownership of the big business groups may be very considerable also. That is bound to mean some watering down of family control over at least some of the more lucrative enterprises, either by way of share sales on the stock exchanges or by bringing in cashed-up partners as co-owners. Such changes are likely to imply broader shifts over the course of time in the direction of more modern, corporate business management and practices.

Third, Thailand's urgent need for any foreign capital it can get since the collapse of the 1986 to 1997 boom, and that of its business firms to diversify their sources of finance so as to reduce their dependence on a single bank or joint-venture partner, suggests a number of lines of enquiry that might be pursued into the financial strategies of both LSEs and SMEs in the post-crisis era. It can be hypothesized that the patterns likely to be discerned after 1997 – and the impact on ownership structures – are likely to be very different from those of the boom years, and earlier. However, we can barely guess how they will differ until fuller information is available.

Finally, amazingly little is known about the SME sector, either Sino-Thai or ethnic Thai firms, or the inter-ethnic relations between them, apart from the study by Szanton (1983). Fuller information about the overall structure of the SME sector, sources of capital at different levels, use of family labor, or the extent of Sino-Thai firms' reliance on the traditional forms of networks recorded in the earlier literature, would be illuminating. Most valuable of all would be any enquiry into the extent to which SMEs are still anchored in traditional Chinese business practices or are starting to move towards more modern corporate, non-familistic styles of operation and management.

4

The Philippines

Theresa Chong Carino

Brief History of Ethnic Chinese Business

Let me begin by asserting that the contribution of ethnically-based business networks and Confucian culture to the growth of Chinese capital in Southeast Asia has been over-rated. Chinese business development in Southeast Asia has depended primarily on the prevailing domestic conditions, particularly state policies pertaining to the economy and the avenues available to the Chinese to enable them to develop their enterprises. This has certainly been true of the Chinese in the Philippines whose fortunes have been dependent on the rise and decline of the local economy, as well as on the attitude and policies of various government administrations.

State policies had a considerable impact on the size and economic activities of the Chinese. It is not by accident that the Chinese population in the Philippines is numerically one of the smallest in Southeast Asia. Both Spanish and American colonial policies dictated that the Chinese alien population remain small and within the bounds of colonial control and management. During the Spanish colonial era (1521–1898), periodic expulsions, massacres and strict immigration laws kept the Chinese population sizeable enough to serve the needs of the Spaniards, but not large enough to be an economic or political threat. The population size of Chinese immigrants was officially limited to 6,000, but actual numbers often exceeded this figure. When the population size of ethnic Chinese exceeded what the Spanish authorities could handle, mass expulsions or deportations were carried out (see Guerrero 1969). Further limits on the growth of the Chinese population were imposed through strict residency laws. Through the royal decree of 1608, Chinese residents were confined to the *parian*, an enclosed or fortified area, where the Chinese were required to stay during the night under penalty of death (Guerrero 1969). Movement restrictions on the Chinese meant that until the second half of the 19th century, at least 90 per cent of the Chinese were concentrated in Manila (Guerrero 1969).

Spanish policies also encouraged the formation of a distinct class of Chinese mestizos, the offsprings from inter-marriages between Catholic Chinese and Catholic Indios. Spanish priests actively tried to convert the Chinese to Catholicism, and those who were converted were encouraged to marry Christianized indigenous women and live in special communities apart from non-Christian Chinese. As a result, the Chinese assimilated rapidly into Filipino society and by the mid-19th century Chinese mestizos greatly outnumbered the Spanish mestizos. By the mid-19th century, there were 240,000 Chinese mestizos compared to less than 10,000 Spanish mestizos (Tan 1985). During the 19th century, within the economy, the Chinese mestizos began to compete with the Chinese and usurped their place in retail trade and other businesses whenever there were mass expulsions or deportations of the Chinese by Spanish authorities. Culturally and politically, the Chinese mestizos are regarded as Filipino and distinct from the Chinese. They are thus not quite comparable to the Peranakans in Indonesia or the Babas and Nonyas in Malaysia who are still regarded as Chinese by the indigenous population. Many wealthy Chinese mestizo families became part of the Filipino indigenous landowning elites.

Under Spanish rule, the colonial authorities distrusted the Chinese but tolerated them because they provided some of the basic services necessary for the sustenance of the colonial governing class. At the same time, the Chinese were willing to engage in trade and other economic activities that the Filipinos were incapable of participating in or were not interested in pursuing. For example, the Chinese had been responsible for introducing sugar refining devices, new construction techniques, moveable type printing and bronze making. The Chinese were also fishermen, gardeners, artisans and traders (Fukuda 1995).

Historically, the Chinese went into business because, as aliens, they were prohibited from owning land. The only route out of poverty was to become self-employed as vendors, retailers, traders, collectors and distributors of goods. During the colonial period and even in the early days of World War II, their lack of access to land for farming made self-employment in petty trade the only channel for upward mobility. The small Chinese population and their concentration in Manila was further reinforced by limited Spanish interest in developing agriculture in the Philippines until the late 18th century. However, in Baguio, some market-gardening was done by the Chinese, though this was less land intensive and more capital and labor intensive than rice farming (Fukuda 1995).

During the Spanish era, those Chinese who could be classified as workers were made up of artisans, servants and cooks who were domestically employed. After 1850, however, demand for Chinese workers grew in the services sector, especially in shipping ports and warehouses (see Go 1996). Following US occupation of the Philippines in 1898, the Chinese Exclusion Act was enforced, effectively prohibiting the importation of Chinese labor to develop the Philippines. The American colonial administration (1898–1945) was more interested in using the Chinese trading network for the marketing and distribution of American products in the Philippines and the exportation of raw materials. Thus, following the implementation of the Chinese Exclusion Act, Chinese traders were not included in the list of Chinese barred from entering the Philippines. Instead, Chinese immigration was restricted to a small quota, consisting mainly of traders and teachers. As a result of such colonial policies, only a very small section of the Chinese community had proletarian origins.

The various restrictions on Chinese immigration imposed by the Spanish authorities and subsequently by the American colonial administration have limited the population size of this ethnic community in the Philippines. By the end of the 1990s, ethnic Chinese constituted less than two per cent (or below one million) of the total Filipino population of 68 million. Numerically, the Philippines has one of the smallest ethnic Chinese populations in Southeast Asia. The Chinese community is also less diversified in terms of dialect groups. The pattern of Chinese immigration was such that the majority of them originated from Fujian province, particularly from the areas around Quanzhou and Xiamen. During the 1930s, it was estimated that 80 per cent of the Chinese in the Philippines were Hokkien while a bulk of the remaining 20 per cent were Cantonese (Hicks 1993). According to Fukuda (1995), the Hokkiens tended to run capital intensive businesses such as banks, international trade, rice mills and general stores while the Cantonese concentrated in the hotel, restaurant and laundry enterprises. Presently, one of the unique features of the Chinese population in the Philippines is their relative homogeneity. In contrast to the Chinese population in most other parts of Southeast Asia, more than 85 per cent of Chinese Filipino are Hokkien and even those of other dialect groups, such as the Cantonese and Hakka, have adopted Hokkien as the lingua franca in the Chinese community.

Since many of the early Chinese migrants to the Philippines were traders, they tended to be active in business. By the end of the 19th century, the Chinese had managed to emerge as a community that had some economic strength, although their capital base was very modest compared to that owned by American and European enterprises. In 1930, although Chinese share of trade was only 13 per cent of total Philippine trade, their position in retail trade, however, was regarded as "truly impressive," as they controlled 90 per cent of domestic retail trade (Fukuda 1995). The Chinese were also active in banking and insurance. China Banking Corporation (which still continues to operate), with its headquarters in Manila and a capital base of 10 million pesos, had branches in Xiamen, Shanghai and Hong Kong in the 1930s. The Mercantile Bank of China, with a capitalization of two million pesos, had branches in Beijing, Shanghai, Hong Kong and Xiamen (Fukuda, 1995). There were also Chinese investments in marine insurance. Fukuda (1995) observed that the Chinese extended fairly large credit to the Filipinos at lower interest rates than anywhere else in Southeast Asia; this was attributed to their wealth and the "richness of Philippine productivity" at the time. Nevertheless, Chinese participation in the financial sector of the economy was rather minimal compared to their involvement in the commercial sector: whereas Chinese investments in the commercial sector totalled approximately 100 million pesos in 1930, investment in banking was only about eight million pesos (Fukuda 1995).

The Chinese suffered during the years of the world economic depression of the late 1920s, which also coincided with a drive by indigenous Filipinos for control of the economy. State measures were instituted to confine river navigation to the Filipinos, alternative distribution networks were set up, and agricultural warehouses, rice and corn companies were established to challenge Chinese dominance of retail and distribution. In the 1930s, the Chinese community's boycott of Japanese goods ironically allowed the Japanese in the Philippines to make inroads into the Filipino economy. Between 1932 and 1934, the number of Japanese merchants actually outnumbered the Chinese in retail trade. Except for this period, the Chinese dominated retail and wholesale trade before the World War II, and in the early post-War years, they began to resume their dominance in retail trade. However, after 1954, with the rise of Philippine economic nationalism and the passage of the Retail Trade Nationalization Law, the Chinese were pressured to move out of the retail sector. The introduction of the Retail Trade Nationalization Law in particular was a significant blow to the Chinese community. Since most Chinese did not have Filipino citizenship, as aliens, they were barred from retail trade by this legislation (see Agpalo 1962; Tang 1988). The owners of larger Chinese businesses circumvented the Retail Trade Nationalization Law by acquiring citizenship for some family members through naturalization, but this was a long, difficult and expensive process that not many Chinese could afford.

There were other restrictions on Chinese economic activities. By restricting land ownership to Filipino citizens, the Chinese were prevented from owning land. Import controls had been imposed after 1949 to limit Chinese, while increasing Filipino, involvement in the import sector (Yoshihara 1994). In 1960, the Rice and Corn Nationalization Law was passed, restricting to Filipinos the trading, milling and warehousing of rice and corn, activities in which the Chinese then had a significant presence (Jiang 1974).

Conditions for Chinese involvement in business improved considerably during the regime of President Ferdinand Marcos (1966–1986), especially after 1975 until his ouster in 1986. As part of an effort to establish diplomatic relations with the People's Republic of China in 1975, Marcos had to resolve the issue of citizenship for the Chinese minority. This Marcos accomplished by issuing a presidential decree, Letter of Instruction 270, which converted the legal procedure of naturalization of aliens into an administrative one. In effect, it simplified the naturalization process, allowing a substantial majority of the ethnic Chinese population to acquire citizenship in a very short time (see Quisumbing 1983). This was a historic turning point for the Chinese as it freed them from the numerous restrictions that had curbed their participation in economic activities.

This presidential decree laid the foundation for the rise of a new breed of Chinese capitalists, some of whom became closely associated with Marcos. By lifting the restrictions on the Chinese, Marcos believed he could use their economic influence as a counter weight to the power of the landowning 'old rich' who were opposed to him (Yoshihara 1994). Among the ethnic Chinese businessmen who emerged under Marcos' patronage and were reputedly his cronies included Ralph Nubla, Jose Campos and Lucio Tan (Yoshihara 1994; Carino 1998). Ralph Nubla was President of the Federation of Filipino-Chinese Chambers of Commerce and Industry (FCCCI) and Board Chairman of the Philippine Bank of Communications (Carino 1998). Jose Campos owned the largest drug company in the Philippines. Lucio Tan, who started out with a small foothold in the cigarette industry, joined the big business league after he went into banking in 1977. Marcos was believed to have been behind Tan's venture into banking as the latter's bank, Allied Banking Corporation, received large infusions of low-interest loans from the Central Bank (Yoshihara 1994). Tan, whose flagship company Fortune Tobacco controls the largest market share of cigarette distribution in the country, is presently one of the richest men in the Philippines (Rivera and Koike 1995).

Under Marcos, the Chinese regained their dominance over the retail sector. In the 1980s, the most dramatic development involving the Chinese was their participation in large-scale retailing. Until the late 1970s, non-Chinese, like Tantoco, a mestizo and a crony of Marcos, had owned the largest and most prestigious department stores, like Rustan's. By the 1980s, however, ethnic Chinese had emerged as owners of the largest department stores in the Philippines. Henry Sy's Shoe Mart and John Gokongwei's Robinson's had expanded rapidly, evolving into huge shopping malls in various parts of Metro-Manila (Yoshihara 1994; Rivera and Koike 1995).

The restrictions on ethnic Chinese economic activities, especially in the two decades between 1954 and 1974, pushed those who had the necessary capital into manufacturing. Most of these industries were import-substituting activities, since such manufacturing ventures were given incentives under the import-substitution industrialization strategy promoted in the Philippines until the 1980s. President Marcos paid lip-service to an export-oriented industrialization strategy in the 1980s but did not push hard enough for its implementation because of resistance from monopolists and oligopolists, many of whom were his cronies. In 1965, ethnic Chinese owned 32 per cent of the largest manufacturing firms in the Philippines. Most of these companies were involved in light industries, producing tobacco, paper, paper products, metal fabrication, soap, cosmetics and rubber products (Yoshihara 1985). By 1986, Chinese Filipino owned 45 per cent of the top 120 domestic manufacturing companies. While these firms were predominantly involved in tobacco and cigarettes, textiles and rubber footwear, the Chinese also controlled a significant share of the steel industry as well as the processing of coconut products, flour and food products (see Rivera and Koike 1995). In a 1990 study of the top 1,000 firms in the Philippines, 37 per cent of the firms in the manufacturing sector were owned by Chinese (Palanca 1995). Many of these companies were in textiles, leather, wood products, paper and publishing, paints, rubber products, plastic products and steel and metal products (Palanca 1995). By 1990, the Chinese had expanded their manufacturing activities to relatively heavier industries, such as steel and metal products.

Despite this active participation in the manufacturing sector, Palanca (1995) noted that between 1980 and 1990, Chinese ownership of manufacturing companies decreased from 48 per cent in 1980 to around 37 per cent in 1990. Meanwhile, Chinese engagement in the services sector grew from an insignificant 1.2 per cent in 1980 to 13.8 per cent in 1990. Such changes in Chinese ownership of economic sectors may be related to the mass naturalization of the Chinese in 1975 and the easing of restrictions on their participation in the economy under Marcos. After 1975, there was rapid expansion of Chinese participation in the banking, hotels and real estate sector, while a number of the larger Chinese-owned businesses began to diversify extensively.

Chinese Participation in the Philippine Economy: A Profile

Top firms

In spite of the economic downturn in the Philippines from 1983 until 1992, some of the larger Chinese-owned companies, most of which are essentially family firms, have diversified and grown into large conglomerates. John Gokongwei, owner of one of the six largest Chinese conglomerates, for instance, started out in food processing in the 1950s, ventured into textile manufacturing in the early 1970s, then became active in real estate development and hotel management in the late 1970s. Gokongwei's group established the Manila Midtown Hotels in 1976 and now runs the Cebu Midtown hotel chain and the Manila Galeria Suites (Rivera and Koike 1995). Gokongwei's group has also acquired a significant interest in PCI Bank and Far East Bank. Lucio Tan started out in tobacco and cigarette manufacturing, and moved into the financial sector when he took over the General Bank and Trust Company in 1977 and turned it into Allied Bank. Tan has since diversified further into real estate and property development, hotels (Century Park Sheraton) and owns a majority interest in Philippine Airlines (PAL). Henry Sy, who built an empire out of his Shoe Mart department store chain, has expanded into real estate development and banking. Sy's group is now the majority owner of Banco de Oro, a commercial bank, and has a substantial interest in China Banking Corporation (Rivera and Koike 1995).

In 1992, of the top 500 companies on the Philippines stock exchange, roughly one-third was Chinese-owned (FFCCCI 1994). Palanca's (1995) study of the top 1,000 firms in the Philippines in 1990 indicated that Chinese Filipinos owned 36 per cent of these companies, while 35 per cent were owned by non-Chinese Filipinos, i.e. indigenous Filipinos as well as Spanish- and Chinese-mestizos (who, as mentioned, are not regarded as Chinese), and 29 per cent by foreigners. Among the top 100 corporations, 43 per cent were owned by Chinese Filipinos, 30 per cent by non-Chinese Filipinos and 27 per cent by foreigners. However, among the top 30 companies, non-Chinese Filipino-owned firms were thrice as many as those owned by Chinese Filipinos. This meant that the leading Filipino companies were still dominated by non-Chinese Filipinos particularly Spanish-mestizo families, such as the Sorianos, Lopezes and Ayalas, and Chinese-mestizo families, like the Cojuangcos and Concepcions.

This highlights one of the unique features of the Philippines: unlike most other Southeast Asian countries where ethnic Chinese have ownership of some of the major enterprises, a strong, dominant class of Filipino entrepreneurs have continued to dominate the economy, retaining ownership and control of the largest enterprises in the country; this class of business elites comprises Chinese-mestizo and Spanish-mestizo families who also remain a powerful political force. For example, a comparison of the Chinese communities in Thailand and the Philippines indicates that while the Sino-Thais own almost all large domestic companies in Thailand, Chinese Filipinos are a less dominant economic force in the Philippines (see Yoshihara 1994). Since the 1980s, however, the situation has begun to change, and a few Chinese Filipinos have shown a capacity to begin challenging the dominance of the traditional Filipino business elites. For example, in late 1992, Lucio Tan outbid an alliance of the Ayalas and Cojuangcos to take control of Philippine Airlines. The assets of J.G. Summit, controlled by the John Gokongwei group, was estimated to be one third of the capital of the Ayala conglomerate and one fourth of San Miguel's in 1993 (Carino 1995). In the same year, in the real estate sector, the Gotianuns (counted among the top six Chinese-owned businesses in the Philippines) who own Filinvest Company outbid the well-established Ayalas for the development of the Alabang Stock Farm (Carino 1995).

Manufacturing

The Chinese appear to have developed an advantage in textiles, garments, dyeing, construction materials, steel and hardware manufacturing, as well as in sugar refining and timber processing. Some Chinese-owned companies are engaged in the manufacture of steel and hardware, with technology from Taiwan. Textiles and garments were the Philippines' top exports in 1993, and of the large-scale garment factories in Metro-Manila, 25 are owned by the ethnic Chinese with a total capitalization of 25 billion pesos (or roughly US$1 billion in 1994). Approximately 200 Chinese-owned firms are involved in the assembly of electronic and electrical products (FFCCCI 1994).

The Chinese are also involved in the processing and distribution of pharmaceutical products. Of the approximately 1,000 firms involved in this industry, most are small and medium-sized companies with a total capitalization of 1.2 billion pesos. The Chinese are active in food-processing as well, with approximately 200 firms engaged in this industry, exporting their products to Hong Kong, Singapore and Taiwan. In the tobacco industry, there are six Chinese-owned firms. Of these, Lucio Tan's Fortune Tobacco is said to control the largest market share in the country (Rivera and Koike 1995). There are also more than 200 companies engaged in the production of paper, paper-products, fertilisers, cosmetics, rubber products and plastics (FFCCCI 1994). In spite of their active involvement in manufacturing, Rivera and Koike (1995) noted that the Chinese are not as involved in export-oriented industries, nor are they into technology-intensive industries; these manufacturing sectors have tended to be dominated by foreign MNCs.

Inter-Island Shipping

There are 12 Chinese Filipino families engaged in inter-island transport and shipping, particularly the shipping of food products requiring refrigeration, with a capitalization of 10 billion pesos. Taiwanese investors have participated in some joint enterprises, and have opened up a direct route between Manila and Cebu. This has facilitated the export of shrimps and other seafoods, vegetables and fruits. In this sector, there is more evidence of joint-ventures between Chinese Filipino firms and non-Chinese Filipino firms or MNCs rather than between Chinese Filipino firms.

Retail Trade, Restaurants

As mentioned, since the 1970s, the Chinese have managed to re-establish their dominance over retail trade. It has been estimated that there are around 8,500 Chinese-owned retail and wholesale firms (FFCCCI 1994). It should be noted, however, that Henry Sy's Shoe Mart chain alone accounts for 49.45 per cent of the total assets of all firms in the wholesale and retail sector (Rivera and Koike 1995). The retail sector appears to be dominated by a few large firms that include Sy's Shoe Mart and Gokongwei's Robinson's, which collectively have thousands of very small retail outlets. There are also roughly 3,000 restaurants and fastfood outlets, one-third of which are based in Metro-Manila. The others are in Cebu, Naga City and Baguio. These fastfood and restaurant outlets, especially those specializing in Chinese cuisine, have attracted investments from Hong Kong and Taiwan (FFCCCI 1994).

Banking and Insurance

There are nine banks where the majority shareholder is Chinese Filipino. These banks include the Metrobank, Allied Banking, China Bank, Equitable Bank, Philippine Bank of Communication, Rizal Commercial Banking Corporation, Philbanking, Philippine Trust and Producers' Bank (Go 1995). Most of these banks constitute part of a family-owned conglomerate. The total assets of these nine banks are estimated to exceed 100 billion pesos (FFCCCI 1994). There are also more than 23 Chinese-owned insurance companies, some with branches overseas and in Hong Kong (FFCCCI 1994).

The Chinese have been in the banking sector since the early part of the 20th century. The two earliest Chinese-owned banks in the Philippines were China Bank and the Mercantile Bank of China, established in 1920 and 1924 respectively. Of the two, China Bank survived the depression years only because its founder, Dee C. Chuan, realizing they required superior expertise in banking, hired two Americans as managers (Go 1995).

Real Estate

In Metro-Manila, 120 Chinese-owned companies are in real estate and construction, while there are about just over 500 firms in the entire Philippines (FFCCCI 1994).

These figures reveal that the Chinese are active in almost every major area of the Philippine economy. Chinese share of the top 1,000 corporations has remained relatively constant at around 35 per cent, and they continue to dominate retail trade, while their influence in the banking sector remains significant. However, the majority of the Chinese seem to be engaged in small and medium-scale enterprises with relatively low levels of capitalization. Among the big Chinese-owned businesses, there is more evidence of competition rather than cooperation. Where there have been joint-ventures, these have been with big non-Chinese Filipino companies or MNCs. Joint-ventures between Chinese Filipino companies and firms from Hong Kong and Taiwan were formed more because of the expertise, technology and capital the latter contributed rather than because of common ethnic ties. Their active involvement in manufacturing shows that Chinese business in the Philippines has a productive dimension although they have been weak in research and development.

Chinese Organizations, Networks and Business Development

Since the Chinese constitute less than two per cent of the total population, their strong presence in many sectors of the Philippine economy is particularly significant. The development of Chinese enterprises in the Philippine economy has been attributed primarily to the evolution of ethnically-based social and business networks. There has, however, not been much research that shows how these ethnically-based networks actually generate capital or play a crucial role in linking up Chinese companies. There is evidence of numerous types of Chinese-based organizations, some of which can be used for business advantage, though most of them perform social rather than economic functions. Contrary to popular perception, Chinese-based organizations are *not* price-fixing cartels nor are they mutual aid societies that pool capital, undertake cooperative buying and selling, provide loans or share business secrets (Omohundro 1983). Even the Chinese chambers of commerce are primarily organized for 'defense' or charitable purposes rather than to enhance business opportunities for its members. Historically, these chambers of commerce have been organized as a means to check corruption among members and to act as a pressure group against particular government policies.

In fact, in spite of the small Chinese population, there has been a proliferation of Chinese organizations, which reflects the competition and rivalry among different groups. There are at least two major Chinese Chambers of Commerce that compete for political leadership among the Chinese – the Federation of Filipino-Chinese Chambers of Commerce and Industry (FFCCCI) and the Philippine-Chinese General Chamber of Commerce (Carino 1998). A third chamber or major business club is now in the process of being formed as a means to challenge the FFCCCI and the Philippine-Chinese General Chamber of Commerce. Many of these communally-based organizations are divided along generational and ideological lines and do not cooperate well at all. The FFCCCI was formed in 1954 as a result of a split in the Philippine-Chinese General Chamber of Commerce, and even the passage of the 1954 Retail Trade Nationalization Law, which seriously threatened ethnic Chinese business interests, failed to bring together the two rival organizations.

Family associations have very little to do with business; instead, they generally perform charitable and social functions. Business interests are pursued informally rather than formally. In his classic study of Chinese merchants in Iloilo, Omohundro (1983) describes how a family association officially refused an application for a loan by one of its members on the grounds that it would set a dangerous precedent. In private, however, the applicant was able to secure some loans from individual members of the association for the expansion of his business.

According to Wickberg (1992), Chinese organizations are not usually a means for upward mobility for those at the bottom of the social ladder. Members join only *after* they have established themselves and have achieved a modicum of respectability. Most businessmen join organizations like the Federation of Filipino-Chinese Chambers of Commerce and Industry or the smaller trade organizations more for reasons of prestige than for economic gain. In fact, membership in such organizations, especially the larger and more prestigious ones, can be rather costly for leaders since they are required to give generous contributions to social and charitable projects, not to mention politicians and political parties to fund election campaigns. Thus, while large organizations exist for the prestige they confer on members, especially leaders, small ones exist mainly to provide comradeship and mutual aid (Wickberg 1992).

Nevertheless, these large organizations have the capacity to become important vehicles for facilitating the business of their members. Wickberg (1992) also argues that although corporate deals are never on the official agenda, the social links established in these organizations could help build up important contacts that can be transformed into business ties. Chinese kin and social networks may also be indirect sources of labor, credit, information, market outlets and security. There is, however, no empirical research to support the hypothesis that business deals have emanated through ties established in such organizations and networks.

In addition to the existence of the more traditional types of Chinese organizations, new forms of organization and networking are beginning to emerge among a younger generation of, usually locally-born, ethnic Chinese. Wickberg (1992) noted the growing popularity of membership in the Kiwanis, Lions, Jaycees and Rotary clubs among this generation of Chinese who feel more comfortable in these organizations than in the traditional clan associations and Chinese chambers of commerce. These 'modern associations' are almost exclusively Chinese in composition and exist for two purposes: conspicuous social service and avid 'business networking'; membership in these organizations also allow them the possibility of securing business contacts that transcend ethnic lines (Wickberg 1992).

In a study of Chinese merchants in Iloilo, Omohundro (1983) discovered that at least 50 per cent of a merchant's contacts were *not* related to him in any way. The successful merchants not only use more social connections in business, but also have slightly more fictive kinsmen as benefactors than the poorer merchants. These fictive kin are usually Filipino or Chinese godparents. This bears out Wong's (1993) contention that in the conduct of business by the Chinese, *personalistic* rather than *kinship* ties have been more important (see also Mackie 1995). Omohundro's (1983) study also noted the increasing importance of classmate connections, which are replacing kinship links in Chinese business ties in the Philippines.

It is also significant that Omohundro (1983) found that those Chinese businessmen who have become affluent establish corporate ties *more* with Filipino 'friends' later in their careers. The unsuccessful businessmen tended to rely on ties related to clans, lineage and hometown associations, indicating that social networks with an ethnic base do not in themselves guarantee business success. A review of the biographies of more successful businessmen has revealed that most of them avoided close contact with Filipinos early in their careers, but once successful, establish alliances with Filipinos of high status and political power. Therefore, as Chinese businessmen become more successful, they include more 'outsiders,' for example, Filipino compadres, friends and foreigners in their business ventures (Omohundro 1983).

Inter-Ethnic Links and Corporate Development

There is evidence that the Chinese businessmen most successful in developing large enterprises have been those who have relied *least* on Chinese networks. In a study of six of the richest Chinese 'taipans' in the Philippines, it was pointed out that one outstanding feature of the development of their enterprises has been "the skillful cultivation of partnerships and social linkages with key indigenous elites at crucial times in their business careers" (Rivera and Koike 1995). Business linkages with local non-Chinese Filipino elites, rather than intra-ethnic Chinese networks, seem to have been the key to the growth of Chinese Filipino enterprises.

Among the leading taipans, George Ty established Metrobank, now one of the top banks in the Philippines, with a "formidable array of former leading public officials" (Rivera and Koike 1995). These officials have included a former Central Bank governor, a former president of the Philippine National Bank, and former premier Cesar Virata, all of who are members of Metrobank's board of directors. Alfredo Yuchengco had close ties with the former Foreign Minister Carlos Romulo, Cesar Virata (Prime Minister during the Marcos era) and Siguon Reyna who owns one of the leading legal firms in the country. A former Customs commissioner presently heads Fortune Tobacco, the flagship firm of Lucio Tan who is reputedly a crony of former president Marcos. Andrew Gotianun, another taipan whose core company is in real estate, is related by marriage to the Consunji family, a Filipino family who owns one of the largest construction companies in the Philippines. Gotianun's son is married to the daughter of Cosunji. John Gokongwei is linked with Eugenio Lopez, head of one of the largest conglomerates in the Philippines, in a number of joint-ventures. Henry Sy has Jose Cuisia, former governor of the Central Bank, as vice-chairman of his main holding company, SM Holdings (Rivera and Koike 1995).

Rivera and Koike (1995) also noted that of these top six Chinese taipans, only one had his business origins in the pre-World War II period. Most of the remaining five taipans established their enterprises after the war, specifically during the 1960s. Four of them had their origins in finance and commerce while two had their base in manufacturing (Rivera and Koike 1995). It is significant that among these six leading taipans, only Lucio Tan is an active member of a Chinese organization, the Federation of Filipino-Chinese Chambers of Commerce and Industry, an umbrella organization organized mainly for 'defense' purposes. The rest of the leading taipans have kept aloof from such communally-based organizations and their activities.

These leading taipans have also established fairly extensive international business linkages. There is no indication that these six taipans have established business linkages on the basis of common ethnic ties; most joint-ventures they have set up involve non-Chinese MNCs, usually forged because the latter provided the needed capital and technological expertise. Yuchengco, who has been around the longest and whose core company can be traced to the pre-war period, has the most extensive links with foreign investors, especially with Japanese corporations. Gokongwei, whose business was established in the 1950s, has joint-ventures and licensing agreements with American, British and Japanese companies. George Ty has established companies with Toyota and Mitsui, which have branches in Xiamen, Beijing, New York, Guam, Taiwan and Hong Kong (Rivera and Koike 1995). It appears that the longer these businessmen have been in business and the larger their enterprise, the greater the variety of international linkages established by them. More recent research also indicates that partners of Japanese investments in the Philippines have been, in many cases, the Chinese Filipinos (see Palanca 1995). For example, when the Philippine-based Toyota Corporation was established in 1988, the company was 40 per cent Japanese-owned while a Chinese Filipino held the remaining equity. On the other hand, American firms tend to have Filipinos as their local partners.

Changing Characteristics of Chinese Family Firms

All major Chinese companies are essentially family firms that remain under the control of their founders or their families. Another characteristic these large Chinese firms share is that they have become conglomerates, with diversified interests, in banking and finance, real estate, manufacturing, agribusiness and transport.

A comparison of Chinese-owned family firms (including four companies owned by taipans) and Spanish-mestizo-owned family enterprises (specifically the Ayala family conglomerate) concluded that there did not appear to be very unique differences in the business style of the Chinese and non-Chinese entrepreneurs (Rivera and Koike 1995). In both cases, family members maintained control over their companies and rapid diversification was the pattern of corporate growth. However, in the non-Chinese Filipino firm, decision-making was much more complex as highly trained professionals were part of the management team. In the case of the Chinese companies, management control was exerted through trusted family members, who headed operations and were responsible for decision-making of core companies and subsidiaries.

Rivera and Koike (1995) believe that the greater reliance on non-family members in management among the Ayalas was attributable to the fact that Jaime Zobel has only two sons but a very extensive corporate empire. Otherwise, there was a possibility that, like Chinese-owned firms, Ayala family members would have held key management posts in this Zobel-controlled conglomerate. There is also some evidence that as Chinese family businesses expand, there seems to be growing recognition of the need to professionalize the management of their operations. Family members involved in big Chinese companies are increasingly more highly educated, often holding management degrees from top universities in the US or the Philippines.

Interestingly too, there have been deviations from the more traditional Chinese practice of business inheritance. Among many of the top Chinese family firms, the transfer of control is being determined not by order of birth, but by education and expertise. Thus, it is not always true that the eldest son will inherit the family business. Rather, it is increasingly the practice to pass on the business to the one most capable of developing the enterprise.

Noteworthy too is the rapidly changing attitude towards the involvement of female family members in the family businesses. One interesting finding in Rivera and Koike's (1995) comparative study is that Jaime Zobel Ayala has not involved any of his five daughters in the family business. In contrast to this, the Chinese taipans have tended to involve their daughters as top executives and managers of various divisions of their conglomerates. Gokongwei's daughter, Robina, is actively involved, and has been delegated much responsibility, in his extensive business operations. In the case of Tan Yu, it is obvious that he has fully entrusted his business empire to his daughter Bien Bien Roxas. Apart from daughters, there is growing evidence that among the Chinese Filipinos, the wives of the owners, whether ethnic

Chinese or not, have become more active in the family business and are often responsible for the management of a branch of the family firm.

Certainly, one of the most interesting developments in recent years has been the growing number of Chinese Filipino women entrepreneurs. Since the mid-1990s, a few Chinese Filipino women have been breaking traditional barriers to become members of what used to be exclusively male enclaves, such as the powerful Federation of Filipino-Chinese Chambers of Commerce and Industry.

Chinese Economic Behavior and International Networks

The investment patterns and form of corporate development of Chinese enterprises have been determined by a strong sense of insecurity. This insecurity has also influenced the pattern of capital accumulation of Chinese businessmen. High rates of savings and high levels of liquidity are said to characterize Chinese enterprise. There might be some cultural propensities for such business practices, but political factors, particularly the periodic occurrence of mass expulsions of the Chinese during the colonial era and the early years of intense nationalism in Southeast Asia, have perpetuated a general sense of uncertainty and insecurity among Chinese Filipinos. In recent years, periodic outbursts of anti-Chinese violence in some Southeast Asian countries, including the fact that the Chinese have become the target of kidnappings in the Philippines, has reinforced this sense of insecurity.

This sense of insecurity is also probably one reason for the diversification of Chinese businesses. Among a number of Chinese companies, there is very little vertical integration of their activities (Mackie 1995). Business diversification does not appear to be a method of rationalizing a business, but seems basically a hedge against economic downturns or vulnerability in situations where there are high levels of political and economic volatility.

Interestingly, however, it appears that the growing number of cases of the internationalization of Chinese businesses has not been due to this insecurity, but is the result of the geographical mobility of the Chinese and the opening up of more economic opportunities. Remigration from Southeast Asia to the US, Canada, Australia and New Zealand, for a variety of reasons, has fuelled the emergence of international networks, normally based on family ties. Based on his more recent study of Chinese organizations in the Philippines,

Wickberg (1992) noted this trend towards internationalization among a number of associations including those based on clan and locality, as well as the Lions Clubs and alumni associations. A variety of reasons have been cited for this development. Some internationalization of organizations may have emerged for the purpose of attending international conventions. Others may be the result of secondary overseas migration; for example, the Philippine Cultural High School Alumni Association has a branch in Vancouver. Yet others may have been formed with the aim of having formal exchanges with organizations in China and Taiwan (Wickberg 1992). Whatever may have been the reasons for the internationalization of these organizations, their effectiveness in affecting the flow of Chinese capital and the degree of Chinese business networking they have generated remains to be studied.

In some of the writings on Chinese business networks in recent years, the impression has been created that there exist tightly-knit, interlocking global networks of Chinese enterprises capable of wielding enormous economic power. Writers, like Seagrave (1995), who make sweeping allusions to extensive, elaborate, global Chinese networks also tend to describe them as exclusive, secretive and manipulative. Some of the negative sentiments towards ethnic Chinese business may be traced to fears of China's emergence as an economic and political power. An article by *Time* (10/5/93) magazine in 1993 described the Chinese diaspora as China's 'secret weapon'. Among Southeast Asian governments, especially in the Philippines and Indonesia, fears have been expressed that China's rise may rekindle patriotic sentiments among the ethnic Chinese and lead to some form of resinification. In 1995, Jose Almonte, the highly influential security adviser of former president Fidel Ramos and director-general of the National Security Council of the Philippines, bluntly warned the Chinese, in an address to the Federation of Filipino-Chinese Chambers of Commerce and Industry (FFCCCI), that "[h]istorically, heightened national feeling in China has resonated strongly among the overseas Chinese communities. If it does so again in our time, then it will complicate our own societies, in which the *huaquiao* are a dominant economic and cultural factor" (quoted in Almonte 1995). Underlying this sentiment is the lingering suspicion among indigenous communities in Southeast Asia that ethnic Chinese political loyalties are still suspect even if they have acquired citizenship in these countries; this sentiment has been strongly disputed by ethnic Chinese in Southeast Asia.

118

Investments in China

The Philippine government does not prohibit ethnic Chinese investments in China, but the authorities frown upon such investments. In view of this negative attitude towards investments in China by the Philippine government, the amount of Chinese Filipino investments in the mainland is difficult to assess since those businessmen who have invested there prefer to keep a low profile. When President Ramos went to China in 1993, with the top six Chinese Filipino taipans in tow, he openly stressed the point in Beijing that the primary role of Filipino businessmen, whether Chinese or non-Chinese, was to reinvest in the Philippines. Ramos also pressured these Chinese Filipino businessmen into forming a corporation that is supposed to invest in infrastructure development in the Philippines. The Emerging Dragon Corporation was eventually formed with Yuchengco as the chairman of the board of directors, with the other five taipans as directors of the company (Carino 1995). To date, this artificially contrived alliance, which brings together business rivals and competitors, has been fraught with difficulties. The Emerging Dragon Corp's plans for the expansion of the airport in Manila is still on the drawing board, withheld from full implementation because of competing plans to develop a new airport at Subic Bay.

Interestingly enough, San Miguel, a huge non-Chinese Filipino firm, is one of the largest investors in China. San Miguel has prawn farms in Xiamen, a feeds factory in Sichuan, a brewery in Guangzhou, and has yet more plans for further expansion into China. Among the big Chinese Filipino firms, a number of them have invested in Xiamen in particular, partly because of the incentives this region offers as a Special Economic Zone and partly due to the historical links of Chinese Filipinos to this area. Lucio Tan, for example, has invested in real estate in Xiamen, while his Allied Bank has established a branch there. Similarly, Henry Sy has invested in real estate and has plans to develop a mall in Xiamen. Gokongwei has a food-processing factory in Xiamen. George Ty is establishing bank branches in Xiamen, Beijing and Shanghai (Suryadinata 1995).

Do these investments mean that these Chinese Filipinos have political loyalties to China? There is little evidence of this. It should be noted that when China was undertaking economic reforms and offering favorable incentives to investors in the 1980s, the Philippine economy was in crisis. Both push and pull factors probably came into play in the decision to invest in China. Investing in China could also be the route for Chinese Filipinos – and other Filipino firms – to expand their operations abroad. During the last two decades, Western firms, for a variety of reasons, had avoided investing in Southeast Asian countries that had socialist regimes, even in those that were shifting towards market economies. As a result, Southeast Asian firms had access to markets in countries such as China, Vietnam, Cambodia, Laos and Myanmar where they did not have to compete with the larger, global companies. Moreover, the governments in Myanmar and Vietnam, as in China, have attracted investment through generous incentives and lower labor costs. Hardly any research has been done into the factors that have encouraged Chinese Filipino companies to invest abroad. Such studies would help shed some light on the role of ethnic Chinese businesses in integrating the economies in the region.

Ethnicity and Investments in ASEAN Countries

How effective have Chinese Filipinos been in attracting foreign investments into the Philippines, especially from Taiwan, Singapore, Malaysia and Hong Kong? Has common ethnicity been an important factor for the link up between ethnic Chinese firms from different countries in East and Southeast Asia? To what extent have ethnic Chinese contributed to the process of economic integration among the ASEAN (Association of Southeast Asian Nations) countries? In the Philippines, the Federation of Filipino-Chinese Chambers of Commerce and Industry (FFCCCI) has always seen as important its own role in attracting investments to the Philippines. The FFCCCI has also been acutely conscious of its ASEAN identity since its formation, using this as a means to bring together businessmen in the region. In 1978, the FFCCCI organized the first ASEAN traders' conference in Manila and annually sends delegations to visit ASEAN countries.

In analyzing some of the reasons why Thailand overtook the Philippines in terms of economic growth since the 1970s, Yoshihara (1994) asserted that Thailand's larger Chinese population – about 10 per cent of the Thai population – was a major factor that gave Thailand an edge. Yoshihara (1994) argues that ethnic Chinese business networks were important in attracting foreign capital, especially ethnic Chinese capital to Thailand. In Thailand, in view of their larger Chinese population size and the greater concentration of economic wealth among members of this ethnic community, as well as the relative lack of discriminatory legislation against them, the Sino-Thais had stronger networks which were "informal, independent of

120

each other but based on trustworthiness and performance" (Yoshihara 1994). Those who belonged to these networks had access to credit, received price discounts and could exchange information. In contrast, in the Philippines, legislation against the Chinese, such as the Retail Trade Nationalization Law of 1954, had "damaged" Chinese networks there; the more efficient networks that the Chinese had built were replaced by less efficient, artificially contrived networks set up by the Philippine government and non-Chinese Filipino (Yoshihara 1994). As a result of the damaged networks, Chinese Filipinos have been much less successful than Sino-Thais in attracting ethnic Chinese investments from abroad. For instance, between 1987 and 1990, Taiwanese companies invested US$2 billion in Thailand, and Hong Kong became Thailand's biggest investor in 1991 (Yoshihara 1994). In contrast to this, Taiwanese investments in the Philippines amounted to a paltry US$9 million in 1987 and grew to only around US$100 million during the period 1988 to 1990 (Wang 1995).

Ethnic connections may have played a role in attracting Taiwan- or Hong Kong-based capital to Thailand but one can also argue that the overall economic conditions in the Philippines over the same period were much less conducive to foreign investments. Political instability, natural calamities, the energy crisis and the spate of kidnappings of the Chinese all contributed to making the Philippines a much less attractive destination for foreign capital from 1983 to 1993. Chinese-based institutions can be good vehicles for attracting more capital to the Philippines, but other conditions have to be in place for them to operate effectively.

Conclusion

The future of Chinese economic activities in Southeast Asia depends on a combination of market forces and state policies. In the Philippines, the development of Chinese business has been partly shaped by legislation imposed by various administrations from the Spanish colonial period to the present government, and partly by economic conditions in the country. In contrast to its Southeast Asian neighbors, the Philippines granted citizenship status to most of its ethnic Chinese population rather late – two to three decades after it had already been done in Malaysia, Indonesia and Thailand. Until 1975, the Chinese, as 'aliens,' were barred from many types of economic activities. Under such conditions, Chinese big business in the Philippines may be considered as something of a 'late bloomer' in the region. This fact and the relatively small size of the ethnic Chinese population have imposed limits on the development of their enterprises.

Chinese Filipino ties to Fujian province and with Taiwan have been particularly strong. In the first two decades after World War II, when the Philippines was economically more advanced than its neighboring countries, Chinese businessmen maintained strong links with Taiwan and invested in the Taiwanese economy. These economic ties have continued until the present and are probably better documented in Chinese language sources published in Taiwan and on the Chinese mainland. Extremely little has been written in English about both the political and economic links between Taiwan and ethnic Chinese in the Philippines. This is an area where translations of Chinese sources would contribute greatly to our knowledge of such intra-ethnic ties. Chinese language sources also provide a wealth of information on the forms of business links established between the Fujianese and Chinese Filipinos. Such Chinese-language sources also provide insights into issues such as migration; for example, on the North Point area in Hong Kong which even today continues to serve as a connecting point in the flow of new migrants from China to the Philippines.

From recent studies of the Chinese Filipinos, one cannot unequivocally conclude that Chinese-based organizations and their business networks have been primarily responsible for Chinese corporate development. While they can function as a medium for social contacts, prestige-building and networking, most of the largest Chinese firms have had to develop strategic linkages with the indigenous political elites and non-ethnic Chinese businessmen at various stages of their development. These inter-ethnic links appear more crucial than intra-ethnic ties in explaining Chinese business development in the Philippines, and requires further study.

Comparative studies of Chinese and non-Chinese Filipino business firms, such as has been initiated by Rivera and Koike (1995), will be useful in clarifying whether business methods and operations unique to the Chinese have been employed in the development of their companies. This will help shed more light on whether factors related to ethnicity and culture are crucial for capital accumulation. It should be stressed that the studies undertaken so far of the enterprises owned by the top six Chinese taipans in the Philippines have indicated that there are already substantial departures from Chinese traditions in their pattern of business. Such departures include the greater involvement of women in management, changing patterns of business inheritances and the fact that the younger generation Chinese taking over business firms are being trained in some of the best business schools in the United States. In view of this, Wong Siu Lun's (1993) observation that the Chinese are strong in entrepreneurship but weak in management may no longer hold true, but this point requires further research. Chinese big businesses are sharply aware of the need to gear up for stronger competition in the midst of further economic liberalization in the region and the rapid globalization of the economy. One area of possible research is to find out how they are preparing for this and in this context, to assess the importance of ethnic Chinese networks in further promoting their enterprises.

There are evidently limits to the usefulness of Chinese networks. In an increasingly internationalized environment, Chinese businessmen will seek new ways of doing business more effectively and successfully. This would probably entail greater inter-ethnic linkages, and there is a need to determine at what levels this is happening. Rohwer (1996) has noted that Liem Sioe Leong of Indonesia's Salim Group has allowed a Filipino professional manager, Manuel Pangili-gan, to run a subsidiary, First Pacific, and to turn it into a conglomerate, even to the extent of sometimes overriding family decisions. It should be noted, however, Pangiligan was a classmate of Salim's son, an indication that 'old school ties' may be more important than ethnic ties (Rohwer 1996).

Finally, what does globalization mean for the majority of Chinese-owned firms that are small and medium-scale enterprises (SMEs) in the Philippines? For the larger companies, there are opportunities for joint-ventures with foreign partners. For the SMEs, however, the entry of foreign competition is not always welcome. In the retail sector, even big Chinese-owned companies are protesting against rapid economic liberalization. When the bill on retail trade liberalization was proposed in Congress in 1994, it was strongly opposed by the Philippine Department Store Owners Association among whose members are the owners of Shoe Mart, Robinson's, Fairmart and Isetann, the biggest department store chains in the country (See 1997). How small and medium-scale enterprises are coping with economic liberalization and global competition should be an important area for further research.

5

Indonesia

Diao Ai Lien and Mely Tan

This chapter, through a literature review of some major studies on Indonesia's political economy, provides an overview of the state of research on Indonesian Chinese enterprise. For this review, we have made extensive use of the article by Dede Oetomo, entitled 'The Ethnic Chinese in Indonesia,' published in Leo Suryadinata's 1989 edited volume, *The Ethnic Chinese in the Asean States: Bibliographical Essays*.[1] This article by Oetomo, based on a review of publications from 1945 to 1986, provides a comprehensive picture of all aspects of the situation of ethnic Chinese in Indonesia. Oetomo's article includes a bibliography of about 520 entries, but we will only review those articles on the economic activities of ethnic Chinese. In addition, we have referred to a number of publications on the Chinese in Indonesia in the last decade, continuing where Oetomo left off in 1986. These publications include articles in newspapers and economic and business magazines. We have also undertaken a review of unpublished materials, such as theses, dissertations and seminar papers.

This paper consists of two parts. The first section provides a brief history of the Chinese in Indonesia. The second part provides a discussion on the problems in defining 'Chineseness' and 'Chinese business' in Indonesia as well as the constraints on researching on Chinese business in the country. The chapter concludes with a section on our suggestions for further research on this topic. An updated bibliography of publications on the economic activities of ethnic Chinese in Indonesia is also provided in the list of references in this volume.

Chinese Business in Indonesia

The Colonial Period

Under Dutch colonial rule of Indonesia, which started from the mid-17th century and ended in 1941 with the Japanese invasion of the Dutch East Indies during World War II,[2] the Chinese played the role of economic middlemen. Buying produce cultivated by the indigenous Indonesian population, the Chinese sold them to the Dutch colonial masters, who shipped them to Europe. The proceeds from the sale of these goods filled the coffers of the Dutch to overflowing. Ricklefs (1981) noted that between the early 1830s and late 1870s, the Dutch government had secured revenues totalling almost 832 million guilders from its colonial territories in this region; by 1860, it was estimated that this Dutch colony was providing almost a third of Holland's state revenues.

The middleman role played by the Chinese was reflected in their position in the social stratification of colonial Indonesia. The Dutch were the overlords, the Chinese formed the middle level, and the indigenous Indonesian occupied the bottom level. A more elevated space was, however, given to the indigenous nobility, that is the sultans and rajas spread over various parts of the archipelago. Selected indigenous people were appointed to rule over the indigenous population, through an 'indirect rule system'. This economic, social and legal division by race practiced by the Dutch was popularly known as the 'divide and rule' system.

The Chinese were part of the category of 'foreign orientals,' which also included Arabs and Indians of South Asia; in terms of numbers, however, the Chinese were the largest population. In the beginning of colonial rule, the Chinese were allowed to own land, and some of those who accumulated huge properties eventually emerged as powerful landlords. In 1860, however, the Agrarian Law was enacted by the Dutch to bar the Chinese from owning land. The Chinese could not, therefore, be directly involved in agriculture, although there were – and there still are – Chinese engaged in farming, especially vegetable and fruit, in some parts of Java and on some of the other islands. The Chinese were also excluded from becoming civil servants, as they were barred from taking the civil servant examination. Hence, as a source of livelihood and income, the Chinese had few alternatives but to engage in trade and business. As a result of events that occurred during colonial rule, the Chinese became very adept in economic activities;

125

they continue to dominate trade in agricultural produce and also control the domestic distribution and retail market.

Chinese control of the distribution and retail market was concentrated in the towns and villages in Java, as well as some of the other islands. Most of these Chinese retailers, who dealt in foodstuff and daily household necessities, operated out of 'shop-houses,' with the shops on the ground floor and the living quarters on the upper floor. Such shop-houses were commonly located on the main streets of towns, ingraining in the minds of the indigenous community a sense of the ubiquitous presence of Chinese enterprises.

While most Chinese were involved in small-scale retailing during the colonial period, in one particular area of the economy, revenue farming, some Chinese were able to accumulate wealth. Revenue farming involved the parcelling out of certain economic activities, such as the sale and distribution of opium and the operation of local markets, by the Dutch colonialists to wealthy Chinese businessmen.[3] Through this farming out system, the colonial government was assured of receipt of payment of taxes on these activities. However, since revenue farming activities included tax and debt collection by some Chinese, the indigenous community soon came to have a hostile view of Chinese enterprise; this image was not helped by Chinese dominance of the retailing of basic commodities.

There are a number of important studies depicting the economic activities of the Chinese in the colonial economy, especially in their role as middleman. One of the best pre-World War II studies, though in the Dutch language, is the edited volume by J.L. Vleming, *Het Chineesche Zakenleven in Nederlandsch-Indie* (Business Activities of the Chinese in the Netherlands Indies), published in 1926. Vleming, the head of the Indies Revenue Auditing Service, edited this highly informative book on the economic activities and practices of the Chinese in the Netherlands East Indies in the 1920s. Another important study on the Chinese, by a Dutch civil servant and scholar, P.H. Fromberg, was *Verspreide Geschriften* (Miscellaneous Writings), a compilation of writings also published in 1926. The most well-known pre-World War II study on Chinese enterprise published in English (in 1936) was by J.W. Cator, *The Economic Position of the Chinese in the Netherlands Indies*, which is still considered a classic on the topic.

Special note should be taken of a publication on the Chinese in the pre-World War II period that was written and published in Holland during the war (in 1943) by an Indonesian-born Chinese, Ong Eng

Die. This study, Ong's doctoral dissertation entitled *Chineezen in Nederlandsch-Indie: Sociografie van een Indonesische Bevolkingsgroep* (The Chinese in the Netherlands-Indies: A Sociography of an Indonesian Population Group), is virtually the only sociological study on the Chinese during the pre-World War II period. It covers all aspects of life of the Chinese, commencing with a demographic overview of the spread of the Chinese over the archipelago, and providing a number of chapters on their economic role, business activities and practices and form of entrepreneurship. Unfortunately, the more typically sociological aspects, such as social stratification and leadership patterns are not dealt with at all. Interestingly, Ong moved into mainstream politics after Indonesia declared Independence in 1945. Ong had returned to Indonesia that year, became involved in politics by joining the major political party, Partai Nasional Indonesia (PNI) (1947–1948), and in 1955 became Minister of Finance in the Cabinet of Ali Sastroamidjojo. At the time, there was another minister of Chinese origin, Dr Lie Kiat Teng, who occupied the post of Minister of Health from 1953 to 1955.

The picture we get of the economic role of the Chinese in the colonial period is that of a small ethnic community that was given a niche in Indonesian society by the Dutch, especially in revenue farming activities. The Dutch had, however, distributed revenue farming licences to a relatively small number of Chinese while simultaneously restricting the participation of the Chinese in other areas of the economy. Most Chinese remained small-scale retailers (see Table 5.1), while those Chinese who had managed to accumulate some wealth were unable to expand their business beyond their revenue farming activities. The interpretation, however, by certain ethnic Indonesian writers of the place of the Chinese under Dutch rule was that of a group that enjoyed certain privileges, in the economy and in their legal position, which was superior to that of the indigenous Indonesians (see, among others, *KENSI Berjuang*). This, they contended, allowed the Chinese to have a head start in business, enabling them to secure a dominant presence in a number of sectors of the Indonesian economy. This legacy of the colonial period, they maintained, had to be remedied, as it was untenable that ethnic Indonesians who, with Independence, were masters of their own country, but had not achieved ownership and control of any segment of the economy. Hence, the grip on the economy by the Chinese had to be broken, by implementing policies that would protect and enhance the economic activities of indigenous Indonesians.

Table 5.1 Control of Economic Sectors by Ethnic Groups in Java, 1930

Sector	Indigenous Indonesians		Chinese		Europeans	
	Number	%	Number	%	Number	%
Wholesale and intermediate trade	6,551	0.7	1,892	1.8	3,498	37.0
Retail trade	837,200	92.1	92,849	88.1	2,957	31.3
Credit and loan	13,725	1.5	5,336	5.0	1,798	19.1
Other trades	51,464	5.7	5,365	5.1	1,194	12.6
Total	908,940	100.0	105,442	100.0	9,447	100.0

Source: Suryadinata 1992: 82

Beginning of the Republic

In the early 1950s, the government issued policies clearly geared towards this objective of developing indigenous businessmen with some influence in the economy. During this period, the 'Benteng'[4] program was introduced, aimed at providing special opportunities for indigenous Indonesians to participate in the economy. This program proved unsuccessful, and led to practices where business licenses issued to ethnic Indonesians were channelled to companies financed and managed by ethnic Chinese. Many of the ethnic Indonesians who were recipients of such licences were 'straw-men,' whose names were on the licence, but who were usually merely receiving an attractive remuneration as a director of the company with little or no active participation in the enterprise. Such practices led to a widespread belief that ethnic Indonesians were not adept in doing business though there have been no conclusive studies examining this contention.

There had been a number of well-established companies owned by indigenous Indonesian during colonial rule and in the early period of the Republic. Companies such as Dassaad-Musin and Djohan Djohor are still remembered as among the largest indigenous Indonesian firms of the colonial period. However, only a few of these companies survived the fierce competition that ensued in the late 1950s, while the nationalization policy implemented subsequently by the government led to the creation of state enterprises. It is also quite probable that under the Benteng program, those ethnic Indonesians who became 'straw-men' had been selected as business partners by the Chinese precisely because they had no interest in developing an enterprise and would therefore not interfere in the management and development of the company. This remains an under-researched topic that is also relevant in the present period.

With the Benteng program a failure, and as ethnic Chinese continued to dominate the private sector, ethnic Indonesians made more demands for some form of state intervention in the economy. Such sentiments were manifested in writings published in 1956. One example was the piece written by Assaat, entitled *Perlindungan Khusus bagi Usaha Nasional* (Special Protection for National Enterprises); another publication was by the Badan Pekerja KENSI Pusat (an organization of ethnic Indonesian businessmen), entitled *KENSI Berjuang* (The Struggle of KENSI). Obviously, the term 'national enterprises' was meant solely for enterprises owned by indigenous Indonesians.

One reason for this call for the state to provide avenues to increase equity ownership by the indigenous Indonesians was that during the 1950s the Dual Nationality Treaty between Indonesia and the People's Republic of China had not been implemented. Until the end of the 1950s, the citizenship position of the Chinese inhabitants was unclear.[5] This Dual Nationality Treaty was signed in 1955 between both countries to resolve the problem faced by ethnic Chinese in Indonesia of dual citizenship (in China and Indonesia). This treaty was applicable to those people living in Indonesia whose father was recognized to be Chinese or of Chinese origin. This treaty was only enacted in 1960, and for a two-year period, ethnic Chinese were required to go to court to fill in a form rejecting Chinese citizenship if they wanted to have only Indonesian citizenship. According to Heidhues (1998), when ethnic Chinese in Indonesia were asked to make a choice of their citizenship, "the majority elected to be Indonesian citizens, but about one-third opted for Chinese citizenship, thus raising the number of aliens. Only a few individuals were naturalized as citizens, so over 60 per cent of the ethnic Chinese in Indonesia remained aliens up to the 1980s."[6]

This uncertainty over the citizenship of ethnic Chinese contributed to criticisms by ethnic Indonesians that the former had no right to take over industries that were traditionally in the hands of the indigenous community, such as the batik, cigarette (especially clove cigarette) and textile industries (see, for example, Castles 1967). This led to demands by the indigenous community that the Chinese be excluded from owning or operating in certain industries. During the 1950s, ethnic Chinese also continued to face discrimination in the form of restrictions on landholdings, a policy introduced during the colonial period.

In spite of the restrictions and impediments to the development of Chinese capital, and although the state had been able to curb the growth of such ethnic enterprise, there was widespread perception among ethnic Indonesians that the Chinese occupied a position in the economy that was not commensurate with their population size; this has given rise to what is referred to as the *masalah Tionghoa* or *masalah Cina*, or 'the Chinese problem'. Of Indonesia's total population of 200 million, ethnic Chinese are estimated to constitute about three percent of the population, or about six million people. The Chinese, however, are well-dispersed throughout the main islands of the archipelago, and are primarily concentrated in the cities of Jakarta (in Java), Medan (in Sumatra) and Pontianak (in Kalimantan). Even though a majority of ethnic Chinese has rejected PRC citizenship and opted to be Indonesian citizens, the view of many ethnic Indonesians was that the Chinese were a minority of foreign origin, and therefore 'not one of us'. This view has changed, depending on the general situation in society: whenever there is a condition of social or economic discontent, Chinese businesses usually are one of the first victims of the social unrest that may ensue. This has been repeatedly seen in Indonesia's history. The Chinese had been subjected to some form of violence during the Japanese Occupation (1942–45), the Indonesian revolution (1945–49), the period following the abortive coup in 1965 and in May 1998 during the fall of the Soeharto regime.

The New Order Government of Soeharto

In the aftermath of the abortive coup of 30 September 1965, attributed to the Indonesian Communist Party, the government of President Soekarno was replaced by Soeharto. In spite of the dire economic conditions that were a legacy of the Soekarno government, by 1968, the inflation rate had been reduced to manageable proportions, after reaching about 650 per cent by the time of the upheaval in 1965. This achievement was attributed primarily to Soeharto's economic advisors, a group of Berkeley-trained, young economists, under the leadership of Professor Widjojo Nitisastro and his colleagues of the University of Indonesia.

In 1967, in an attempt to rehabilitate the ailing economy, the government had adopted the policy of inviting direct investment from abroad, with the requirement that such investments be undertaken through joint ventures with local companies. At the time, the local companies that were in a viable economic position to participate in business ventures with foreign investors were those owned by ethnic Chinese. Most of the Chinese-owned companies that emerged as 'conglomerates' had their beginnings precisely at the inception of the New Order government of President Soeharto. It was during the Soeharto regime that the presence of ethnic Chinese in most economic sectors increased tremendously. The Chinese had moved beyond the retail business, into manufacturing, banking and finance, property development, hotels, telecommunications and forestry, with some Chinese emerging as owners of large, well-diversified enterprises. These Chinese-owned conglomerates are popularly referred to in the media as 'konglomerat' (which in the press parlance also refers to the owner of the enterprise).

One of the most comprehensive books discussing the pattern of development, as well as the political links, of some of the largest conglomerates is that of Richard Robison's *Indonesia: The Rise of Capital*, published in 1986. The largest enterprises include Sudono Salim (Liem Sioe Liong)'s Salim Group – Liem is considered one of the wealthiest ethnic Chinese in Asia – Mochtar Ryadi and son James Ryadi's Lippo Group, Eka Tjipta Widjaja and his family's Sinar Mas Group, William Soeryadjaja and sons' Astra Group and Muhamad (Bob) Hasan's Nusamba Group. Robison based his study on an analysis of published documents on company files and documents of firms that have been publicly-listed on the Jakarta Stock Exchange (JSE), combined with perceptive interviews with knowledgeable persons. Robison provides an insightful and revealing analysis of how these big businesses operate and relate with the power holders (see also Supriatma 1996).

Liem is the most prominent member of the Chinese capitalists who emerged under the Soeharto regime. Liem is reputed to have benefited from his close association with Soeharto who gave him access to credit and licences to establish an interest in banking, logging, clove imports, flour-milling and cement production. Operating through his main investment arm, the Salim Group, reputedly once the world's largest Chinese-owned conglomerate, Liem has expanded his business overseas securing lucrative interests holdings in Singapore, the Philippines, Hong Kong and in the US. In 1990, the Salim Group alone accounted for at least five per cent of Indonesia's GDP, while the group's turnover totalled almost US$8 billion, making it Indonesia's largest and most important conglomerate. The Liem-Soeharto tie has constantly been used to indicate two important aspects of Indonesia's political economy, i.e. the heavy reliance of most businessmen on the government for support and that business groups are subject to government intervention.

A more recent publication on the political economy of big business in Indonesia is the volume by Adam Schwarz, *A Nation in Waiting: Indonesia in the 1990s*, published in 1994. This highly perceptive analysis of the political economy of Indonesia is the product of Schwarz' research while stationed in Jakarta from 1988 to 1992 as correspondent for the *Far Eastern Economic Review*. Schwarz provides insightful views on the development of the role of Islam in politics and in the economy and of how President Soeharto's children, as well as their spouses, and even one of his grandsons, had managed to secure control over a huge corporate base through companies under their ownership. There is also a chapter in Schwarz' volume on the rise of ethnic Chinese conglomerates and of their relationship with the Soeharto family and other influential people in government and the armed forces. Schwarz suggests that the rapid development of conglomerates by members of the Soeharto family and some Chinese businessmen was due to a form of state patronage that is now popularly termed 'cronyism'.

There are, however, structural reasons that help explain how Chinese enterprises have been developed in Indonesia. Following the state's decision to embrace the market system, the New Order government realized that it would be detrimental to economic growth if Chinese business activities were heavily restricted. The expansion of Chinese enterprise in the Indonesian economy during the New Order era was primarily due to the opportunities accorded to such businesses by the government, including by making it easier for them to acquire credit from state banks. In contrast to this, under the Soekarno government, regulations had been introduced to curb the rise of Chinese capital. For example, in the late 1950s, the government introduced legislation to prevent all foreigners not born in Indonesia (and this included many ethnic Chinese) from being involved in the retail sector outside the cities. Foreigners were also subsequently prevented from settling in rural areas, contributing to the concentration of ethnic Chinese in towns, particularly in the major cities in Java, Sumatra and Kalimantan. The strategic location of Chinese companies in towns also facilitated the development of their business in a period of rapid economic expansion during the Soeharto era. However, in spite of the favorable support that Chinese firms, particularly the largest companies, received from the state, the Soeharto government also insisted that such enterprises set up programs, referred to as 'partnership programs,' to assist the development of medium and small ethnic Indonesian business and cooperatives.

Studies on some of the major Chinese enterprises also argue that their development style indicates an entrepreneurial dimension (see, for example, Sato 1993). There are those who attribute the development of large enterprises by these businessmen to their cultural background, pointing out that the 'economic tigers' in Asia all have one thing in common, i.e. the Confucian tradition, or their sinitic heritage (see, for example, Redding 1990; Seagrave 1995). Others argue that the historical network of business and trade relations that have been developed across national boundaries, operating in a 'borderless world,' is a crucial factor in explaining the prominence of Chinese enterprise in Indonesia and Southeast Asia (Ohmae 1995; Fukuyama 1995; Hamilton 1991). There is, however, insufficient empirical evidence to substantiate these arguments. There is also some evidence that suggests that ethnic Chinese have been able to thrive only in those areas where the local population has not had a strong tradition of active engagement in trade and business, as for example in Java.

Fall of Soeharto and Rise of Habibie

On 21 May 1998, in an unprecedented ceremony, Soeharto, two months into his seventh term in office as president announced his resignation and immediately transferred power to Vice-President B.J. Habibie.[7] This dramatic event marked the end of a 32-year rule that started with the upheaval of 1965, following the killing of six top generals and the subsequent fall of Soekarno.

Soeharto's resignation was preceded by a series of unsettling events precipitated by a financial crisis that had adversely affected the Indonesian economy. Thailand had been the first Southeast Asian country to be affected by this crisis that began with a precipitous fall in the exchange rate of the Thai currency, the baht, against the US dollar in July 1997. In Indonesia, the crisis also commenced with a rapid decline of the value of its currency, the rupiah. In July 1997, the exchange rate of the Indonesian currency was Rp.2.400 to one US dollar; by the end of August, it had declined to Rp.3.000, before weakening further to Rp.4.000 at the end of November; by the first week of December, it was down to Rp.6.000.[8]

The free fall in the international value of the rupiah had a devastating effect on the corporate sector, especially on the banking industry. Pangestu and Soesastro (1999: 8), while assessing the role of the International Monetary Fund (IMF), which had started to assist Indonesia in October 1997, observed that by 1999 the volume of total private debt in the local banking sector was still an estimated US$74 billion, and a large number of companies continued to be in no position to service their debts.

In actual fact, the 'ordinary' people in Indonesia did not feel the impact of the crisis until the first week of January 1998, when there was a sudden run on supermarkets, mostly by well-off housewives. Within a few days, even the shelves of the huge hypermarkets were empty. By this time, the rupiah had fallen to Rp.10.000 to the dollar, and on 22 January it hit Rp.17.000 (Pangestu and Soesastro 1999: 12).[9] The run on supermarkets arose following persistent rumors that the stock of basic commodities would soon be depleted and that the factories producing such staples would have difficulty shipping the products to their distributors. Consequently, the price of these commodities rose significantly, and the government had to set up special distribution points to sell at a low price the three basic commodities of rice, cooking oil and sugar. Food lines appeared, with people standing in queues for hours to get their rationed share; jostling and fights were reported in some of these food lines.

The print and electronic media were soon filled with reports of shops in small towns along the northern coast of Java being attacked, ransacked, looted and burnt down. The attackers had accused the shopowners of hoarding basic necessities and selling them at inflated prices. In some cases, the attackers took the goods out of the store, heaped them in the middle of the road and burnt them, prohibiting onlookers from taking them away. This was, ostensibly, to show that they were not looters, only wanting to punish the shopowners for hoarding goods. The owners of most of these shops were ethnic Chinese.

The Chinese, as noted earlier, dominate retail trade in small towns in Java, and in particular along the northern coast of the island, among the earliest Chinese settlements. Their enterprises, commonly located along the main road of the towns, were predominantly small grocery shops. Most of these enterprises were family businesses, with the husband, wife and children minding the store, sometimes aided by a few sales staff, usually young ethnic Indonesian girls. Their customers were mostly the local ethnic Indonesians with whom the Chinese shopowners appeared to have a good relationship. However, in times of general discontent generating social unrest leading to outbursts of violence, the Chinese easily became the target for ethnic Indonesians to vent their anger on.

There are several reasons why the Chinese are normally targetted by ethnic Indonesians during turbulent periods. Since the Chinese enterprises are concentrated in main shopping districts, they are a highly visible community. They sell goods that people need on a daily basis, making the Chinese vulnerable when prices of these commodities suddenly rise. They have no political power and therefore no one to protect their interests or voice their concerns in government (Tan 1998).

There was little attempt on the part of the ethnic Chinese to participate in political activities, nor did the government or the larger society encourage such activities by this community. Moreover, among the leading Indonesian capitalists who had emerged during the Soeharto era were a significant number of ethnic Chinese who had managed to create, within a few decades, large corporate bases. Among these corporate groups, some of which secured much state patronage, included those owned by the Liem, Riady and Widjaja families. Widespread public knowledge of the corporate equity owned by these leading Chinese capitalists contributed to the belief that ethnic Chinese dominated the economy.

These factors contributed to the appalling violence perpetrated against the Chinese during the 13–15 May 1998 riots in Jakarta, as well as in Solo in Central Java and also in Medan in North Sumatra. For three days, mobs went on a rampage that was clearly directed at businesses, shopping centers and residential areas with a high concentration of ethnic Chinese. Huge shopping malls were looted and then burnt down. More than a thousand people, mostly looters among who included women and children, were killed in the process.

These events were preceded by demonstrations by university students demanding the resignation of Soeharto. On 12 May, these demonstrations led to the fatal shooting by uniformed men of four students at the private Trisakti University, even though the students had already entered the campus.[10] The three days of mayhem culminated in the sit-in on the Parliament grounds and eventual invasion of the building by the students. More tense days followed until the resignation of Soeharto on 21 May 1998 and the installation of Habibie as President.

The euphoria that followed Soeharto's departure soon gave way to concern, and even alarm, as the magnitude of the economic disarray was brought into the open, especially in the banking system and the corporate sector; this eventually led to huge lay-offs in all sectors of the economy. The tenuous economic condition was aggravated by uncertainty in the political arena, due to liberalization of political activities after the fall of the Soeharto government. Political liberalization led to a proliferation of new political parties. While only three parties were allowed to function under the Soeharto regime, during the parliamentary election scheduled for 7 June1999, 48 parties were eligible to participate in the polls. One party, Partai Bhineka Tunggal Ika (PBI), was reputedly established to represent Chinese interests. The leader of this party is ethnic Chinese, but membership is open to all Indonesians.

The parliamentary election itself was conducted without any incidence of violence, and according to the evaluations of both the foreign and local monitoring groups, voting was carried out in a remarkably free and fair manner.[11] The results of the June election favored the Indonesian Democratic Party for Struggle (PDI-Perjuangan), led by Megawati Soekarnoputri, which secured 33.7 per cent of the total votes cast. The Golkar, the ruling party, which secured the second largest volume of support, obtained just 22.46 per cent of the total votes cast, while all but one of the other parties secured less than 10 per cent of the votes (*Kompas* 27/7/99).[12] Since no party won a clear majority, this has led to the need to form coalitions. This situation, however, generated debates, primarily involving accusations of 'money politics,' which contributed to deep feelings among the population of instability in the political arena.

The validity of concerns about 'money politics' was confirmed following disclosure of irregularities involving the Bank Bali and treasurers of the Golkar. It was alleged that public funds meant for the recapitalization of Bank Bali were diverted to a company owned by the treasurer of the Golkar to fund Habibie's campaign during the presidential elections, scheduled for November 1999.[13] Bank Bali is associated with the Ramli family, who are Chinese-Indonesians, while its chief executive officer was Rudy Ramli before management of the bank has been taken over by the Standard Chartered Bank.

Ethnic Chinese had dominated the domestic banking sector. The biggest private banks are the Bank Central Asia (BCA), associated with Liem Sioe Liong and his son Anthony Salim; the Lippo Bank, associated with the Lippo Group controlled by the Riady family; the Bank Internasional Indonesia (BII), associated with Eka Tjipta Widjaja who controls the Sinar Mas Group; and the Bank Danamon, associated with Usman Atmaja. During the restructuring of the banking sector, however, of these four banks, the BCA and Danamon Bank were taken over by the government,[14] as was Bank Bali. BII and

Lippo Bank continue to function on their own as they have managed to fulfill their recapitalization requirements.

The way in which ethnic Chinese have coped with the political and economic crises reflects the remarkable resilience of this community. After the riots in May, many of the affected Chinese sought refuge in hotels or in other areas of Jakarta, or within Indonesia, considered safe. Those who could afford it went abroad, mainly to Singapore or Australia. However, within weeks of the crisis, many Chinese had returned, although often without their family. The shopping areas that were not hit during the looting were reopened, and within a few months, the businessmen who owned stores in buildings that were burnt down restarted their business in new premises (*Kompas* 26/3/99).

Among the large Chinese-owned conglomerates, those that rely on foreign imports for the production of their commodities are still in a state of paralysis. However, those companies involved in agri-industry or agri-business continue to operate relatively well. Some companies that operate in areas outside Java are even thriving, for example in North Sulawesi, where they deal in cloves, copra, vanila, corn and fish and fish products, and in Bangka, especially in the pepper and tin sectors. In these two areas, export of their products has increased appreciably because of the high exchange rate of the dollar to the rupiah.[15]

Meanwhile, a number of ethnic Chinese have emerged from the traumatic experience of the May riots more assertive of their political rights as Indonesian citizens. Admittedly, these 'activists' constitute a minority of the Chinese-Indonesian population, but they are articulate, have strong media exposure and have entered mainstream politics through political parties. At least three Chinese-led political parties have been formed, but eventually only one, the Partai Bhineka Tunggal Ika, or PBI, applied to the Komisi Pemilihan Umum (KPU, or National Election Commission) and passed the qualifying requirements to participate in the June 1999 parliamentary election. As mentioned, even though an ethnic Chinese, who has a thriving travel business, leads the PBI, membership in the party is open to all ethnic groups.

Four categories of 'activists' can be distinguished among Chinese-Indonesians: (i) those who have set up a political party; (ii) those who have established pressure groups, usually referred to as a forum or a 'gerakan' (movement), such as the Forum Kerukunan Bangsa (Forum for the Harmony of the Nation) and the Gerakan Perjuangan Anti-Diskriminasi (Movement for the Struggle Against Discrimination) and the INTI (Perhimpunan Indonesia Tionghoa, or Chinese Indonesian Association); (iii) those who have set up mutual aid associations, usually referred to as 'paguyuban', e.g. the Paguyuban Sosial Marga Tionghoa Indonesia (Association of Chinese Indonesians); and (iv) those who are members of one of the three existing Chinese parties or of the other 45 newly-established political parties. People in the fourth category include three well-known ethnic Chinese, Christianto Wibisono, a Protestant, K. Sindhunata, a Catholic, and Junus Jahya, a Muslim, who have joined PAN, which is headed by Amien Rais, a professor in political science at the Gadjah Mada University. Kwik Kian Gie, a prominent economist, is a leading member of Megawati's PDI-P, while Henry Kuok, a young, articulate ethnic Chinese, is active in the Partai Rakyat Demokratik (PRD, or People's Democratic Party); Kuok represents his party in the National Election Commission (Tan 1999).

Another new development among ethnic Chinese is the expression of their ideas by publishing tabloids and magazines run and read mainly by ethnic Chinese. Among these publications are the tabloids *Nagapos* and *Suara 168* and the magazine *Media Sinergi Bangsa*, or *Sinergi*. A community bulletin, the *Glodok Standard*, has also been published.[16]

A number of books have also been published on Chinese-Indonesians. Among these publications include *Kapok Jadi Nonpri: Warga Tionghoa Mencari Keadilan* (Fed Up With Being a Non-Pri: Ethnic Chinese Citizens in Search of Justice), edited by Alfian Hamzah in 1998. This volume is a compilation of articles written by a number of well-known figures, both ethnic Chinese and ethnic Indonesians, regarding their views on the riots of May 1998 and the position of ethnic Chinese in its aftermath. Such publications reveal that the perception among ethnic Indonesians of these events in May 1998, for example the alleged gang rape of ethnic Chinese women and girls,[17] are varied, from believing without any reservation that such assaults occurred to expressing grave doubts about these incidents.

Another publication dealing with reactions to the May 1998 riots is a volume based of the proceedings of a seminar on ethnic Chinese, organized by the Centre for International and Development Studies (Cides), of the Ikatan Cendekiawan Muslim Indonesia or ICMI (Association of Muslim Intellectuals), held in October 1997. This volume, edited by Moch. Sa'dun M. and entitled *Pri-Non-Pri: Mencari Format Baru Pembauran* (Pri-Non-Pri: In Search of a New Format of Assimilation), also includes a selection of articles that appeared in various media until August 1998. In March 1999, a reader edited by I. Wibowo, entitled *Retrospeksi dan Rekontekstualisasi Masalah Cina* (Retrospection and Recontextualization of the Chinese Problem), was published, with contributions by political scientists, historians and sociologists, both ethnic Chinese and ethnic Indonesians. The thrust of the book is a fresh look at the role of ethnic Chinese in Indonesian society, away from the restricting format of the Soeharto government, i.e. of the concept of assimilation as defined by the government, which according to some of the authors, has influenced the approach of scholarly research on the community in Indonesia.

There have been some encouraging signs of the beginning of a more open attitude by the government and of the society at large towards the ethnic Chinese. There is also some evidence of growing confidence among ethnic Chinese of being accepted as Indonesian citizens. However, social and economic problems continue to arise which impair the transition to democracy and the creation of a more open and tolerant society.[18]

Definitional and Research Problems: Ethnic Chinese and Chinese Business

From this brief historical profile of the Chinese in Indonesia, it is clear that there is a need to differentiate between the various types of Chinese who live in Indonesia. The major distinction has to do with the period when the Chinese migrated to Indonesia. Among the early Chinese migrants, most of whom were males, there was much inter-marriage with local women; this formed the nucleus of the 'peranakan' community, i.e. ethnic Chinese who had assimilated into Indonesian society, adopting the local language and customs.[19] The more recent Chinese migrants, which form a distinct community from the peranakans, are known as 'totoks,' which means 'pure'. Even among the recent migrants, there are sub-ethnic distinctions that need to be recognized. There are also class differences between the peranakans and totoks, as well as between the owners of major enterprises and small and medium-scale companies. This distinction, however, between the peranakans and totoks is becoming increasingly blurred, not in the least because since the 1965 upheaval Chinese-language schools have been banned.

These nuances need to be recognized in an analysis of the Chinese. However, most of the literature in the English language on Chinese communities outside China and Taiwan, in particular those written by non-Chinese, tend to regard the Chinese residing outside these countries, or those of Chinese origin, as a monolithic group, collectively referred to as 'Overseas Chinese' (see, for example, Kotkin 1992; East Asia Analytical Unit 1995). This is incorrect, as the term 'Overseas Chinese' is a translation of the Chinese word, *huaqiao*, which literally translated means 'sojourners'. The term, *huaqiao*, was used by the government of China, and later the Taiwanese government, in reference to the Chinese residing outside these two countries. The term *huaqiao* seems to have been imposed by these two governments with political intentions, as it is based on the principle of 'jus sanguinis,' thus stipulating that anyone born of a father recognized as Chinese is a Chinese citizen. Since *huaqiao* also means 'sojourner,' it carries the suggestion of a person who has only left the country to seek work or a livelihood, but with the intention of eventually returning to his 'homeland'. This term would probably be valid for most ethnic Chinese outside the PRC in the pre-World War II period, when the citizenship status of Chinese in the colonies in Southeast Asia was not clear. This term, however, is no longer applicable to most ethnic Chinese who are now citizens of these Southeast Asian countries. The term *huaqiao* is only valid for those Chinese citizens of the PRC or Taiwan who reside outside these countries. For those Chinese who are citizens of the country they live in, it has become more customary to use the term 'ethnic Chinese'. In Indonesia, for example, ethnic Chinese are referred to as 'Chinese-Indonesians' or 'Sino-Indonesians', similar to Thailand where the term used is 'Sino-Thai'.

When we talk about Chinese in business in Indonesia, there is also a need to make a distinction between firms controlled by the peranakans and the totoks. Some peranakans had emerged as owners of major enterprises during the colonial period, though most of them eventually lost control of their business interests. Presently, most of the largest Chinese enterprises are owned by totoks.

Moreover, when talking about Chinese business two things need to be clarified. The first is about the concept of 'Chinese business'. What is meant by this term? Are we assuming that there is something unique about the way ethnic Chinese do business that is different from, say, the Americans, Japanese or Dutch? Are we referring to the substance of the business or the style of developing an enterprise? If our concern is with the substance, we have to compare the characteristics of the business itself as well as the ownership structure of Chinese companies. For example, are Chinese firms predominantly closed family businesses or publicly-listed enterprises? In which economic sectors are Chinese enterprises concentrated in – trade, investment, banking and finance, services or manufacturing? If our concern is with the style of doing business, the focus is more on management style and the form of relationship with other companies owned by co-ethnics as well as non-Chinese. Most of the literature on Chinese business has concentrated on the style of business. There is a need to focus more attention on Chinese business involvement in particular economic sectors. There is a also a need to differentiate between the activities of large-scale enterprises and small and medium-scale companies as there appears to be significant differences in management style by the owners of these enterprises, even though much of the current literature on Chinese business suggests otherwise.

As in the case in most societies where entrepreneurial activities are undertaken as a family business, there is a tendency for ethnic Chinese in business to function like a closed society, making it difficult to have access to them for research purposes. Moreover, in Indonesia, Chinese businessmen are generally reluctant to participate in a research project. This is primarily due to their vulnerable position in the economy; members of the indigenous community, especially ethnic Indonesians who are in business, tend to be adamant about the need to check the role of ethnic Chinese in the economy. There are also those in government who see the ethnic Chinese businessmen as potential 'donors' for their 'projects,' be they of a personal or public nature.

Suggestions for Further Research

In view of such research problems, most studies on Chinese enterprise in Indonesia have focused primarily on the largest enterprises. There is still very limited research on the development of Chinese small- and medium-scale companies even though these enterprises have received little support from the state and have been most exposed to hostility by ethnic Indonesians, particularly during periods of crisis. There has been almost no research on how such firms operate their business, and of the factors that have helped them to sustain their enterprise.

There has been no comparative research of businesses run by different ethnic communities in Indonesians. Nor has there been any comparative research of companies owned by the peranakans and the totoks or between the different sub-ethnic groups. This type of research is important to determine if cultural traits particular to the Chinese have been a factor in helping them develop their enterprise.

The connections between leading Chinese businessmen and people holding power in government have been repeatedly mentioned as one crucial factor aiding the development of Chinese enterprise in Indonesia. For example, some Chinese have benefited very favorably from their ties with people in power during Dutch colonial rule and the New Order era (1966–1998). During the Japanese occupation of Indonesia and under the Soekarno government, however, the Chinese were not provided with a conducive environment to conduct business. Does this suggest that the most crucial factor determining the growth of a Chinese business elite in Indonesia is political connections? If the answer to this question is yes, does this mean that if ethnic Indonesians were privy to the same opportunities and if political patronage for Chinese business were reduced, Chinese enterprises would experience a major downturn in business fortunes? The failure of the Benteng program to increase the participation of ethnic Indonesians in business and reduce the economic influence of the Chinese showed that this is not the case. Moreover, the second generation of Chinese businessmen appears increasingly less dependent on political power-holders for economic concessions (Mackie 1992). This younger generation also seems to be adopting a more professional business approach, though this assumption has not been proven yet with detailed case studies.

History reveals that the Javanese were farmers or employed in low-level bureaucratic positions during the Dutch colonial period, and hence were not involved much in commercial activities. Could this be one reason for the failure of the Javanese to develop a significant interest in the corporate sector? According to Suryadinata (1978), the failure of the Benteng program was caused by, among other things, the lack of business experience of indigenous Indonesians. The question is whom Suryadinata meant by indigenous Indonesians? Are they only the Javanese? Some ethnic Indonesians, like the Minang and Bugis/Makasar ethnic groups, are known for their trading skills. In fact, members of the Minang and Makasar ethnic communities, i.e. Hasyim Ning and Abdul Latief, who are Minangs and Jusuf Kalla who is a Makasarese, own three conglomerates in Indonesia.

There are different sizes of business, i.e. small, medium, and large enterprises. Do ethnic Indonesians and Chinese have different levels of entrepreneurial skills in these three types of companies? What are the key differences and commonalities among these three types of companies? Most of the literature on Chinese entrepreneurship in Indonesia adopts a cultural perspective as an explanatory framework. The main contention by these studies is that the Chinese have a good measure of business acumen and deal-making skills, are known for their frugality and strong work ethos, value trust and have a flexible financial structure. These ideas have not been tested in a comparative study of Chinese business enterprises of different sizes; nor have there been studies comparing corporate activities of the Chinese with that of other ethnic communities, to determine if such 'values' are unique to the Chinese.

In terms of business links between Indonesian businessmen and foreign investors, particularly those from Korea, Japan, Taiwan and Hong Kong, existing data indicate that most linkages forged by these foreigners are with ethnic Chinese. There is still no in-depth study to determine the reasons why foreign investors prefer to work with the Chinese rather than with ethnic Indonesians. It appears that such collaborative ties are due to the wider range of business and political ties that leading Chinese businessmen have managed to develop. Foreign investors probably believe that the political ties that leading Chinese businessmen have would provide them with valuable and greater access to business-related information, policy-makers and capital; these business links also provide foreign investors with access to a wider market and facilitate the employment of local labor. Foreign investors also seem to prefer to work with the Chinese because they appear to share a common business style and aspire to develop the joint-venture enterprises that they have established. These ideas have not been proven with detailed studies of business links between foreign investors and ethnic Chinese businessmen.

All these factors, i.e. international trading networks, political ties, entrepreneurial skills, business experience, work ethics and value systems, have been cited as factors that have enabled the Chinese to secure a much more significant degree of ownership and control of economic sectors compared to ethnic Indonesians. Another related issue is the impact of the development of Chinese enterprises in Indonesia on the government and indigenous people. Ethnic Chinese businessmen are basically in a tenuous position. The loyalty of ethnic Chinese Indonesian citizens has repeatedly been subject to question. One example was the reaction by the indigenous community to newspaper reports about investments in China by 'overseas Chinese,' including Chinese Indonesians. The news coverage of the Second World Chinese Entrepreneurs convention that was held in Hong Kong in November 1993 exposed most cogently the questioning of the loyalty of Chinese Indonesians to their country by ethnic Indonesians (see, for example, *Tempo* 27/11/93).

The greater degree of ownership of corporate stock by ethnic Chinese has generated social problems, particularly in view of the socio-economic gaps between them and the non-Chinese communities. The implications of limiting the access of ethnic Chinese to business opportunities have been publicly discussed, but have not been researched adequately. The events of May 1998 have shown how ethnic Chinese have responded to exclusion and attacks on their property and their lives, raising anguished questions about identity and their place in Indonesian society. This is related to the question of their 'national' orientation: will they be more Indonesian-oriented, Chinese-oriented or adopt a view of themselves as borderless world citizens, with their only consideration being the desire to do well in business. This issue needs further investigation if one wants to solve or reduce tension and conflicts between the ethnic Chinese and ethnic Indonesians.

The above discussion suggests several major research topics:

A. To examine what really is 'Chinese business':

- This could be determined through a comparative study of opportunity and constraint factors available to the ethnic Chinese as well as ethnic Indonesians:
    - internal factors (values, characteristics, ethnicity, religions, skills, knowledge, etc);
    - external factors (networks, deal-making activities, market system, etc)

  Studies are required of the process of a family business developing into a public-listed enterprise; the orientation of the younger generation business people towards corporate activities; pattern of business development and management styles (differentiating between big, medium and small firms) among ethnic Chinese business people; social and marriage ties among families in big business, within the country and outside; and gender studies of the Chinese business.
- Comparative study of national orientation of ethnic Chinese and different indigenous communities in their business ventures.

B. To analyze the impact of state intervention in the economy on Chinese business:

- This could involve an evaluation of policies or programs (for example, the 'partnership programs') that were introduced to encourage economic cooperation between ethnic Chinese and Indonesians:

- factors inhibiting and contributing to policy or program implementation; infrastructure, mentality, political factors, perceptions of the policy or program, etc;
- the quantitative and qualitative impact of policies or intervention programs on the target groups.
- Studies on government policies towards ethnic Chinese economic activities.[20]
- Comparative studies of government policies towards ethnic Chinese.

C. To obtain a comprehensive picture of the contribution by ethnic Chinese in shaping Indonesian society:

- Evaluation of their quantitative and qualitative achievements in and through business:
  - economic achievements: development of business enterprise, contribution to development of brand products, employment creation and foreign investments.
  - social achievements: national and international awards received for their innovations in business and management. Human resource development, role in promoting joint business activities with indigenous communities.

C. To obtain a comprehensive picture of the societal gaps existing between ethnic Chinese and indigenous Indonesians.

- Studies on inter-ethnic conflict and inter-ethnic harmony;
- Studies on income and occupational disparities between these two groups;

E. To gain a better understanding of ethnic Chinese communities through comparative studies across countries.

6

Taiwanese Business in Southeast Asia

I-Chun Kung

Introduction

Investment by Taiwanese companies in Southeast Asia has grown significantly since the late 1980s. From being a meager investor in Southeast Asia prior to 1986, Taiwanese firms have emerged as one of the largest investors in this region. Between 1959 to 1996, in terms of investment in approved projects, Taiwanese companies ranked second among the top ten foreign investors in Malaysia, second in Thailand, third in Philippines, seventh in Indonesia and the first in Vietnam (see Table 6.1) (Hsiao and Kung 1998).

Although investment abroad by Taiwanese companies is a relatively new phenomenon, the limited academic attention on this subject is surprising. Studies that have been undertaken of Taiwanese investments abroad are disproportionately in the disciplines of economics and international trade, concentrating primarily on the economic conditions of the home and host countries and of the factors motivating such foreign direct investment (FDI) (see, for example, Chen et al. 1995; Lee 1994; Hsu 1994). The issue whether the social and cultural conditions of a country also influence decision-making by Taiwanese firms interested in investing abroad has been neglected in these studies. This study analyses the transnationalization of the Taiwanese small- and medium-sized enterprises (SMEs), concentrating on why such companies have ventured abroad and how they have survived in their host countries. This study will also examine the characteristics of Taiwanese SMEs and whether specific features facilitated the expansion of their businesses into Southeast Asia. The empirical foundation on which the arguments here are based is several case studies of Taiwanese FDI and my own fieldwork in Malaysia. This study is organized in two sections. The first section examines the factors encouraging Taiwanese SMEs to invest abroad. The second part analyses Malaysian economic and social conditions that attract Taiwanese SME investment. The central issue is to determine if Taiwanese firms invest in a specific country based exclusively on economic factors, or if the prevalence of common cultural practices and ethnically-based business networks also influences decision-making.

Foreign Direct Investment by Taiwanese SMEs

Growing FDI by Taiwanese firms in Southeast Asia after 1987 has been attributed by many economists primarily to the changing economic environment in both Taiwan and in the host countries (see Hsu 1994; Lee 1994; Chen et al. 1995). The argument made by most economists has focused on the abrupt appreciation of the Taiwanese currency, the New Taiwan (NT) dollar, in the late 1980s, creating problems for many SMEs involved in export-oriented and labor-intensive industries. The problems ensuing from the appreciation of the NT dollar compelled SMEs to venture overseas, as a means to find avenues to reduce production costs. Since the 1970s, Taiwan's price competitiveness in export was assisted by the government's protection of the NT dollar from any surge against major foreign currencies, especially the US dollar. However, as the Taiwan-US trade surplus grew, the US pressured the Taiwanese government to

Table 6.1 Taiwanese Investment in Southeast Asian Countries (1959–96)

Country	Number of cases	Total amount (US$ million)	Top ten rank	Average capital (US$ million)
Malaysia	1454	7940.6	2	5.46
Thailand	1345	9477.8	2	7.04
Indonesia	506	9253.2	7	18.28
Philippines	815	968.9	3	1.18
Singapore	201	846.7	–	4.21
Vietnam	297	4423.0	1	14.89
Cambodia	9	10.6	–	1.17

Source: Hsiao and Kung (1998)

147

liberalize foreign trade and let the NT dollar appreciate in value. The NT dollar subsequently rose 22.4 per cent (from NT$36.00 to NT$28.95) against the US dollar in 1987.

Apart from the favorable price factor, another competitive advantage domestic manufacturers in Taiwan's export-oriented industries had was low labor costs. In mid-1980s, however, wage rates in Taiwan increased appreciably. The average monthly wage in the manufacturing sector rose from US$353 in 1985 to US$821 in 1990, and then to US$1,086 in 1992 (Hsing 1998: 13). This significant rise in wage rates undermined the competitiveness of labor-intensive SMEs.

To maintain industrial competitiveness, in 1987[1] the government launched a series of economic reforms to encourage Taiwanese firms to invest abroad. For example, in July 1987, the Taiwan government lifted foreign exchange control restrictions and allowed each citizen to remit abroad a maximum of US$5 million per year. The tax law was revised to exempt foreign-sourced individual income from personal income tax, whereas corporate income tax was to be assessed on consolidated global income. These provisions, initially designed to encourage Taiwanese citizens to remit their overseas earnings to Taiwan during a period of foreign exchange shortage, became a measure encouraging personalized FDI.

Apart from this, in the mid-1980s, Southeast Asian governments introduced favorable polices to encourage FDI as a means to promote economic growth following a severe economic recession; these incentives attracted much investment from SMEs in Taiwan. From the late 1980s, as FDI began to emerge as a primary factor expediting the rapid development of Southeast Asian economies, governments in this region began to introduce additional incentives to attract more investments. In short, there were a number of economic factors encouraging Taiwanese SMEs to invest in Southeast Asia: currencies were at appropriate levels, lucrative business opportunities were available, highly attractive investment incentives (including tax holidays, investment tax credits and export incentives) were being offered, Free Trade Zones were being established, and a relatively inexpensive labor force, through control of labor unions, was available (Tzeng 1997: 4–5).

Although most studies argue that the changing economic environment in Taiwan and in Southeast Asia drove Taiwanese firms to invest in the region (see Chen et al. 1996; Lee 1994; Shu 1994), favorable structural conditions were not sufficient reasons to explain why a large number of Taiwanese enterprises began to invest abroad. Moreover, since most economic analyses of foreign investment are based on the study of large-sized corporations, it is questionable if the factors that encouraged investment by such enterprises were also applicable to the SMEs. Furthermore, the structural constraints on SMEs to engage in FDI have not been fully probed.

A well-accepted assumption is that SMEs face several disadvantages when they invest abroad, including an inadequate supply of capital and managerial resources and limited risk-absorbing capacity, which can jeopardize the overseas operation. Capital shortage could lead to under-investment or could force SMEs into joint-ventures that can bring about negative consequences. A shortage of managerial resources can limit a small firm's scope for internationalization and impair their decision-making system, which may be influenced by individual perceptions rather than rational evaluations. Ill-planned administrative procedures and an inadequate use of business strategies, like in-depth market analysis and proper cost allocations and budgeting, can force small firms to take shortcuts in decision-making and information-gathering, which sometimes may lead to disastrous outcomes (Chen et al. 1995).

Although problems like limited capital and managerial resources can hinder an SME from venturing abroad, these limitations do not appear to have impeded Taiwanese SME investment abroad. FDI by SMEs constitutes a large portion of total overseas investment by Taiwanese enterprises. From 1986 to 1992, Thailand, Malaysia, Indonesia, Vietnam and the Philippines approved a total of 2,780 project proposals by Taiwanese companies, involving investments amounting to US$14.1 billion. Of these investment proposals, no more than 200 projects were proposed by large firms, i.e. companies with annual sales in 1986 exceeding 500 million NT dollars (approximately US$14 million at that time). The SMEs were presumably responsible for implementing the rest of the proposed projects (Chen 1995).

Between 1987 to1993, Taiwan was the eighth largest FDI country in terms of capital outflow (Lin 1998), and such foreign investment disproportionately came from SMEs. What made Taiwanese SMEs outward looking or transnationalist? Were decisions to venture abroad by Taiwanese SMEs merely the result of utilitarian calculations of a capital venture, or were these decisions also embedded in reasons pertaining to social structure and social relations? The concept of 'embeddedness' was developed by Granovetter (1985) to refer to the fact that economic transactions in pre-market as well as in capitalist societies exist within social structures that give them their shape and influence their outcomes. In other words, were such transnational investments dependent on social and historical factors, and were they also embedded in the network of social relationships?

From a historical perspective, transnational tendencies among Taiwanese enterprises, in terms of the willingness to invest overseas and engage in foreign trade, can be traced to the early 17th century. Taiwan was brought into the international trading market circuits by Europeans who saw the island as a 'flying territory' of Fujianese patricorporations that dominated a coastal trading zone running from Nagasaki to Manila and the ports of mainland Southeast Asia. Taiwan's strategic geographic location bolstered its international trade links. Situated between the Malay archipelago and China and Japan, Taiwan has had an eventful past. As early as the second half of the 16th century, Taiwan was used by the Europeans, Chinese and Japanese as a base to transfer their commodities to third countries or to trade with Taiwanese aborigines. In order to trade with China, the Dutch colonized the southern part of Taiwan in 1624. Two years later, the Spanish arrived, occupying the northern part of the country. In 1642, the Dutch expelled the Spanish, and by 1650 managed to occupy the whole island. The Dutch exported bukskin, venison, dried fish and sugar to Japan in exchange for Japanese silver. These commodities, along with spices, which were purchased in Southeast Asia, were also shipped to Holland from Taiwan.

During the Dutch occupation from 1624 to1661, trading activities in Taiwan were very lucrative. In 1624, the Dutch reported that among their trading activities in 19 ports in Asia, the Taiwanese trade alone earned them 25.6 per cent of the total profits, next only to the trade with Japan (Hsiao and Hsiao 1996). In 1661, after being defeated by the ascending Ch'ing dynasty, the Chinese Ming loyalist Zheng Cheng Kung and his troops fled to Taiwan, drove away the Dutch, and established the Kingdom of Zheng, or the Kingdom of Formosa, as it was called by the British. The government welcomed trading with all countries except Holland and the Ch'ing dynasty. The Zheng government also increased its trading activities in Southeast Asian ports. One or two Taiwanese ships annually sailed to Luzon, Cambodia, Thailand, Malacca and Batavia. During this period, the British replaced the Dutch as the dominant European traders in Taiwan.

In 1683, Ch'ing conquered Taiwan. Before the formal opening of Tamsui and Anping harbors under the Peking Treaty in 1860,

Taiwanese trade with China was confined mostly to people in Fujian province. After 1860, European trade in Taiwan increased, and as might be expected, this openness of trade reduced the importance of China as Taiwan's trading partner, and restructured Taiwan's trading pattern. During this period, some Taiwanese merchants were able to learn the trading system from the Europeans and started their own trading companies that eventually performed better than the European trading houses. For example, by 1881, almost 90 per cent of Taiwanese tea was exported by Taiwanese merchants (Hsiao and Hsiao 1996).

From 1895, Taiwan became a Japanese colony, and emerged as a strategic base of Japan's Southward movement that aimed to colonize Southeast Asian countries and establish the 'Greater East Asia Co-Prosperity Sphere'. Taiwanese businessmen followed in the steps of the Japanese empire, penetrating into most Southeast Asian countries, including Indonesia, Singapore, Thailand, the Philippines and Indo-china (Lim 1996: 11).

These experiences in trade imply a mind set among Taiwanese, i.e. a willingness to undertake transnational business ventures. Following Japan's defeat in World War II, Taiwan became one of the provinces of the Republic of China in 1949, ruled by the Kuomintang (KMT) regime. During KMT rule from mainland China, other structural factors emerged which began pushing Taiwanese SMEs to adopt a more 'outward looking' perspective.

As mentioned earlier, SMEs play a dominant role in Taiwan's economy, given their very pervasive presence in the country's industrial sector. According to the definition provided by the government in 1967, an SME in the manufacturing sector was an enterprise having total assets of less than NT$5 million (about US$0.15 million) with not more than 100 persons regularly employed; or a commercial firm having an annual turnover of not more than NT$5 million with less than 50 persons regularly employed (Hsiao and Hsiao 1996). Since then, this definition of what constitutes an SME has been changed six times – in 1973, 1977, 1979, 1982, 1991 and 1995. In 1995, the total asset volume in the SME definition increased to NT$60 million, and the maximum number of employees increased to 300. In spite of the various changes to the definition of what constitutes an SME, the number of companies in the manufacturing sector between 1961 and 1989 that can be termed as an SME constituted almost 99 per cent of total firms in this sector.

In spite of this, the domestic market is dominated either by government enterprises or by large private companies, for example,

Formosa Plastics Corporation, Tatung Co., Yulon Motor, Far East Textile and Cathay Life Insurance Co. The dominant position of state-owned and large private enterprises in the Taiwanese economy squeezed most of the SMEs out of the domestic market. After its defeat by the Communist Party in China, the KMT leadership led by Chiang Kai Shek, along with approximately two million soldiers and civilian followers, migrated to Taiwan. In the early period of KMT rule in Taiwan, public enterprises emerged as the central vehicle to promote growth as well as to consolidate the party's position. Public enterprises had two primary objectives: to produce goods directly for state use and to employ a large number of the KMT followers in order to retain their loyalty. The state controlled the services and utilities sectors – railways, electricity, telecommunications – the financial system, the media, particularly broadcasting networks, and mono-polized cement, metals and petroleum production. A very large segment of the Taiwan economy quickly came under the control of state-owned enterprises, and the profits from all such enterprises, properties and monopolies accounted for roughly one-fourth of the national revenue throughout the 1950s, 1960s and the early 1970s (Gates 1996). Meanwhile, Taiwan's large private enterprises aligned themselves with the KMT through complex, particularistic and patrilineal connections in order to secure privileged access to the domestic market. In other words, these large-sized private enterprises emerged as clients of the state, subordinate to KMT control. In this relationship, the large private enterprises were protected and permitted a share of the domestic market by the state.

In this economic environment, Taiwanese SMEs were forced to explore avenues to help them develop their enterprise. One strategy used by the SMEs was to integrate themselves into an efficient flexible production network, which consisted of a variety of SMEs at different levels of production. These SMEs were independent, but shared production and market information that enabled them to increase flexibility and capacity to cope with rapid change in technology and demands in the world market. Taiwan's export-oriented industrializa-tion was underpinned by this kind of production network. In the 1980s, 70 per cent of SME output was for export, constituting 60 per cent of Taiwan's total exports (Chou 1989). In 1981, 68 per cent of total exports, valued at NT$15.3 billion, was contributed by SMEs; in 1986, it was 66 per cent and worth NT$26 billion, and in 1989, 62 per cent and worth NT$41 billion (Hsiao and Hsiao 1996: 7).

State Policy and Taiwanese FDI in Southeast Asia

Many analysts have argued that state policies, principally those introduced after 1986, have played a significant role in encouraging Taiwanese SMEs to invest abroad. Among the policies most cited was the 'Southward Policy,' an attempt to encourage Taiwanese firms to invest in Southeast Asia. Since 1994, the KMT government has been actively implementing its 'Southward Policy' to check an over-concentration of Taiwanese business investment in China. After the mid-1980s, Taiwanese companies had begun to aggressively invest in the mainland. More than 160 companies quoted on Taiwan's stock market – or about 40 per cent of total listed companies – have operations in the mainland. This massive investment by Taiwanese companies in China raised concern among KMT officials that local enterprises might become too dependent on the mainland for their business. The KMT was also worried that this would enable Beijing to gain political leverage over Taipei. Through its Southward Policy, the government selected the Philippines, Indonesia and Vietnam as new frontier bases of transnational industrial development. The KMT also provided economic aid to these three Southeast Asian countries to help them set up industrial parks, in which Taiwanese enterprises could establish manufacturing-based ventures.

To what extent have FDI by Taiwanese SMEs been influenced by this state policy? Table 6.2 provides several economic indicators of Taiwanese FDI in Southeast Asia between 1959 and 1996. Investment patterns by Taiwanese SMEs have changed considerably since 1988, when unprecedented investment in Southeast Asian countries began. The Southward Policy was, however, only inaugurated in 1994, six years after Taiwanese companies had begun to invest heavily in Southeast Asia. This time lag suggests that the state was a follower rather than an initiator of this process of Taiwanese FDI flows into Southeast Asia. The enterprises that seem to have been most influenced by the Southward Policy are the large private enterprises, state-owned firms and KMT-owned companies. These companies tend to abide by state policies because of their alliances with the KMT and in order to secure economic privileges from the government. The Land Development & Management Corporation, established by the Ministry of Economic Affairs, for example, has helped to facilitate collaborative ventures among state-owned companies, KMT-owned corporations and large private enterprises to develop the Batam Industrial Park in Indonesia. The investment pattern of Taiwanese companies reflects the limited capacity of the KMT government to regulate investment abroad.

That Taiwanese investors have chosen Malaysia rather than Indonesia, the Philippines or Vietnam as the country to invest in also reflects the failure of the KMT government in directing Taiwanese foreign investment. Table 6.2 compares the FDI figures approved by Southeast Asian countries. Between 1987 and 1996, compared to Indonesia, the Philippines, Thailand and Vietnam, Malaysia attracted the largest volume of investments from Taiwan, in terms of the number of investment projects. Malaysia was not one of the primary locations selected by the KMT government as the new frontier bases of transnational industrial development. What then encouraged Taiwanese companies to invest in Malaysia?

Taiwanese Business in Malaysia

Economists have argued that a dearth of resources and high transaction costs compelled Taiwanese SMEs to invest overseas (see, for example, Chen 1994). It is also probable that countries that have geographical proximity, and share cultural and structural similarities, with Taiwan are potential venues of investment to Taiwanese SMEs. Close proximity and similarities in culture and market structure can also help reduce transaction costs as well as provide access to managerial resources needed to run viable transnational operations. There is evidence that even large firms prefer to operate in a nearby and familiar environment. A study by Yonekura (1988) indicates that over 70 per cent of Japanese electronic subsidiaries are located in Asia. Yonekura further indicates that, while large Japanese firms locate their subsidiaries around the world, medium-sized firms cluster their overseas operation in Taiwan, Korea and Singapore, while small-sized firms concentrate mainly in Taiwan. These Asian countries offer a pro-FDI policy environment, Taiwan and Korea also possess a sizeable Japanese-speaking population and certain Japanese-style industrial infrastructures can be traced back to the Japanese colonial era.

We can use the above arguments to hypothesize why Taiwanese SMEs have invested primarily in Southeast Asian countries and China. Apart from their geographical proximity, since these are countries where many ethnic Chinese reside, Taiwanese businessmen presume that the common language and similar cultural background they share with a section of the population can facilitate the establishment and

Table 6.2 Taiwanese FDI in Southeast Asian Countries (in US$ million)

Country Year	Malaysia			Thailand			Indonesia			The Philippines			Singapore			Vietnam		
	Case number	Invested amount	Average Investment	Case number	Invested amount	Average Investment	Case number	Invested amount	Average Investment	Case number	Invested amount	Average Investment	Case number	Invested amount	Average Investment	Case number	Invested amount	Average Investment
1959–87	175	141.39	0.80	259	855.03	3.30	27	2223.40	82.34	97	16.87	0.17	–	–	–	0	0	0.0
1988	111	313.00	2.81	308	859.94	2.79	16	913.00	57.06	86	109.87	1.27	3	1	0.3	0	0	0.0
1989	191	815.00	4.26	214	892.20	4.16	19	157.00	8.26	190	148.69	0.78	1	1	1.0	0	0	0.0
1990	270	2383.00	8.82	144	782.69	5.43	94	618.30	6.57	158	140.65	0.89	3	3	1.0	11	176.10	16.00
1991	182	1314.21	7.22	69	583.46	8.45	58	1057.30	18.22	109	11.61	0.10	4	24	6.0	20	561.36	28.06
1992	137	602.00	4.40	44	289.92	6.58	23	563.30	24.49	27	9.27	0.34	1	0	0.0	22	602.05	27.36
1993	86	346.50	4.39	61	215.00	3.52	21	131.40	6.25	21	5.37	0.25	1	0	0.0	44	499.78	11.35
1994	100	1149.60	11.50	88	477.48	5.42	48	2487.50	51.82	42	292.37	6.96	0	0	0.0	76	524.01	6.89
1995	123	565.49	4.59	102	1803.91	17.7	89	576.40	6.47	63	181.55	2.88	–	–	–	63	1215.10	19.28
1996	79	310.40	3.92	56	2688.20	48.0	111	534.60	4.81	22	52.70	2.93	–	–	–	61	844.61	13.84
Total	1454	7940.59	5.46	1345	9477.83	7.04	506	9253.20	18.28	815	968.94	1.18	201	846.7	4.21	297	4423.01	14.89

Source: Hsiao and Kung (1998)

running of business enterprises. This hypothesis suggests that the decision to invest abroad can be determined by the social and cultural context of the host countries. Taiwanese SME cross-border investments are as much determined by economic factors as cultural considerations as businessmen recognize that certain common features they share with members of the host country can be exploited to help develop their enterprise.

Let us now examine whether common social and cultural factors influence investment by Taiwanese SMEs in Malaysia. Table 6.3 presents the distribution of Taiwanese firms investing in Malaysia in 1993, the size of which is determined by the number of employees. 44 per cent of these firms employed less than 100 workers, and 77 per cent of them employed less than 300 workers. Table 6.4 shows the same tendency in 1998 among the sample base of Taiwanese companies investing in the state of Malacca, i.e. 60 per cent of the firms employed less than 100 workers and 87 per cent of them employed less than 300 workers. 68.2 per cent of these Taiwanese firms commenced business with a capital investment of less than US$1 million (see Table 6.5). This means that most Taiwanese firms in Malaysia are still SMEs. As we noted above, if limited capital and management resources could impede transnational investment by SMEs, what unique comparative advantages does Malaysia offer to such Taiwanese firms?

The Chung-Hua Institution for Economic Research (CIER), based in Taipei, has done a survey to answer this question. 300

Table 6.3 Distribution of Size of Taiwanese Firms by Number of Employees in Malaysia (1993)

Number of Employees	Number of Firms	Percentage
<50	26	21.1
50–99	28	22.8
100–149	11	8.9
150–199	13	10.6
200–299	17	13.8
300–499	10	8.1
500–999	10	8.1
1000+	8	6.5
Total	123	100

Note: An SME is defined as one that has less than 300 employees
Source: Chen et al. (1995: 144)

Table 6.4 Distribution of Size of Taiwanese Firms by Number of Employees in Malacca (1998)

Number of Employees	Number of Firms	Percentage
<50	10	43.5
50–99	4	17.4
100–149	4	17.4
150–199	1	4.3
200–299	1	4.3
300–499	2	8.7
500+	1	4.3
Total	23	100.0

Source: Author's own survey

Table 6.5 Distribution of Size of Taiwanese Firms by Starting Capital in Malacca (1998)

Start Capital	Number of Firms	Percentage
Below US$1 million	15	68.2
Above US$1 million	7	31.8
Total	22	100.0

Source: Author's own survey

questionnaires were sent to potential respondents who were registered members of the Taipei Investors Association. The survey was carried out in mid-1994, yielding 126 responses. I also conducted interviews with Taiwanese investors in Malaysia.[2] The results from the survey and the interviews indicate that the main reasons for deciding to invest in Malaysia were political stability, good infrastructure, language and communication convenience, and the favorable status for companies producing goods for export. There was no mention that Taiwanese businessmen had been able to establish business networks with ethnic Chinese in Malaysia.[3] One investor I interviewed in Malacca in 1998 recalled his reason for investing in Malaysia:

> *My company is very small. We could not afford to undertake an oversesas market survey before approving a transnational investment like big enterprises do . . . The main reason I chose to invest in Malaysia is that there are a lot of ethnic Chinese here with whom I can communicate. Otherwise, I would feel uneasy.*[4]

Another Taiwanese investor, the owner of a furniture firm, felt that Malaysia shared some characteristics similar to that of Taiwan:

> *For us, being in Malaysia is just like being in our own country, because its population includes Chinese. And this similarity in culture makes me feel comfortable doing business here.*

Other Taiwanese investors expressed similar sentiments. One Taiwanese businessman cited the anti-Chinese riots in Indonesia as a deciding factor for investing in Malaysia rather than Indonesia, although the cost of labor and land was much cheaper in Indonesia. Among Southeast Asian countries, Malaysia has the second largest ethnic Chinese population, next to Indonesia. However, while only three per cent of Indonesia's population is ethnic Chinese, in Malaysia this community constitutes about 28 per cent of the country's population. Malaysia is one of the few Southeast Asian countries that still allows Chinese-medium schools to operate, i.e. institutions that offer lessons in the Chinese language; this is another factor which appealed to Taiwanese investors. These factors suggest that favorable economic incentives are not the sole impetus encouraging capital mobility. The availability of common cultural and ethnic resources, for example, a common language, are also important factors that influence decision-making.

More details on the survey conducted by CIER to determine the reasons why Taiwanese businessmen chose Malaysia over other Southeast Asian countries as a venue of capital investment are provided in Table 6.6. The results of this survey in Table 6.6 suggest that the rationale for investing in Malaysia vary with the size of the firm. Most small-sized firms, i.e. companies with less than 300 employees, reported "good potential for their products in the local Malaysian market" and having "cultural similarities with local entrepreneurs or people" as the reasons for choosing Malaysia. On the other hand, a high proportion of large-sized firms reported "cheap labor" as the primary reason for pursuing FDI in this country (Chen et al. 1995: 131).

If cultural similarities with Malaysian businessmen and people are a major concern of Taiwanese investors, who are these Malaysians that Taiwanese investors can identify with? And what is the nature their relationship? What role do these Malaysians play in Taiwanese companies with investments in Malaysia? Tables 6.7 and 6.8 provide a breakdown of the roles played by Malaysians in helping to attract Taiwanese investments and of the role they play in these companies.

Table 6.6 Reasons for Choosing to Invest in Malaysia rather than other Southeast Asian Countries (by Size of Firms)

Reasons	Size of firms	<300	300+	Total
Cheap labor		25.5	46.4	29.8
Political stability		81.9	100.0	85.5
Good infrastructure		52.1	64.3	55.6
Sound legal framework and commercial practices		35.1	50.0	38.7
Racial homogeneity		46.8	53.6	48.4
Good supporting industries		24.5	21.4	24.2
Good potential for products in local market		48.9	25.0	43.5
Have cultural similarities with entrepreneurs or people		29.8	10.7	26.6
High level of education		11.7	28.6	15.3
Attractive fiscal incentives		29.8	53.6	35.5
Favorable status for exporting to third party countries		18.1	32.1	21.8
Little government intervention		6.4	3.6	5.6
Others		5.3	7.1	5.6

Source: Chen *et al.* (1995)

Table 6.7 Role Malaysian Chinese Play in Taiwanese Companies in Malaysia (Percentages)

1. Providing information	26	(70.3)
2. Serving as managerial staff	20	(54.1)
3. Helping to establish marketing channels	15	(40.5)
4. Supplying material	8	(21.6)
5. Providing technology	2	(5.4)
6. Providing financial support	4	(10.8)
7. Serving as partners	12	(32.4)
8. Building ties with government	21	(56.8)
9. Helping to establish satellite factors	4	(10.8)
10. Building customer relations	11	(29.7)
11. Without any help	3	(8.1)
Sample size	37	

Source: Liu (1994)

Tables 6.7 and 6.8 indicate that Malaysian Chinese play different roles in Taiwanese firms. "Providing information" is the most frequently mentioned point by the Taiwanese investors, while the next two are "building relations with government" and "serving as managerial staff" (see Table 6.7). Table 6.8 further distinguishes the

Table 6.8 Role Different Ethnic Groups Play in Taiwanese Firms in Malacca (1998) Unit: Number of Firms

Ethnicity The role different ethnic groups play in Taiwanese firms in Malacca	Taiwanese	Chinese	Malay	Indian	Bangladeshi	Indonesia Malay
As co-partner	13	5	1	0	0	0
As supplier or subcontractor	13	3	0	0	0	0
As office staff	3	23	0	0	0	0
As manual worker	0	4	14	4	14	3
Sample Size			23			

Source: Author's own research.

roles of different ethnic groups in Taiwanese companies. The office personnel are mostly ethnic Chinese, not Malays and Indian. All the 23 Taiwanese firms I interviewed in Malacca hired ethnic Chinese as office staff, but none of them hired Malays or Indians to serve in the same position. Most Malays and Indians work as manual labor in these firms. One interesting finding is that most Taiwanese investors prefer hiring foreign workers from Bangladesh to Malay or even Indonesian workers. The reasons why Taiwanese investors prefer Bangladeshi workers rather than Malay or Indonesian workers are still unclear and requires further research, but most Taiwanese investors I interviewed mentioned that Bangladeshi workers "work better than locals and Indonesians," "they are hard-working," and "they are always eager to work overtime". One investor even claimed that "without the Bangladeshi workers, my company would have had to close."[5]

These figures in Tables 6.7 and 6.8 suggest that co-ethnic identity tends to facilitate cooperative relations between Taiwanese investors and Malaysian Chinese because it can be mutually beneficial. Similar ethnic characteristics, such as common language, religion and educational background, have helped strengthened the capacity of Taiwanese investors to cope in an unfamiliar environment. During my research, I noted that most Taiwanese investors could not speak English, and only two of them could speak some Malay. On the other hand, ethnic Chinese in Malaysia often can speak Malay, English, Mandarin and various Chinese dialects. Most Taiwanese investors have to depend on local ethnic Chinese employees to communicate with the Malaysian government and their non-Chinese workers. The need to create links with Malaysian Chinese, by employing them or using the professional services they provide. Although this is an important strategy for the Taiwanese SMEs to survive in Malaysia, this, however, does not mean that such co-ethnic ties are devoid of tension.

Business cooperation between Taiwanese and Malaysian Chinese was very limited before the mid-1980s. It was only after the emergence of massive Taiwanese FDI in Malaysia that the interactions between Taiwanese and Malaysia Chinese become more pronounced. Such intra-ethnic cooperation, however, has been very unstable, and disputes have often occurred. Disputes in land transactions are particularly common, since Taiwanese investors often use Malaysian Chinese to acquire land on their behalf, given the restrictions imposed by the Malaysian government on land ownership by foreigners. Table 6.8 indicates that business cooperation between Taiwanese investors and local Chinese are limited. Of the total 23 Taiwanese firms in my sample, only five of them have local Chinese partners and only three of them have local Chinese suppliers or subcontractors.

There are, however, some cases where long-term cooperative links have been maintained. What are the differences between the firms that successfully built cooperative links with Malaysian Chinese and those that did not? The relationship between Taiwanese and Malaysian Chinese is not based primarily on common clan or dialect group ties. Common ethnicity cannot automatically ensure successful business cooperation, particularly when they do not have previous experience working together. The available empirical evidence indicates that the most important factor in cases where a cooperative relationship has been forged between Malaysian Chinese and Taiwanese investors was previous "Taiwanese experience".[6] The most important of such previous "Taiwanese experience" is that the Malaysian Chinese partner would have spent two to five years in Taiwan, usually while pursuing tertiary education.

Since the mid-1950s, higher learning institutions in Taiwan have been admitting Malaysian Chinese students. Table 6.9 shows that among the ethnic Chinese students from Southeast Asia in Taiwan's higher learning institutions, Malaysian Chinese constitute the largest number. This is probably because most of these Malaysian Chinese students would have been educated in Chinese-medium schools, while the medium of education in Malaysian tertiary institutions is Malay and, for some courses, in English. Inevitably, Malaysian Chinese who have been educated in Chinese-medium schools find it difficult pursuing tertiary education in Malaysian universities. Moreover, since entry into tertiary institutions in Malaysia is regulated by a quota system that heavily favors the indigenous community, there is much competition among Malaysian Chinese for entry into Malaysian universities. This situation has compelled many Malaysian Chinese students to pursue tertiary education abroad. For many Malaysians who were educated in the Chinese medium, Taiwanese universities and colleges have proven a viable alternative to other foreign tertiary institutions. On the other hand, for political reasons, the KMT government provided many incentives to ethnic Chinese students to encourage them to study in Taiwan.

By the late 1990s, there were more than 30,000 Taiwan-educated college graduates in Malaysia, and at least 700 more will continue to return to Malaysia every year. Since the Malaysian government does not recognize most of the college degrees awarded by Taiwanese institutions, students educated in Taiwan are discriminated against in the job market. However, as the number of Taiwanese companies investing in Malaysia grew after the mid-1980s, employment in such enterprises has become an important alternative for Malaysian graduates from Taiwan.

The research I did in Malacca revealed that in most Taiwanese firms, there was much overlap between ownership and management. Only seven of the 23 Taiwanese firms in my sample separated management from ownership; among these seven non-owner managers, two were Taiwanese and the remaining five Malaysian Chinese. Of these five Malaysian Chinese managers, four were Taiwan-educated graduates.

Many Taiwanese investors I interviewed said that they were inclined to hire Taiwan-educated graduates due to a sense of "closeness," by which I took to mean that these Malaysians were familiar with Taiwanese culture. One investor told me that:

Taiwan-educated graduates have stayed in Taiwan for at least three years. They are more familiar with Taiwanese culture and understand what we want. Besides, the pace in Taiwan is quicker than in Malaysia, and Taiwan-educated graduates can catch up with our pace better than other local people.

Another manufacturer, in the electronics sector, mentioned that most managerial staff in his company were Taiwan graduates due to their more active working style:

Table 6.9 Southeast Asian Chinese Students in Taiwanese Higher Education Institutions (1953–1994)

Country Year	Malaysia	Indonesia	Vietnam	Philippines	Singapore	Thailand	Cambodia	Brunei	Myanmar
Before 1955	11	11	24	11	4	8	1	–	2
1956–60	297	190	230	96	75	19	12	12	23
1961–65	1,454	773	609	157	122	71	53	45	40
1966–70	2,355	744	648	49	18	153	50	52	204
1971–75	2,407	672	760	58	54	182	30	50	448
1976–80	2,502	547	773	28	28	247	102	55	521
1981–85	3,543	736	279	23	123	361	136	69	511
1986–90	3,254	838	223	39	123	428	43	79	794
1991–94	2,822	393	59	28	106	212	11	71	575
Total	18,645	4,904	3,605	489	653	1,681	437	433	3,118

Source: Calculated from Overseas Chinese Education Commission, Department of Education, Taipei (1996: 105–107)

Business conditions in Taiwanese firms are more competitive and aggressive. Things should be done within a very short period. According to my observation, the attitude of local people to work is more passive and they can't match our speed. I must watch them all the time to keep them on track.

Lee Fang Hsin, the owner of a famous Taiwanese pharmaceutical manufacturing firm with 7,000 retail clients in Malaysia, claimed that his company employed many Taiwan graduates, the number big enough to lead to the rise of two factions – the Tai-Da faction (comprising graduates from National Taiwan University) and Chun-Hsin faction (National Chun-Hsin University graduates) (see *Excellence Magazine* April 1996).

I also interviewed some Malaysian graduates from universities in Taiwan working for Taiwanese companies in Malaysia. One interviewee, a manager of a Taiwanese metal servicing company, believed that common language, an ease in communicating with staff, and a lower salary expectation were the reasons why Taiwan graduates were attractive to Taiwanese employers. Another interviewee, working for a large Taiwanese company with 7,000 workers, told me that his firm recruited him in 1990 before he graduated from the National Taiwan University. After he was given the job, he recommended that more than ten Malaysian graduates from Taiwan join the company. Six of them are still working for the company and in senior executive positions, while he is managing the company's branch. Such evidence suggest that Malaysian Chinese do play an important role in Taiwanese enterprises in Malaysia, but the primary factor that has facilitated this link is not co-ethnic identity, but the "Taiwanese experience" of Malaysian Chinese.

Conclusion and Implications for Research

In this chapter, we have explored some aspects of the transnationalization of Taiwanese SMEs in Southeast Asia. The decision by Taiwanese firms to invest abroad is determined by a combination of issues, including economic and social-cultural factors. Although transnationalization has become an important alternative to Taiwanese businessmen, especially owners of SMEs, to develop their enterprise, the factors that encourage investment abroad still need further research. The growing volume of literature which argue that common ethnic and cultural identity is the key factor that facilitates such transnational investment have misrepresented the key issues that encourage such capital movement across borders.

Common language and cultural practices between Taiwanese investors and Malaysian Chinese have, undoubtedly, helped facilitate a faster process of cross-border capital flows. This does not, however, imply that common ethnic identity also expedites cooperative business ventures between Chinese from Taiwan and Malaysia. Although Taiwanese investors depend on local Chinese to function as middleman to negotiate with the host government and non-Chinese workers, there are limited cases of joint-ventures between Taiwanese and Malaysian Chinese companies. There were only three cases of joint Taiwanese-Malaysian Chinese ownership of a company in my sample of 23 Taiwanese firms in Malacca. In fact, Taiwanese investors tend to depend more on other Taiwanese firms in business deals in Malaysia. I found that a number of Taiwanese SMEs, and not Malaysian Chinese firms, were subcontractors of larger Taiwanese firms in Malacca. Why was this the case? I was surprised by the two answers given by my informants: the Taiwanese do not trust Malaysian Chinese and that there were different business operation and management styles between Taiwanese and Malaysian Chinese. Taiwanese investors also complained that Malaysian Chinese usually misinterpreted their words to third parties and showed a lack of flexibility in business deals between them.

In this regard, this preliminary study has generated more questions than answers. Why is it that Taiwanese and Malaysian Chinese do not trust each other? What are the differences in business style between these two Chinese communities? From these questions, we can take issue with popular notions of "co-ethnic business networks" and "Chinese commonwealth". In particular, it is questionable if the presumed "Chineseness" shared among ethnic Chinese of diaspora has contributed to the establishment of extensive Chinese interlocking business networks. From the empirical evidence I have gathered of Taiwanese investments in Malaysia, there are limited business own-ership ties between Taiwanese and Malaysian Chinese. There is also evidence that although both communities share a common ethnic identity, their "Chineseness" does not guarantee smooth business cooperation. In this study, shared "Taiwanese experience," rather than common Chinese identity, offered a stronger basis for business cooperation. Such questions suggest that much more research is required before we can determine the factors that have enabled Chinese capital in transnational contexts to develop their enterprise.

Notes

————◆◆◆————

Introduction

1 Apart from such dialect- and clan-based organizations, by 1997, four World Chinese Entrepreneurs' Conventions and 21 World Chinese Traders' Conferences had been convened and attended by Chinese from all continents. Liu (1998) provides a detailed discussion on the impact of these conventions which have been used to try and establish internationally-based Chinese organizations.

2 Yoshihara's 1994 publication, *The Nation and Economic Growth: The Philippines and Thailand*, although a study of the political economies of these two countries, provides useful, but brief, insights on the history of Sino-Thais and Filipino Chinese. Carino's 1998 publication, *Chinese Big Business in the Philippines: Political Leadership and Change*, is a study of the institutions created by the major ethnic Chinese capitalists to promote their economic interests and secure an avenue to try and influence policy decisions in government.

3 Between 1985 and 1994, Malaysia had been the largest recipient of FDI among the rapidly developing Southeast Asian economies. During this ten-year period, FDI in Malaysia increased from US$695 million to US$4,348 million; FDI in Malaysia had peaked at US$5,183 million in 1992. Indonesia was the second largest recipient of such FDI in Southeast Asia; compared to the total volume of US$310 million in 1985, in 1994, FDI peaked at US$2,109 million (World Bank 1996: 28).

Taiwanese investments in Indonesia had also been growing during the early 1990s, much of which was channelled into small manufacturing ventures. These enterprises were labor-intensive which helped absorb the country's labor force which had been growing at a rate of around 2.2 million annually (*Far Eastern Economic Review* 30/7/98). It was hoped that the paper on Taiwanese investments in Southeast Asia would generate ideas on the importance of structural factors in pulling such investments.

166

4 Peranakan men are known as 'baba,' and the women 'nonya'. The term, 'baba,' is, however, used collectively when referring to the community. Skinner (1996) provides a comprehensive discussion of the creolized Chinese in Malaysia, Indonesia and the Philippines in his article 'Creolized Chinese Societies in Southeast Asia'.

5 The term *huaren* is now also commonly used to refer to ethnic Chinese of the diaspora.

6 These three terms, *huaqiao*, *huaren* and *huayi*, still commonly in use by the authorities in China when referring to the Chinese diaspora, suggests that all ethnic Chinese still view China as their 'motherland'. This view has been contested by a number of scholars (see, for example, Suryadinata 1997). For a more detailed discussion of the use of the terms *huaqiao*, *huaren* and *huayi*, see Wang (1992: 1–10, 1994, 1995, 1996).

7 The breakdown of sub-ethnic Chinese communities in Malaysia does not include the ethnic Chinese population in Sabah and Sarawak. In Sabah, the Hakka are the largest sub-ethnic community, comprising 57 per cent of the Chinese population, while the Cantonese make up 14.4 per cent, the Hokkien 13.2 per cent, the Teochew 5.2 per cent, the Hainanese 3.5 per cent and the Foochow 2.4 per cent. In Sarawak, the Foochow community is the largest sub-ethnic group, constituting 33.5 per cent of the total population, the Hakka 32 per cent, the Hokkien 13.3 per cent, the Teochew 8.1 per cent and the Cantonese 6.2 per cent (Niew 1998: 183–86).

8 A comprehensive review of the reasons why these sub-ethnic groups lost control of the economic sectors they controlled has still not been undertaken. A historical review of the traditional economic activities these sub-ethnic groups would also help provide the context for these groups contemporary economic activities.

9 According to the *Far Eastern Economic Report* (28/5/98), these figures were secured from the Pusat Data Business Indonesia. There is no information, however, on how these figures have been tabulated.

10 In the Philippines, however, according to one study in the early 1990s by Palanca (1995a: 52–53), ethnic Chinese owned 27 per cent of the top 100 corporations; they owned about 354 companies, or about 36 per cent, of the top 1,000 corporations.

11 See Gomez (1999) for a more detailed discussion on the criticisms made by leaders of political parties of the government's ethnic equity ownership figures. Their main argument is that the amount of corporate holdings attributed to the Chinese was too high, while the quantum of equity ownership by the indigenous community was too low.

12 Chen's volume, *Made in Taiwan: The Story of Acer Computers*, provides a comprehensive history of the development of this company. Chen is the Vice President of Acer.

13 For Biggart (1997), the institutional perspective incorporates important aspects of the market, cultural and political economy approaches in the analysis of business organizations, particularly in comparative perspective. Biggart (1997: 4–5), thus, argues for the use of "an institutional perspective rooted in Weberian sociology in the study of non-Western societies" because this perspective "accounts well for both ideal and material factors, may be used to explain both micro- and macro-level patterns of

organization, may allow for the agency of actors, readily allows comparison, and has no inherent Western bias."

14 Among academics in the fields of sociology, economics and business administration in Taiwan presently, there is a growing desire to engage in research on the involvement of Taiwanese enterprises in the economies of Southeast Asia and China, with an attempt to develop theoretical insights which can be compared with western theories of overseas investment and business organization and management. Several research teams are organized to this end.

15 Members of the second generation Kwek family have denied that divisions have emerged among them. For further reports of the divisions within the Kwek family, see *Far Eastern Economic Review* (22/2/90), *Asiaweek* (15/5/92) and *The Star* (14/4/94).

16 YHS later sold its rights to distribute these drinks in Malaysia to the Antah Group, a company controlled by members of the Negri Sembilan royal house.

17 See Gomez (1999) for case studies of the Berjaya Group and MUI, led by Tan and Khoo respectively. Both Khoo and Tan attempted to merge their enterprises with another major Chinese company, Tan Chin Nam's IGB Corporation Group. The venture failed to materialize and eventually ended in a bitter feud between Khoo and Tan Chin Nam, and later between Vincent Tan and Khoo. At one stage, Vincent Tan came close to implementing a takeover of Khoo's MUI.

18 Contributing to the Salim Group's problems was the cancellation of several key business deals by the Indonesian government, under the new administration of President B.J. Habibie. Apart from this, the BCA bank, controlled by Liem, was taken over by the government following a run on the bank (*Newsweek* 15/6/98).

19 The other companies in this list include Japan's Sony Corporation, Honda Motor Company, Toyota Motor Corporation, Canon Incorporated and Hitachi Ltd, as well as South Korea's Hyundai Motor Corporation, Samsung Electronics Company and Pohang Iron & Steel Company (*Asia, Inc.* June 1997).

Chapter 1

1 Government-linked companies are state-owned enterprises, many of which will be privatized. There are between 500 and 600 such enterprises.

2 For a list of some of the largest Chinese-owned companies in Singapore, see Introduction, Table I.3.

3 The 'external wing' refers to investments abroad by Singaporean companies to generate income for the local economy.

4 The Central Provident Fund (CPF) manages a forced savings plan for all employees in Singapore, the funds of which can be withdrawn by members on retirement; both the employee and his employer are required to make monthly contributions to employee's CPF account (see Ng 1996). Members of the CPF can withdraw part of the funds before their retirement age to purchase HDB flats and houses as well as for share and stock investment.

5 The 'growth triangle' concept was conceived by Singapore Prime Minister Goh Chok Tong to cover Singapore, the state of Johor in Malaysia and the Riau archipelago of Indonesia to exploit their comparative advantage and to encourage foreign investment (see Lee 1991).

6 See Introduction for a more detailed discussion on the YHS takeover by Ng Teng Fong.

7 'Kia-su' is a term in the Hokkien dialect that means 'afraid of losing'.

8 The phenomenon of moral hazard arises from information asymmetries. In this context, the provider (government) institutes a safety net with the objective of providing insurance against risk in the event of business failure arising from an investment. However, after this provision has been provided, the beneficiaries, who are supposed to venture abroad with more confidence, become more risk averse and prefer to stay in the safety net for good. Their behavior works against the common good of the society.

Chapter 2

1 For a comprehensive study of the Baba community in Malaysia, see Tan Chee Beng's *The Babas of Melaka: Culture and Identity of a Chinese Peranakan Community in Malaysia*. See also John R. Clammer's *Straits Chinese Society*.

2 The Hokkiens still constitute the largest sub-ethnic Chinese community in Malaysia, followed by the Cantonese, Hakkas, Teochew and Hainanese. Among the smaller sub-ethnic Chinese groups are the Kwongsai, Hokchiu, Hokchia and Hengwa.

3 For an insightful account of revenue farm activities in Southeast Asia, see James R. Rush's *Opium to Java: Revenue Farming and Chinese Enterprise in Colonial Indonesia, 1860–1910* and Carl A. Trocki's *Opium and Empire: Chinese Society in Colonial Singapore, 1800–1910*.

4 Eu Tong Sen was a tin miner, who ventured into rubber plantations and eventually founded the Lee Wah Bank in Singapore. Lau Pak Kuan, also a tin miner, established two banks, the Chung Khiaw Bank and the Overseas Union Bank, and an insurance company, Public Insurance Company. Chung Thye Phin started out as a revenue farmer and later ventured into the tin mining and rubber plantation sectors. Loke Yew started out in tin mining, then diversified into rubber plantations, tobacco cultivation, trading and banking. He helped found the Kwong Yik Bank, the first Chinese bank to be incorporated in Malaya in 1903. Tan Kah Kee ventured first into rice trading, then diversified into pineapple production, rubber plantations and shipping, emerging eventually as one of the leading businessmen of the colonial era. A further discussion on Tan Kah Kee is provided below. Lee Kong Chian developed a reputation in the rubber industry through his company, the Lee Rubber group, and helped found the Oversea-Chinese Banking Corporation (OCBC), which remains a major Chinese-owned enterprise in Southeast Asia (Chan and Chiang 1994; Lee and Chow 1997).

5 See Heng Pek Koon's *Chinese Politics in Malaysia: A History of the Malaysian Chinese Association* for a detailed account of the factors that led some of the leading Chinese capitalists in Malaya to establish this party.

6 Among the Indian businessmen who have had access to state rents include T. Ananda Krishnan, who controls a number of companies including public-listed Tanjong plc. See Gomez and Jomo (1999) for detailed case studies on Ting Pek Khiing, Vincent Tan Chee Yioun and T. Ananda Krishnan. See Gomez (1999: 163–73) for a case study of YTL Corporation.

7 Among the Chinese-controlled firms identified to help ailing Malay companies were YTL Corporation, the beneficiary of highly profitable privatized power generating licence, and Genting Bhd, which relies on the renewal of its lucrative casino licence to sustain its business (*Far Eastern Economic Review* 19/2/98). This, however, was not the first time UMNO leaders had called upon Chinese businessmen who had benefited from government patronage to bailout well-connected Malay businessmen. In 1994, during the height of the economic boom, Ting Pek Khiing had acquired the public-listed and debt-ridden Granite Industries from the politically well-connected Samsudin Abu Hassan when the latter had run into severe financial and personal problems.

8 When the term, *huaqiao*, came into use at the end of the 19th century, it then had the meaning of a Chinese national temporarily residing abroad. This term, however, also acquired political, legal and emotional overtones, referring to official protection accorded by the Chinese government to ethnic Chinese abroad, with the latter expected to give their primary loyalty to China (Wang 1991: 36).

9 For a discussion on the dynamism of Taiwanese SMEs, see Lam and Lee (1992). See Chew (1988) for a review of the dynamics of SME operations in Singapore, though the emphasis here is not on providing an analysis of corporate development by Chinese-owned enterprises. See Wong (1988) for a discussion on Chinese firms in Hong Kong, developed by migrants from Shanghai.

10 Gomez (1999) noted that among the leading Chinese capitalists in Malaysia, Robert Kuok and his close associate, Khoo Kay Peng of the MUI group, were the only businessmen who had established some longstanding corporate ties with other ethnic Chinese in East and Southeast Asia. Kuok has been a major advocate of the need for Chinese businessmen of the diaspora to cooperate in business as a means to develop their corporate influence in the region.

11 There had been an attempt in 1996 by the Pacific Bank to merge its activities with OCBC's banking operations in Malaysia. This has failed to materialize.

12 See, for example, the interview with the prominent timber merchant in Sarawak, Lau Hui Kang, who suggests that sub-ethnic cooperation had been a factor in helping the Foochows capture control of the timber sector in this state (*The Star* 11/9/91).

Chapter 3

1 For a good short account of the Chinese community in Thailand, see the chapter by Michael Vatikiotis in Pan (1998). The best treatment of the Chinese in Thailand is given by Skinner (1957, 1958), with valuable historical material on their economic roles. More recent studies of Sino-

Thai business groups are by Krirkiat and Yoshihara (1983) and Suehiro (1989, 1992). This article deals only with the situation prior to the 1997 East Asian financial crisis.

2 Estimates of numbers and definitions of 'Sino-Thai' are here taken from Vatikiotis (1998: 218). Suryadinata (1997: 2–9) gives a useful discussion of the citizenship status and identity dilemmas of the Southeast Asian Chinese.

3 See Yoshihara Kunio (1988; 73–4, 165–6) for details of the major ethnic Thai enterprises, and for excellent brief biographical vignettes on the main Sino-Thai capitalists.

4 Cristina Szanton (1983) has given the fullest account yet available on inter-ethnic relations in a Thai small town.

5 In the best prewar estimate of Chinese and other foreign capital in Thailand, Callis (1942: 109) assessed Chinese capital there in 1937 at between US$142–140 million as against US$124 million of Western capital.

6 Suehiro (1989: 83–7) provides an account of the four largest rice-milling groups in the 1920s, of which the largest was the Lee Teck Oh group, said to control 60 per cent of the rice export trade before 1929 but collapsed in the Depression. None of the four were still prominent in the 1930s.

7 The 'Big Five' families which dominated the rice industry between the 1930s to 1940s were the Wanglee, Bulasuk, Bulakun, Iamsuri and Lamsam families, all of which later diversified their business activities in varying degrees with differing degrees of success (Suehiro 1989: 110–22). The Lamsams were of Hakka origin, then the only non-Teochew group, although later intermarried into the Wanglee family, the prominent leaders of the Teochew community. The Lamsams later headed the big Thai Farmers Bank group, which has remained among the foremost Sino-Thai business groups ever since. The Wanglee Bank was one of the largest in the 1950s, but has fallen far behind the leaders since the 1960s.

8 By the late 1970s, and ever since, by far the largest of the local commercial banks were a new 'Big Four' – the Bangkok Bank, Thai Farmers Bank, Bank of Ayudhya and Bangkok Metropolitan Bank, controlled by the Sophonpanich, Lamsam, Ratanarak and Tejaphaibun families respectively. The Bangkok Bank held deposits well in excess of those of all the next three (Suehiro 1989: 248–9). The Bank of Asia, which had been nearly as large as them in the 1950s, later fell far behind the others.

9 The Thai Farmers Bank (TFB) group, headed by the Lamsam family, is unique in that it is the oldest of the major conglomerates, apart from the Wanglee group, now fallen far behind. In the 1930s, it was already one of the Big Five rice milling-trading groups. The TFB group then had close links with some of the 1932 coup leaders, but fell out of favor in the 1940s when they lost power. It has subsequently adapted very successfully to the changing political and economic environment, and is one of the foremost in adopting modern management techniques.

10 Suehiro (1992: 37–40) notes several other characteristics of modern Sino-Thai business organization besides those mentioned here. LSEs were dominant in terms of investment volume and employment creation. They were not dependent on a single source of capital but could draw on the 'tripod structure' of state enterprises, MNCs and domestic private banks.

The bank-based groups grew to be the largest of all. More than 70 per cent of the country's 100 largest enterprises were owned by 16 Sino-Thai groups. Only a small proportion of these were listed on the stock exchange until the late 1980s.

Chapter 5

1 We also consulted Suryadinata's article entitled 'The Ethnic Chinese in the Asean States' in the same publication.
2 Although Independence was declared in August 1945 at the end of World War II, this was only realized in December 1949 after a national revolutionary struggle with the Dutch. The vast Indonesian archipelago is made up of around 13,000 islands, the largest of which are Java, Sumatra, Kalimantan, Sulawesi and Irian Jaya. A majority of the ethnic Chinese population live in the island of Java, while sizeable Chinese communities are also found in cities in Sumatra and Kalimantan.
3 There are two major studies on revenue farm activities in Southeast Asia, that is James R. Rush's *Opium to Java: Revenue Farming and Chinese Enterprise in Colonial Indonesia, 1860–1910* and Carl A. Trocki's *Opium and Empire: Chinese Society in Colonial Singapore, 1800–1910*.
4 'Benteng', literally translated, means 'fortress'.
5 Indonesia has always followed a one-China policy, i.e. recognizing only the PRC, although for 23 years, as of 1967, diplomatic relations were frozen in the aftermath of the abortive coup in 1965, attributed to the Indonesian Communist Party. It was only in August 1990 that diplomatic relations resumed between Indonesia and the PRC.

In spite of an absence of diplomatic relations with Taiwan, Indonesia has a thriving economic relationship with this country, manifested in extensive bilateral trade and investment agreements. Trade links between these two countries are handled through a Taiwanese trade and business representative office, based in Jakarta.

As for Hong Kong, before the hand over of this British colony to China in July 1997, there were normal diplomatic and trade relations between the territory and Indonesia. During the period when relations with the PRC were frozen, Hong Kong functioned as the third country through which economic activities between Indonesia and the PRC were conducted.
6 Heidhues (1998) also states that in 1960 around 100,000 ethnic Chinese left Indonesia, though a majority of them did not return to China, but instead migrated to Australia, North America and Europe.
7 For a fascinating account of the dramatic events leading up to the fall of Soeharto, see Pour's *Jakarta Semasa Lengser Keprabon: 100 Hari Menjelang Peralihan Kekuasaan* (Jakarta in the Period of the Resignation: The Last 100 Days).
8 For a detailed and lucid analysis of the crisis and its early impact on the Indonesian economy, see Pangestu and Soesastro's 'The Role of the IMF in Indonesia: Crisis and Recovery'.
9 Although there were dire predictions that the rupiah would continue to fall to Rp.20.000 to the US dollar, this did not happen. In spite if this, by June 1998, the rupiah had lost 78 per cent of its value on the dollar.

10 A full account of these student demonstrations is provided by A. Zamroni and M. Andin in their volume, *Pahlawan Reformasi: Catatan Peristiwa 12 Mei 1998* (Hero of Reformasi: Notes on the Events of 12 May 1998).

11 However, during the counting of the ballot papers, strong allegations were made of various irregularities. This led to a delay in the announcement of the election results.

12 The party with most support after the Golkar was the PKB (Partai Kebangkitan Bangsa, or National Awakening Party) which secured 12.62 per cent of the votes, while the PPP (Partai Persatuan Pembangunan, or United Development Party) and the PAN (Partai Amanat Nasional, or National Mandate Party) obtained 10.72 per cent and 7.12 per cent respectively of the popular support.

13 For a detailed account of this scandal, see *Tempo* 23–29 August 1999.

14 The government takeover was undertaken through the Indonesian Banking Restructuring Agency (IBRA) which had been established following the financial crisis to help deal with the restructuring of the domestic banking system.

15 This information was obtained from conversations with people in Manado, North Sulawesi in May 1999, and with people in Pangkalpinang, Bangka in November 1998.

16 Glodok refers to the Chinatown area in Jakarta.

17 Following the riots, it was later revealed that more than 100 ethnic Chinese women and girls were sexually assaulted and gang raped.

18 The Bank Bali scandal, for example, revealed that corruption still thrives among state leaders that may continue to impair hopes of improving the financial system to encourage economic recovery. In East Timor, following a referendum on independence held on 30 August 1999 and conducted by a United Nations (UN)-appointed agency (UNAMET), a situation of catastrophic chaos emerged after the results revealed that 78.5 per cent of the East Timorese opted for independence. Armed pro-autonomy (i.e. pro-Indonesia) groups, disappointed with the referendum result, went about unchecked torching and ransacking the capital city of Dili, killing an unknown number of people; the violence quickly spread to other parts of East Timor. These acts, which led to a major refugee crisis, created an international uproar, impelling the UN's Security Council to adopt a resolution to send in multinational peacekeeping troops into East Timor. Given the results of the parliamentary elections, it is still unclear if the presidential elections in November 1999 will lead to the selection of a president who has the support of the majority of the Indonesian population.

19 As in the case of the peranakans in Malaysia and Singapore, most of the members of this community were of Hokkien origin. For a more in-depth discussion on the peranakan community, see Suryadinata's *Peranakan Chinese Politics in Java, 1917–42*. See also Skinner's (1996) article, 'Creolized Chinese Societies in Southeast Asia,' which provides a broad picture of the peranakan community in Southeast Asia.

20 A pertinent example is the policy by the Habibie government, in particular the Ministry of Cooperatives and Small Business headed by Adi Sasono, to develop *Ekonomi Kerakyatan* (Populist Economy). This policy is,

according to critics, actually an attempt to reduce or eliminate ethnic
Chinese domination of retail trade.

Chapter 6

1 During this period, Taiwan's political system was in a state of transition,
from an authoritarian regime dominated by the Chiang family to more
democratic rule.
2 I undertook my study of Taiwanese investors in Malacca and Kuala
Lumpur from August to December 1998. I conducted 23 interviews in
Malacca and 15 in Kuala Lumpur; but the cases I cite in this chapter are
based only on the interviews undertaken in Malacca. By 1998, Taiwanese
companies had emerged as the largest foreign investors in the state of
Malacca in terms of volume of investment (RM$2,430.81million) and in
terms of approved projects (41 firms). The next largest foreign investors in
descending order were Germany, Japan, US and Singapore. This
information was obtained from the Government Homepage of the state
of Malacca. Most Taiwanese investors in Malacca are manufacturers of
wood-related products. All interviews were conducted in Mandarin.
3 During my interview with Wei King Yuan, the executive secretary of
Taiwanese Investor Association in Malaysia, he confirmed that the main
reasons why Taiwanese investors invested in Malaysia were good
infrastructure, political stability and limited communication problems.
4 This company is involved in the manufacture of steeless water towers and
employs about 12 workers.
5 Since the early 1990s, labor shortages have been evident in the Malaysian
manufacturing sector. Initially, Indonesians were recruited, but since 1992,
workers from Bangladesh have come into the country on a large scale. In
December 1994, the Ministry of Human Resources disclosed that there
were 1.5 million migrant workers in Malaysia, of which at least 200,000
were Bangladeshi workers (Rudnick 1996: 40–49). Labor shortages are still
a problem, and according to the head of Association of Taiwanese Investor
in Malaysia, there is an average 20 per cent labor shortage in Taiwanese
firms.
6 This "Taiwanese experience" also works between Taiwanese investors.
Table 6.8 shows that most Taiwanese companies source materials from
other local Taiwanese firms and their co-partners are often Taiwanese.
This issue will be discussed later in the conclusion.

Bibliography

———◆◆◆———

General / Southeast Asia

Akerlof, G.A. (1970) 'The Market for 'Lemons': Qualitative Uncertainty and the Market Mechanism', *Quarterly Journal of Economics* August.

Aldrich, H.E. and R. Waldinger (1990) 'Etnicity and Entrepreneurship', *Annual Review of Sociology* 16.

Aldrich, H. (1995) 'Entrepreneurial Strategies in New Organizational Populations', in I. Bull, H. Thomas and G. Willard (eds) *Entrepreneurship: Perspectives in Theory Building*, Oxford: Pergamon.

Backman, M. (1999) *Asian Eclipse: Exposing the Dark Side of Business in Asia*, Singapore: John Wiley & Sons.

Barth, F. (1967) *The Role of the Entrepreneur in Social Change in Northern Norway*, Bergen: Norwegian University Press.

Biggart, N.W. (1997) 'Explaining Asian Economic Organization: Towards Weberian Institutional Perspective', in Orru, Biggart and Hamilton *The Economic Organization of East Asian Capitalism*.

Bonacich, E. (1973) 'A Theory of Middleman Minoities', *American Sociological Review* 38.

Bonacich, E. and J. Modell (1980) *The Economic Basis of Ethnic Solidarity: Small Business in the Japanese-American Community*, Berkeley: University of California Press.

Brown, R.A. (1994) *Capital and Entrepreneurship in South-East Asia*, New York: St. Martin's Press.

Brown, R.A. (ed.) (1995) *Chinese Business Enterprise in Asia*, London: Routledge.

Brown, R.A. (ed.) (1996) *Chinese Business Enterprise: Critical Perspectives on Business and Management*, London: Routledge.

Brown, R. (1994) *The State and Ethnic Politics in Southeast Asia*, London: Routledge.

Callis, H.G. (1942) *Foreign Capital in Southeast Asia*, New York: Institute of Pacific Relations.

Bibliography

Caplen, B. and M. Levin (1992) 'The New Pacific Capitalism: Chinese Families are Changing Business on Both Sides of the Ocean', *Asian Business* 28 (8).

Chan, A.B. (1996) *Li Ka-shing: Hong Kong's Elusive Billionaire*, Hong Kong: Oxford University Press.

Chan, W.K.K. (1982) 'The Organizational Structure of the Traditional Chinese Firm and its Modern Reform', *Business History Review* LVI (2).

Chan, W.K.K. (1992) 'Chinese Business Networking and the Pacific Rim: The Family Firm's Roles Past and Present', *Journal of American-East Asian Relations* 1 (2).

Chan, K.B. (ed.) (1999) *Chinese Business Networks: State, Economy and Culture*, Singapore: Prentice Hall and Nordic Institute of Asian Studies.

Chandler, A.D., Jr. (1962) *Strategy and Structure: Chapters in the History of the American Industrial Enterprise*, Cambridge: MIT Press.

Chandler, A.D., Jr. (1977) *The Visible Hand: The Managerial Revolution in American Business*, Cambridge: Harvard University Press.

Chen, R. H. (1996) *Made in Taiwan: The Story of Acer Computers*, Taipei: McGraw-Hill.

Chen, T.J. (1994) 'FDI by Small and Medium-Sized Enterprises from Taiwan: A Survey of Parent Firms', paper presented at the workshop on 'Taiwan's Small and Medium-Sized Firms' Direct Investment in Southeast Asia', organized by the Chung-Hua Institute for Economic Research, November 18–19, Taipei.

Chen, T.J., et al. (1995) *Taiwan's Small-and Medium-Sized Firms' Direct Investment in Southeast Asia*, Taipei: Chung-Hua Institute for Economic Research.

Chia, F. (1994) *The Babas Revisited*, Singapore: Heinemann Asia.

Chirot, D. and A. Reid (eds) (1997) *Essential Outsiders: Chinese and Jews in the Modern Transformation of Southeast Asia and Central Europe*, Seattle: University of Washington Press.

Chou, T.C. (1989) 'The Powerless Medium and Small-Sized Enterprises' (in Chinese), in M.H.H. Hsiao (ed.) *Monopoly and Exploitation* (in Chinese), Taipei: Taiwan Research Foundation.

Clad, J. (1989) *Behind the Myth: Business, Money and Power in Southeast Asia*, London: Unwin Hyman.

Clark, C. and S. Chan (eds) (1992) *The Evolving Pacific Basin in the Global Political Economy*, Boulder: Lynne Rienner.

Clegg, S.R., S.G. Redding and M. Cartner (eds) (1990) *Capitalism in Contrasting Cultures*, Berlin: Walter de Gruyter.

Clegg, S.R. and S.G. Redding (1990) 'Introduction: Capitalism in Contrasting Cultures', in Clegg, Redding and Cartner (eds) *Capitalism in Contrasting Cultures*.

Coppel, C. and H. Mabbett (1972) 'The Chinese in Indonesia, the Philippines and Malaysia', London: Minority Rights Group Report No. 10.

Crouch, H. and J.W. Morley (1998) 'The Dynamics of Political Change', in J.W. Morley (ed.) *Driven by Growth: Political Change in the Asia-Pacific Region*, Armonk: M. E. Sharpe.

Cushman, J.W. and Wang Gungwu (eds) (1988) *Changing Ethnic Identities of the Southeast Asian Chinese Since World War II*, Hong Kong: Hong Kong University Press.

Deyo, F.C. (1983) 'Chinese Management Practices and Work Commitment in Comparative Perspective', in Lim and Gosling (eds) *The Chinese in Southeast Asia: Volume 2.*

Dirlik, A. (1997) 'Critical Reflections on "Chinese Capitalism" as a Paradigm', *Identities* 3 (3).

Dobbin, C. (1996) *Asian Entrepreneurial Minorities: Conjoint Communities in the Making of the World Economy, 1570–1940*, London: Curzon.

East Asian Analytical Unit (1995) *Overseas Chinese Business Networks in Asia*, Parkes: Department of Foreign Affairs and Trade, Commonwealth of Australia.

Esman, M. (1985) 'The Chinese Diaspora in Southeast Asia', in G. Sheffer (ed.) *Modern Diasporas in International Politics*, London: Croom Helm.

Freedman, M. (ed.) (1970) *Family and Kinship in Chinese Society*, Stanford: Stanford University Press.

Freedman, M. (1971) *Chinese Lineage and Society: Fukien and Kwangtung*, London: The Althone Press.

Freedman, M. (1979) *The Study of Chinese Society*, Stanford: Stanford University Press.

Fukuda S. (1995) *With Sweat and Abacus: Economic Roles of Southeast Asian Chinese on the Eve of World War II*, Singapore: Select Books.

Fukuyama, F. (1995) *Trust: The Social Virtues and the Creation of Prosperity*, London: Hamish Hamilton.

Gates, H. (1996) *China's Motor: A Thousand Years of Petty Capitalism*, Ithaca: Cornell University Press.

Godley, M.R. (1981) *The Mandarin-Capitalists From Nanyang: Overseas Chinese Enterprise in the Modernization of China, 1893–1911*, Cambridge: Cambridge University Press.

Golay, F.H., R. Anspach, M.R. Pfanner and E.B. Ayal (1969) *Underdevelopment and Economic Nationalism in Southeast Asia*, Ithaca: Cornell University Press.

Gold, T. (1986) *State and Society in the Taiwan Miracle*, New York: M.E.Sharpe.

Goldberg, M.A. (1985) *The Chinese Connection: Getting Plugged into Pacific Rim Real Estate, Trade and Capital Markets*, BC: University of British Columbia Press.

Goody, J. (1996) *The East in the West*, Cambridge: Cambridge University Press.

Gosling, L.A.P. (1983) 'Changing Chinese Identities in Southeast Asia: An Introductory Review', in Lim and Gosling (eds), *The Chinese in Southeast Asia: Volume 2.*

Granovetter, M. (1995) 'Economic Action and Social Structure: The Problem of Embeddedness', *American Journal of Sociology* 91.

Hamilton, G.G. and C.S. Kao (1990) 'The Institutional Foundations of Chinese Business: The Family Firm in Taiwan', *Comparative Social Research* 12.

Hamilton, G.G. (ed.) (1991) *Business Networks and Economic Development in East and Southeast Asia*, Hong Kong: Centre for Asian Studies.

Hamilton, G.G. (1996a) 'Competition and Organization: A Reexamination of Chinese Business Practices', *Journal of Asian Business* 12 (1).

Bibliography

Hamilton, G.G. (ed.) (1996b) *Asian Business Networks*, Berlin: Walter de Gruyter.

Hicks, G.L. (ed.) (1993) *Overseas Chinese Remittances from Southeast Asia 1910–1940*, Singapore: Select Books.

Hicks, G.L. (ed.) (1996) *Chinese Organisations in Southeast Asia in the 1930s*, Singapore: Select Books.

Hiscock, G. (1997) *Asia's Wealth Club*, London: Nicholas Breasley.

Hodder, R. (1996) *Merchant Princes of the East: Cultural Delusions, Economic Success and the Overseas Chinese in Southeast Asia*, Chichester: John Wiley & Sons.

Hsiao, M.H.H. and Kung I-Chun (1998) 'The Business Network Between Taiwanese Investors and Ethnic Chinese in Southeast Asia' (in Chinese), paper presented at the international conference on 'Economic Development and Interaction between Taiwan and Southeast Asian Chinese', Taipei: The Institute of Taiwan Economic Studies.

Hsiao, F.S. and W.M.C. Hsiao (1996) 'The Historical Traditions of Taiwanese Small-and-Medium Enterprises', paper presented at the conference on 'Commercial Tradition of Taiwan', Academia Sinica, Taipei.

Hsing, Y.T. (1998) *Making Capitalism in China: The Taiwan Connection*, New York: Oxford University Press.

Hseuh Chi (1994) 'Southward Policy and Asian-Pacific Regional Operation Center' (in Chinese), paper presented at the conference on 'Southward Policy and the Future of Taiwan Economy', New Society Foundation, Taipei.

Hsu, P.S. (1994) 'The Difference in Investment Patterns of Taiwanese Small and Medium-Sized Enterprises in Philippines, Indonesia, Malaysia and Thailand' (in Chinese), Taipei: TIER.

Kao, J. (1993) 'The Worldwide Web of Chinese Business', *Harvard Business Review*, March–April.

King, A.Y.C. (1994) 'Kuan-shi and Network Building: A Sociological Interpretation', in Tu (ed.) *The Living Tree: The Changing Meaning of Being Chinese Today*.

Kotkin, J. (1993) *Tribes: How Race, Religion, and Identity Determine Success in the New Global Economy*, New York: Random House.

Lam, D.K.K. and I. Lee (1992) 'Guerrilla Capitalism and the Limits of Statist Theory: Comparing the Chinese NICs', in Clark and Chan (eds) *The Evolving Pacific Basin in the Global Political Economy*.

Landa, J.T. (1981) 'A Theory of the Ethnically Homogenous Middleman Group: An Institutional Alternative to Contract Law', *The Journal of Legal Studies* X.

Landa, J.T. (1983) 'The Political Economy of the Ethnically Homogeneous Chinese Middleman Group in Southeast Asia: Ethnicity and Entrepreneurship in a Plural Society', in Lim and Gosling (eds) *The Chinese in Southeast Asia: Volume I*.

Lee, Y.C. (1993) 'The Impact of Taiwanese Foreign Investment on Taiwan's Manufacturing Industry', (in Chinese), Taipei: TIER.

Leff, N.H. (1978) 'Industrial Organisation and Entrepreneurship in the Developing Countries: And Economic Groups', *Economic Development and Cultural Change* 26 (4).

Bibliography

Leff, N.H. (1979) 'Entrepreneurship and Economic Development: The Problem Revisited', *Journal of Economic Literature* 8 (March).

Leong, S.T. (1997) *Migration and Ethnicity in Chinese History: Hakkas, Pengmin and Their Neighbors*, Stanford: Stanford University Press.

Lever-Tracy, C., D. Ip and N. Tracy (1996) *The Chinese Diaspora and Mainland China: An Emerging Economic Synergy*, London: Macmillan.

Light, I. (1972) *Ethnic Enterprise in America*, Berkeley: University of California Press.

Light, I. (1980) 'Asian Enterprise in America: Chinese, Japanese and Koreans in Small Business', in S. Cummings (ed.) *Self-Help in Urban America: Patterns of Minority Economic Development*, Port Washington, NY: Kennikat Press.

Light, I. and E. Bonacich (1988) *Immigrant Entrepreneurs: Koreans in Los Angeles, 1965–1982*, Berkeley: University of California Press.

Light, I. and P. Bhachu (eds) (1993) *Immigration and Entrepreneurship: Culture, Capital and Ethnic Networks*, New Brunswick: Transaction Publishers.

Lim, L.Y.C. and L.A.P. Gosling (eds) (1983) *The Chinese in Southeast Asia, Volumes I and II*, Singapore: Maruzen Asia.

Lim, L.Y.C. (1996) 'The Evolution of Southeast Asian Business Systems', *Journal of Asian Business* 12 (1).

Lim, L.Y.C. and L.A.P. Gosling (1997) 'Strengths and Weaknesses of Minority Status for Southeast Asian Chinese at a Time of Economic Growth and Liberalization', in Chirot and Reid (eds) *Essential Outsiders: Chinese and Jews in the Modern Transformation of Southeast Asia and Central Europe*.

Lim, M.H. (1995) 'Taiwanese Business in Southeast Asia During the Japanese Period' (in Chinese), in *Newsletter of Southeast Area Studies* 1, Program for Southeast Asian Area Studies, Academia Sinica, Taipei.

Limlingan, V.S. (1986) *The Overseas Chinese in ASEAN: Business Strategies and Management Practices*, Manila: Vita Development Corporation.

Lin, W.C. (1997) 'The Attitude and Method of Taiwanese Investors' Trans-Culture Communication' (in Chinese), *National Policy Dynamic Analysis* 172.

Liu Hong (1998) 'Old Linkages, New Networks: The Globalization of Overseas Chinese Voluntary Associations and Its Implications', *The China Quarterly* September (155).

Liu Hong (1999) 'Social Capital and Business Networking: A Case Study of Modern Chinese Transnationalism', unpublished manuscript.

Liu, K.C. (1988) 'Chinese Merchants Guilds: An Historical Inquiry', *Pacific Historical Review* 57 (1).

Mackie, J.A.C. (1988) 'Changing Economic Roles and Ethnic Identities of the Southeast Asian Chinese: A Comparison of Indonesia and Thailand' in Cushman and Wang (eds) *Changing Identities of the Southeast Asian Chinese Since World War II*.

Mackie, J.A.C. (1992a) 'Overseas Chinese Entrepreneurship', *Asia-Pacific Economic Literature* 6 (1).

Mackie, J.A.C. (1992b) 'Changing Patterns of Chinese Big Business in Southeast Asia', in McVey (ed.) *Southeast Asian Capitalists*.

Mackie, J. (1995) 'Economic Systems of the Southeast Asian Chinese' in Suryadinata (ed.) *Southeast Asian Chinese and China: The Politico-Economic Dimension.*

Mackie, J.A.C. (1999), 'The Economic Role of the Southeast Asian Chinese: Information Gaps' in Chan (ed.) *Chinese Business Networks: State, Economy and Culture.*

Mackie, J.A.C. and C.A. Coppel (1976) 'A Preliminary Survey', in Mackie (ed.) *The Chinese in Indonesia.*

McVey, R. (ed.) (1992) *Southeast Asian Capitalists,* Ithaca: Cornell South East Asian Studies Program.

McVey, R. (1992) 'The Materialization of the Southeast Asian Entrepreneur', in McVey (ed.) *Southeast Asian Capitalists.*

Min Chen (1995) *Asian Management Systems: Chinese, Japanese and Korean Styles of Business,* London: Routledge.

Nasbitt, J. (1995) *Megatrends Asia: The Eight Megatrends That Are Changing The World,* London: Nicholas Breasley.

Ng, C.K. (1983) *Trade and Society: The Amoy Network on the China Coast, 1683–1735,* Singapore: Singapore University Press.

Ohmae, K. (1995) *The End of the Nation State: The Rise of Regional Economics,* New York: The Free Press.

Orru, M., N.W. Biggart and G.G. Hamilton (1997) *The Economic Organization of East Asian Capitalism,* London: Sage.

Pan, L. (1990) *Sons of the Yellow Emperor: The Story of the Overseas Chinese,* London: Mandarin.

Pan, L. (ed.) (1998) *The Encyclopedia of the Chinese Overseas,* London: Curzon.

Portes, A. and R.D. Manning (1986) 'The Immigrant Enclave: Theory and Empirical Examples', in S. Olzak and J. Nagel (eds) *Competitive Ethnic Relations,* Orlando, FL: Academic Press.

Purcell, V. (1951) *The Chinese in Southeast Asia,* London: Oxford University Press.

Redding, S.G. (1990) *The Spirit of Chinese Capitalism,* Berlin: Walter de Gruyter.

Redding, S. G. (1996) 'Weak Organizations and Strong Linkages: Managerial Ideology and Chinese Family Business Networks', in Hamilton (ed.) *Asian Business Networks.*

Redding, S.G. (1995) 'Overseas Chinese Networks: Understanding the Enigma', *Long Range Planning* 28 (1).

Reid, A. (ed.) (1996) *Sojourners and Settlers: Histories of Southeast Asia and the Chinese,* Sydney: Allen & Unwin.

Rose, M.B. (1993) 'Beyond Buddenbrooks: The Family Firm and the Management of Succession in Nineteenth-Century Britain', in J. Brown and M.B. Rose (eds) *Entrepreneurship, Networks and Modern Business,* Manchester: Manchester University Press.

Rowher, J. (1995) *Asia Rising,* Singapore: Butterworth-Heinemann Asia.

Rutten, M. (1994) *Asian Capitalists in the European Mirror,* Amsterdam: VU University Press.

Seagrave, S. (1996) *Lords of the Rim: The Invisible Empire of the Overseas Chinese,* London: Corgi Books.

Bibliography

Sender, H. (1991) 'Inside the Overseas Chinese Network', *Institutional Investor* August.

Shen, T.R. (1997) 'The Business Operation of Taiwan's Medium-and Small-Scale Enterprises in Southeast Asia', paper presented at the conference on 'Chinese Business in Southeast Asia', held by Faculty of Economics and Administration, University of Malaya, Kuala Lumpur, Malaysia.

Skeldon, R. (ed.) (1994) *Reluctant Exciles? Migration from Hong Kong and the New Overseas Chinese*, Armonk: M.E. Sharpe.

Skinner, G. W. (1996) 'Creolized Chinese Societies in Southeast Asia, in Reid (ed.) *Sojourners and Settlers: Histories of Southeast Asia and the Chinese*.

Suryadinata, L. (1988) 'Chinese Economic Elites in Indonesia: A Preliminary Study', in Cushman and Wang (eds) *Changing Identities of the Southeast Asian Chinese Since World War II*.

Suryadinata, L. (ed.) (1989) *The Ethnic Chinese in the ASEAN States: Bibliographical Essays*, Singapore: Institute of Southeast Asian Studies.

Suryadinata, L. (1992) *Pribumi Indonesians, the Chinese Minority and China* (3rd edition), Singapore: Heinemann Asia.

Suryadinata, L. (ed.) (1993) *Chinese Adaptation and Diversity: Essays on Society and Literature in Indonesia, Malaysia and Singapore*, Singapore: Singapore University Press.

Suryadinata, L. (1995a) *China and the ASEAN States: The Ethnic Chinese Dimension*, Singapore: Singapore University Press.

Suryadinata, L. (ed.) (1995b) *Southeast Asian Chinese and China: The Socio-Cultural Dimension*, Singapore: Times Academic Press.

Suryadinata, L. (ed.) (1995c) *Southeast Asian Chinese and China: The Politico-Economic Dimension*, Singapore: Times Academic Press.

Suryadinata, L. (ed.) (1997a) *Ethnic Chinese as Southeast Asians*, Singapore: Institute of Southeast Asian Studies.

Suryadinata, L. (1997b) 'Ethnic Chinese in Southeast Asia: Overseas Chinese, Chinese overseas or Southeast Asian', in Suryadinata (ed.) *Ethnic Chinese as Southeast Asians*.

Tanaka, Y., M. Mori and Y. Mori (1992) 'Overseas Chinese Business Community in Southeast Asia: Present Conditions and Future Prospects', *RIM: Pacific Business and Industries* II (16).

Tanzer, A. (1994) 'The Bamboo Network', *Forbes* July 18.

Tu, W.M. (ed.) (1994) *The Living Tree: The Changing Meaning of Being Chinese Today*, Stanford: Stanford University Press.

Tzeng, R.L. (1997) 'Foreign Direct Investment in Southeast Asia Since the 1980s: The Implications of Regional Economic Integration', PROSEA Occasional Paper No.1, Academia Sinica, Taipei.

Wade, R. (1990) *Governing the Market: Economic Theory and the Role of Government in East Asian Industrialization*, Princeton: Princeton University Press.

Waldinger, R., H. Aldrich, R. Ward, et al. (1990) *Ethnic Entrepreneurs: Immigrant Business in Industrial Societies*, London; Sage.

Wang Gungwu (1988) 'Trade and Cultural Values: Australia and the Four Dragons', *ASAA Review* 11 (3).

Wang Gungwu (1991) *China and the Chinese Overseas*, Singapore: Times Academic Press.

Bibliography

Wang Gungwu (1992) *Community and Nation: China, Southeast Asia and Australia*, Sydney: Allen & Unwin.

Wang Gungwu (1994) 'Among Non-Chinese', in Tu (ed.), *The Living Tree: The Changing Meaning of Being Chinese Today*.

Wang Gungwu (1995) 'The Southeast Asian Chinese and the Development of China', in Suryadinata (ed.) *Southeast Asian Chinese and China: The Politico-Economic Dimension*.

Wang Gungwu (1996) 'Sojourning: The Chinese Experience in Southeast Asia', in Reid (ed.) *Sojourners and Settlers: Histories of Southeast Asia and the Chinese*.

Wang, T.P. (1994) *The Origins of Chinese Kongsi*, Petaling Jaya: Pelanduk Publications.

Ward, R. and R. Jenkins (eds) (1984) *Ethnic Communities in Business: Strategies for Economic Survival*, Cambridge: Cambridge University Press.

Watson, J.L. (1982) 'Chinese Kinship Reconsidered: Anthropological Perspectives on Historical Research', *China Quarterly* 92.

Weber, M. (1971) *The Protestant Ethnic and the Spirit of Capitalism*, London: Unwin University Books.

Weidenbaum, M. and S. Hughes (1996) *The Bamboo Network*, New York: The Free Press.

Whitley, R. (1987) 'Taking Firms Seriously as Economic Actors: Towards a Sociology of Firm Behaviour', *Organization Studies* 8.

Whitley, R. (1990) 'Eastern Asian Enterprise Structures and the Comparative Analysis of Forms of Business Organization', *Organization Studies* 11 (1).

Whitley, R. (1991) 'The Social Construction of Business Systems in East Asia', *Organizational Studies* 12 (1).

Whitley, R. (1992) *Business Systems in East Asia: Firms, Markets and Societies*, London: Sage.

Wickberg, E. (1994) 'Overseas Chinese Adaptive Organizations, Past and Present', in Skeldon (ed.) *Reluctant Exiles? Migration from Hong Kong and the New Overseas Chinese*.

Williams, L.E. (1966) *The Future of the Overseas Chinese in Southeast Asia*, New York: McGraw Hill.

Wong, S.L. (1985) 'The Chinese Family Firm: A Model', *British Journal of Sociology* 36 (1).

Wong, S.L. (1988) *Emigrant Entrepreneurs*, Hong Kong: Oxford University Press.

Wong, S.L. (1993) 'Business Networks, Cultural Values and the State in Hong Kong and Singapore', unpublished paper.

Wu, Y.L. and C.H. Wu (1980) *Economic Development in Southeast Asia*, Stanford: Hoover Institute.

Wu, Y.L. (1983) 'Chinese Entrepreneurs in Southeast Asia', *American Economic Review* 73 (2).

Yao Souchou (1997) 'The Romance of Asian Capitalism: Geography, Desire and Chinese Business', in M.T. Berger and D.A. Borer (eds) *The Rise of East Asia: Critical Visions of the Pacific Century*, London: Routledge.

Yong, C.F. (1987) *Tan Kah-Kee: The Making of an Overseas Chinese Legend*, Singapore: Oxford University Press.

Yoshihara, K. (1988) *The Rise of Ersatz Capitalism in South-East Asia*, Singapore: Oxford University Press.

Bibliography

Singapore

Chan, K.B. and S.N.C. Chiang (1994) *Stepping Out: The Making of Chinese Entrepreneurs*, Singapore: Simon & Schuster.

Chan, K.B. and B.K. Ng (1999) 'Myths and Misperceptions of Ethnic Chinese Capitalism', in Chan (ed.) *Chinese Business Networks: State, Economy and Culture*.

Chan, K.B. and C.K. Tong (1999) 'Singapore Chinese Doing Business in China', in Chan (ed.) *Chinese Business Networks: State, Economy and Culture*.

Cheng, L.K. (1985) *Social Change and the Chinese in Singapore*, Singapore: Singapore University Press.

Cheng, L.K. (1995) 'Chinese Clan Associations in Singapore: Social Change and Continuity', in Suryadinata (ed.) *Southeast Asian Chinese and China: The Socio-Cultural Dimension*.

Chew, S.B. (1988) *Small Firms in Singapore*, Singapore: Oxford University Press.

Chew, R. (1996) 'Safety Nets for Entrepreneurship in Singapore', in A.M. Low and W.L. Tan (eds) *Entrepreneurs, Entrepreneurship and Enterprising Culture*, Singapore: Addison Wesley.

Chew, R. (1993) 'Local Chinese Banks in Singapore', in Suryadinata (ed.) *Chinese Adaptation and Diversity: Essays on Society and Literature in Indonesia, Malaysia and Singapore*.

Chiew, S.K. (1997) 'From Overseas Chinese to Chinese Singaporeans', in Suryadinata (ed.) *Ethnic Chinese as Southeast Asians*.

Chong, G.M.A. (1992) 'The Chinese Clan Associations in Singapore: Survival or Demise?' Honours Thesis, Department of Sociology, National University of Singapore.

Chuang, P.M. (1987) 'Mixing Business with Family', Singapore: *Singapore Business* 11 (10).

Clammer, J.R. (1980) *Straits Chinese Society*, Singapore: Singapore University Press.

Clammer, J.R. (1985) *Singapore: Ideology, Society and Culture*, Singapore: Chopmen.

Huff, W.G. (1994) *The Economic Growth of Singapore: Trade and Development in the Twentieth Century*, Cambridge: Cambridge University Press.

Koh, A.T. (1987) 'Saving, Investment and Entrepreneurship," in Krause, Koh and Lee (eds) *The Singapore Economy Reconsidered*.

Krause, L.B., A.T. Koh and T.Y. Lee (eds) (1987) *The Singapore Economy Reconsidered*, Singapore: Institute of Southeast Asian Studies.

Kwok, K.W. (1998) 'Singapore', in Pan (ed.) *The Encyclopedia of the Chinese Overseas*.

Lee, R., Y.L. Chan and K.F. Tang (1999) *The Making of a Technopreneur*, Singapore: ITE Alumni Association.

Lee, S.Y. (1974) *The Monetary and Banking Development of Singapore and Malaysia*, Singapore: Singapore University Press.

Lee, T.Y. (ed.) (1991) *Growth Triangle: The Johor-Singapore-Riau Experience*, Singapore: Institute of Southeast Asian Studies and Institute of Policy Studies.

Bibliography

Lee, T.Y. and L. Low (1990) *Local Entrepreneurship in Singapore: Private & State*, Singapore: Institute of Policy Studies and Times Academic Press.

Leong, W.K. (1998) 'Tan Lark Sye's Name Still Sells', *The Straits Times* 24 April.

Mak, L.F. (1981) *The Sociology of Secret Societies: A Study of Chinese Secret Societies in Singapore and Peninsular Malaysia*, Kuala Lumpur: Oxford University Press.

Menkhoff, T. (1993) *Trade Routes, Trust and Trading Networks: Chinese Small Enterprises in Singapore*, Saarbrucken: Verlag Breitenback Publishers.

Ng, B.K. (1996) 'The Role of the Central Provident Fund in Social Development, Stabilization and Restructuring: Experience from Singapore', in *New Zealand Journal of Business* 18 (1).

Ng, L. (1992) 'Keeping the Family in Business', *Singapore Business* December.

Rodan, G. (1989) *The Political Economy of Singapore's Industrialization: National State and International Capital*, Kuala Lumpur: Forum.

Singapore (1997) *Corporate Handbook Singapore*, Singapore: Thomson Information (S.E. Asia).

Singapore Business (1998) 'The Great Fall – From Rags to Rags', June.

Tan, C.B. (1997) 'Comments', in Suryadinata (ed.) *Ethnic Chinese as Southeast Asians*.

Tan, E.L. (1961) 'The Chinese Banks Incorporated in Singapore and Malaya', in T.H. Silcock (ed.) *Readings in Malayan Economics*, Singapore: Eastern Universities Press.

Tan Hock (1996) 'State Capitalism, Multinational Corporations and Chinese Entrepreneurship in Singapore', in Hamilton (ed.) *Asian Business Networks*.

Tang, H.K. (1996) 'The Ascent of Creative Technology: A Case Study of Technology Entrepreneurship," in B.S. Neo (ed.) *Exploiting Information Technology for Business Competitiveness: Cases and Insights for Singapore-based Organization*.

Toh, M.H. and L. Low (1993) 'Local Enterprises and Investment', in L. Low et.al *Challenge and Response: Thirty Years of the Economic Development Board*, Singapore: Times Academic Press.

Tong, C.K. (1996) 'Centripetal Authority, Differentiated Networks: The Social Organization of Chinese Firms in Singapore', in Hamilton (ed.) *Asian Business Networks*.

Trocki, C.A. (1990) *Opium and Empire: Chinese Society in Colonial Singapore, 1800–1910*, Ithaca: Cornell University Press.

Vasil, R. (1995) *Asianising Singapore: The PAP's Management of Ethnicity*, Singapore: Heinemann Asia.

Wilson, D. (1972) *Solid as a Rock: The First Forty Years of the Oversea-Chinese Banking Corporation*, Singapore: Oversea-Chinese Banking Corporation.

Wong, L.K. (1991) 'Commercial Growth Before the Second World War', in E.C.T. Chiew and E. Lee (eds) *A History of Singapore*. Singapore: Oxford University Press.

Yao Souchou (1987) 'The Fetish of Relationships: Chinese Business Transactions in Singapore', *Sojourn 2*.

Bibliography

Yen, C.H. (1986) *A Social History of the Chinese in Singapore and Malaya*, Singapore: Oxford University Press.

Yen, C.H. (1995) *Community and Politics: The Chinese in Colonial Singapore and Malaysia*, Singapore: Times Academic Press.

Yong, P.A. (1995) 'Singapore's Investments in China', in Suryadinata (ed.) *Southeast Asian Chinese and China: The Politico-Economic Dimension*.

Zheng Minbin (1996) 'Singapore – International Financial Centre' (in Chinese), Singapore: Lizhi Mass Communication Centre.

Malaysia

Bowie, A. (1991) *Crossing the Industrial Divide: State, Society and the Politics of Economic Transformation in Malaysia*, New York: Columbia University Press.

Cheong, S. (1992) *Chinese Controlled Companies in the KLSE: Industrial Counter*, Kuala Lumpur: Corporate Research Services Sdn Bhd.

Cheong, S. (1995) *Changes in Ownership of KLSE Companies*, Kuala Lumpur: Corporate Research Services Sdn Bhd.

Chew, D. (1990) *Chinese Pioneers on the Sarawak Frontier, 1841–1941*, Singapore: Oxford University Press.

Chia, O. P. (1990) 'The Chinese in Kuala Krai: A Study of Commerce and Social Life in a Malaysian Town', PhD diss., University of Malaya, Kuala Lumpur.

Chin, J.M. (1981) *The Sarawak Chinese*, Kuala Lumpur: Oxford University Press.

Gale, B. (1985) *Politics and Business: A Study of Multi-Purpose Holdings Berhad*, Singapore: Eastern Universities Press.

Gill, R. (1985) *The Making of Malaysia Inc.: A Twenty-five Year Review of the Securities Industry of Malaysia and Singapore*, Singapore: Pelanduk Publications.

Gomez, E.T. (1994) *Political Business: Corporate Involvement of Malaysian Political Parties*, Townsville: Centre for Southeast Asian Studies, James Cook University of North Queensland.

Gomez, E.T. (1996a) 'Changing Ownership Patterns, Patronage and the NEP', in Muhammad Ikmal Said and Zahid Emby (eds) *Malaysia: Critical Perspectives*, Petaling Jaya: Malaysian Social Science Association.

Gomez, E.T. (1996b) 'Philanthropy in a Multiethnic Society: The Case of Malaysia', in Tadashi (ed.) *Emerging Civil Society in the Asia Pacific Community*.

Gomez, E.T. (1999) *Chinese Business in Malaysia: Accumulation, Ascendance, Accommodation*, London/Honolulu: Curzon Press/University of Hawai'i Press.

Gomez, E.T. and Jomo K.S. (1999) *Malaysia's Political Economy: Politics, Patronage and Profits*, Cambridge: Cambridge University Press (revised edition).

Hara, F. (1991) 'Malaysia's New Economic Policy and the Chinese Business Community', *The Developing Economies* 29 (4).

Hara, F. (ed.) (1993) *Formation and Restructuring of Business Groups in Malaysia*, Tokyo: Institute of Developing Economies.

Bibliography

Hara, F. (ed.) (1994) *The Development of Bumiputera Enterprises and Sino-Malay Economic Cooperation in Malaysia*, Tokyo: Institute of Developing Economies.

Heng, P.K. (1988) *Chinese Politics in Malaysia: A History of the Malaysian Chinese Association*, Singapore: Oxford University Press.

Heng, P.K. (1992) 'The Chinese Business Elite of Malaysia', in McVey (ed.) *Southeast Asian Capitalists*.

Heng, P.K. (1997) 'The New Economic Policy and the Chinese Community in Peninsular Malaysia', *The Developing Economies* XXXV (3), September.

Ho, K.L. (1995) 'Recent Developments in the Political Economy of China-Malaysia Relations', in Suryadinata (ed.) *Southeast Asian Chinese and China: The Politico-Economic Dimension*.

Hua, W.Y. (1983) *Class and Communalism in Malaysia: Politics in a Dependent Capitalist State*, London: Zed Books.

Jesudason, J.V. (1989) *Ethnicity and the Economy: The State, Chinese Business, and the Multinationals in Malaysia*, Singapore: Oxford University Press.

Jesudason, J.V. (1997) 'Chinese Business and Ethnic Equilibrium in Malaysia', *Development and Change* 28 (1).

Jomo K.S. and E.T. Gomez (1997) 'Rents in Multi-ethnic Malaysia', in M. Aoki, H.K. Kim and M. Okuno-Fujiwara (eds) *The Role of Government in East Asian Economic Development: Comparative Institutional Analysis*, Oxford and Washington D.C.: Clarendon Press and the World Bank.

Jomo K.S. (1997) 'A Specific Idiom of Chinese Capitalism in Southeast Asia: Sino-Malaysian Capital Accumulation in the Face of State Hostility', in Chirot and Reid (eds) *Essential Outsiders: Chinese and Jews in the Modern Transformation of Southeast Asia and Central Europe*.

Khoo, K.K. (1988) 'Chinese Economic Activities in Malaya: A Historical Perspective', in Manning Nash (ed.) *Economic Performance in Malaysia: The Insider's View*, New York: Professors World Peace Academy.

Kuo, E.C.Y. (1996) 'Ethnicity, Polity and Economy: A Case Study of the Mandarin Trade and the Chinese Connection', in Hamilton (ed.) *Asian Business Networks*.

Lee, E. (1976) *The Towkays of Sabah*, Singapore: SingaporeUniversity Press.

Lee, K.H. (1987) 'Three Approaches in Peninsular Malaysian Chinese Politics: The MCA, the DAP and the Gerakan', in Zakaria Haji Ahmad (ed.) *Government and Politics in Malaysia*, Singapore: Oxford University Press.

Lee, K.H. and M.S. Chow (1997) *Biographical Dictionary of the Chinese in Malaysia*, Kuala Lumpur: Institute of Advanced Studies, University of Malaya and Pelanduk Publications.

Lee, P.P. (1978) *Chinese Society in Nineteenth-Century Singapore*, Kuala Lumpur: Oxford University Press.

Leong, S. (1993) 'From Dreamland to Kanzen: A Perfect Switch', in Hara (ed.) *Formation and Restructuring of Business Groups in Malaysia*.

Lim, L.L. (1988) 'The Erosion of the Chinese Economic Position', in L.S. Ling et al. (eds) *The Future of the Malaysian Chinese*, Kuala Lumpur: Malaysian Chinese Association.

Lim, M.H. (1981) *Ownership and Control of the One Hundred Largest Corporations in Malaysia*, Kuala Lumpur: Oxford University Press.

186

Bibliography

Lim, M.H. (1983) 'The Ownership and Control of Large Corporations in Malaysia: The Role of Chinese Businessmen', in Lim and Gosling (eds) *The Chinese in Southeast Asia*.

Loh, K.W. (1982) *The Politics of Chinese Unity in Malaysia: Reform and Conflict in the Malaysian Chinese Association 1971–1973*, Singapore: Institute of Southeast Asian Studies.

Low, K.Y. (1985) 'The Political Economy of Restructuring in Malaysia: A Study of State Policies with Reference to Multinational Corporations', M.Ec. diss., University of Malaya, Kuala Lumpur.

Machado, K.G. (1992) 'ASEAN State Industrial Policies and Japanese Regional Production Strategies: The Case of Malaysia's Motor Vehicle Industry', in Clark and Chan (eds) *The Evolving Pacific Basin in the Global Political Economy*.

Mak, L.F. (1995) *The Dynamics of Chinese Dialect Groups in Early Malaya*, Singapore: Singapore Society of Asian Studies.

Ng, B.K. (1998a) 'The New Economic Policy, 1970–1990', in Pan (ed.) *The Encyclopedia of the Chinese Overseas*.

Ng, B.K. (1988b) 'The New Economic Policy and Chinese in Malaysia: Impact and Responses', *Journal of Malaysian Chinese Studies 2*.

Niew, S.T. (1998) 'Sabah' and 'Sarawak', in Pan (ed.) *The Encyclopedia of the Chinese Overseas*.

Nonini, D. (1997) 'Shifting Identities, Positioned Imaginaries: Transnational Traversals and Reversals by Malaysian Chinese', in A. Ong and D. Nonini (eds) *Ungrounded Empires: The Cultural Politics of Modern Chinese Transnationalism*, New York: Routledge.

Puthucheary, J.J. (1960) *Ownership and Control in the Malayan Economy*, Singapore: Eastern Universities Press.

Rugayah Mohamed (1994) 'Sino-Bumiputera Business Cooperation', in Hara (ed.) *The Development of Bumiputera Enterprises and Sino-Malay Economic Cooperation in Malaysia*.

Searle, P. (1999) *The Riddle of Malaysian Capitalism: Rent-Seekers or Real Capitalists?*, St. Leonards/Honolulu: Allen & Unwin/University of Hawaii Press.

Sia, I. (1993) 'Robert Kuok: Taipan Incorporated', in Hara (ed.) *Formation and Restructuring of Business Groups in Malaysia*.

Sieh L.M.L. (1982) *Ownership and Control of Malaysian Manufacturing Corporations*, Kuala Lumpur: UMBC Publications.

Sieh L.M.L. (1992) 'The Transformation of Malaysian Business Groups', in McVey (ed.) *Southeast Asian Capitalists*.

Snodgrass, D.R. (1980) *Inequality and Economic Development in Malaysia*, Kuala Lumpur: Oxford University Press.

Tan C.B. (1983) 'Acculturation and the Chinese in Melaka: The Expression of Baba Identity Today', in Lim and Gosling (eds) *The Chinese in Southeast Asia*.

Tan, C.B. (1988) *The Baba of Melaka: Cultural and Identity of a Chinese Peranakan Community in Malaysia*, Petaling Jaya: Pelanduk Publications.

Tan, T.W. (1982) *Income Distribution and Determination in West Malaysia*, Kuala Lumpur: Oxford University Press.

Bibliography

Torii, T. (1991) 'Changing the Manufacturing Sector, Reorganizing Automobile Assemblers and Developing the Auto Component Industry under the New Economic Policy', *The Developing Economies* 29 (4).

Wong, T.K., D. (1998) *The Transformation of an Immigrant Society: A Study of the Chinese in Sabah*, London: ASEAN Academic Press.

Yasuda, N. (1991) 'Malaysia's New Economic Policy and the Industrial Coordination Act', *The Developing Economies* 29 (4).

Yeung, H.W.C. (1997) 'Transnational Economic Synergy and Business Networks: The Case of Two-Way Investment Between Malaysia and Singapore', *Regional Studies* 32.8.

Thailand

Chan, K.B. and C.K. Tong (1995), 'Modelling Culture Contact and Chinese Ethnicity in Thailand', *Southeast Asian Journal of Social Science* 23 (1).

Choonhavan, K. (1984) 'The Growth of Domestic Capital and Thai Industrialisation', *Journal of Contemporary Asia* 14.

Coughlin, R.J. (1960) *Double Identity: The Chinese in Modern Thailand*, Hong Kong: University of Hong Kong Press.

Cushman, J.W. (1991) *Family and State: The Formation of a Sino-Thai Tin Mining Dynasty, 1797–1932*, Singapore: Oxford University Press.

Brown, R.A. (1998) 'Overseas Chinese Investments in China – Patterns of Growth, Diversification and Finance: The Case of Charoen Pokphand', *The China Quarterly* September (155).

Hamilton, G.G. and T. Waters (1995) 'Chinese Capitalism in Thailand: Embedded Networks and Industrial Structure', in K.Y. Chen and P. Drysdale (eds) *Corporate Links and Foreign Direct Investments in Asia and the Pacific*, Pymble: HarperEducational.

Handley, P. (1998) 'Charoen Pokphand's Investments in China', in Pan (ed.) *The Encyclopedia of the Chinese Overseas*.

Hewison, K. (1985) 'The State and Capitalist Development in Thailand', in R. Higgott and R. Robison (eds) *Southeast Asia: Essays in the Political Economy of Structural Change*, London: Routledge and Kegan Paul.

Hewison, K. (1989) *Bankers and Bureaucrats: Capital and the Role of the State in Thailand*, New Haven: Yale Southeast Asian Monographs.

Krikiat, P. and K. Yoshihara (1983) *Business Groups in Thailand*, Singapore: Institute of Southeast Asian Studies.

Kulick, E. and D. Wilson (1992) *Thailand's Turn: Profile of a New Dragon*, London: Macmillan.

Laothamatas, A. (1988) 'Business and Politics in Thailand: New Patterns of Influence', *Asian Survey* 28 (4).

Laothamatas, A. (1992) *Business Associations and the New Political Economy of Thailand*, Boulder: Westview.

Muscat, R.J. (1994) *The Fifth Tiger: A Study of Thai Development Policy*, New York: M.E. Sharpe

Phongpaichit, P. and C. Baker (1995) *Thailand: Economy and Politics*, Kuala Lumpur: Oxford University Press.

Phongpaichit, P. and C. Baker (1996) *Thailand's Boom*, Chiang Mai: Earthworm Press.

Bibliography

Reynolds, C. (1996) 'Tycoons and Warlords: Modern Thai Social Formations and Chinese Historical Romance', in Reid (ed.) *Sojourners and Settlers: Histories of Southeast Asia and the Chinese.*

Riggs, F. (1966) *Thailand: The Modernization of a Bureaucratic Polity,* Honolulu: East-West Center Press.

Skinner, G.W. (1957) *Chinese Society in Thailand: An Analytical History,* Ithaca: Cornell University Press.

Skinner, G.W. (1958) *Leadership and Power in the Chinese Community in Thailand,* Ithaca: Cornell University Press.

Skinner, G.W. (1960) 'Change and Persistence in Chinese Culture Overseas: A Comparison of Thailand and Java', *Journal of the South Seas Society* 16.

Suehiro, A. (1989) *Capital Accumulation in Thailand, 1855–1985,* Tokyo: Centre for East Asian Cultural Studies.

Suehiro, A. (1992) 'Capitalist Development in Postwar Thailand: Commercial Bankers, Industrial Elite, and Agribusiness Groups', in McVey (ed.) *Southeast Asian Capitalists.*

Suehiro, A. (1993) 'Family Business Reassessed: Corporate Structure and Late-Starting Industrialization in Thailand', *The Developing Economies* XXXI (4).

Szanton, C.B. (1983), 'Thai and Sino-Thai in Small Town Thailand: Changing Patterns of Interethnic Relations', in Lim and Gosling (eds) *The Chinese in Southeast Asia.*

Tejapira, K. (1997) 'Imagined Uncommunity: The Lookjin Middle Class and Thai Official Nationalism', in Chirot and Reid (eds) *Essential Outsiders: Chinese and Jews in the Modern Transformation of Southeast Asia and Central Europe.*

Vatikiotis, M. (1998) 'Thailand', in Pan (ed.) *The Encyclopedia of the Chinese Overseas.*

Warr, P. (ed.) (1993) *The Thai Economy in Transition,* Cambridge: Cambridge University Press.

The Philippines

Agpalo, R. (1962) *The Political Process and the Nationalization of Retail Trade in the Philippines,* Quezon City: University of the Philippines.

Alip, E.M. (1993) *The Chinese in Manila,* Manila: National Historical Institute.

Ang See, T. (1988) *Crossroads: Short Essays on the Chinese Filipinos,* Manila: Kaisa Para Sa Kaunlaran.

Ang See, T. and B.J. Go (eds) (1994) *The Ethnic Chinese: Proceedings of the International Conference on Changing Identities and Relations in Southeast Asia,* Manila: Kaisa Para Sa Kaunlaran and China Studies Program, De La Salle University.

Ang See, T. (1994) 'Political Participation, Integration and Identity of the Chinese Filipinos', in T. Ang See and B.J. Go (eds) *The Ethnic Chinese: Proceedings of the International Conference on Changing Identities and Relations in Southeast Asia.*

Ang See, T. (1976) 'Research Sudies on the Chinese Minority in the Philippines: A Selected Survey', in W. Villacorta and C. McCarthy (eds)

Bibliography

The Chinese in ASEAN Countries: Changing Roles and Expectations, Philippine Sociological Review 24 (1–4).

Ang See, T. (1995) 'The Chinese in the Philippines: Continuity and Change', in Suryadinata (ed.) *Southeast Asian Chinese: The Socio-Cultural Dimension.*

Ang See, T. (1997) *Chinese in the Philippines* (Volume II), Manila: Kaisa Para Sa Kaunlaran.

Appleton, S. (1959) 'Communism and Chinese in the Philippines', *Pacific Affairs* 32.

Baviera, A. (1994) *Contemporary Political Attitudes and Behaviour of the Chinese in Metro Manila*, Quezon City: Philippine China Development Resource Center.

Baviera, A. and T. Ang See (1991/1992) *China Across the Seas: The Chinese as Filipinos*, Quezon City: Philippine Association for Chinese Studies.

Blaker, J. (1970) 'The Philippine Chinese: A Study of Power and Change', PhD diss., Ohio State University.

Bowring, J. (1859) *A Visit to the Philippine Islands in 1858*, London: Smith, Elder and Co.

Carino, T.C. (1998) *Chinese Big Business in the Philippines: Political Leadership and Change*, Singapore: Times Academic Press.

Carino, T.C. (ed.) (1985) *Chinese in the Philippines*, Manila: China Studies Program, De La Salle University.

Carino, T.C. (1988) 'Political Integration and the Chinese in the Philippines: A Preliminary Investigation', *DLSU Dialogue* XXIII (1), April.

Carino, T.C. (1995) 'The Ethnic Chinese, the Philippine Economy and China', in Suryadinata (ed.) *Southeast Asian Chinese and China: The Politico-Economic Dimension.*

Chen, T.K. (1988) *Fei Hua Fen Fang Lu* (Who's who of Filipino Chinese Since World War II) (Volumes I and II), Taipei: Filipino-Chinese Cultural Foundation.

Chua, L. (1979) 'The Filipinisation of the Chinese Schools in the Philippines: The First Six Years', *Dialogue* (De La Salle University) 15 (1–2).

Churchill, B.R. and T.C. Carino (eds) (1993) *Perspectives on Philippine Policy Towards China*, Manila: Philippine Association for Chinese Studies.

Churchill, B.R. (ed.) (1990) *An Assessment: Philippine-China Relations 1975–1988*, Manila: De La Salle University Press.

Cortes, I. (1978) 'Mass Naturalization by Legislation and the Chinese in the Philippines', *Fookien Times Yearbook.*

Dee, K.C. (1968) 'Feilubin Hua Qiao Shan Ju Gong So Jiu Shi Zhou Nian Ji Nian Kan' (90th Anniversary Year Book of the Philippine-Chinese Charitable Association Inc 1877–1967), Manila: Philippine-Chinese Charitable Association.

D'Mello, M.T. (1978) 'The Chinese Problem and LOT No. 270', M.A. diss., University of the Philippines.

Federation of Filipino-Chinese Chambers of Commerce and Industry (FFCCCI) (1994), *Ruby Anniversary Commemorative Album*. Manila: FFCCCII.

Felix, A. (ed.) (1969) *The Chinese in the Philippines: 1770–1898, Volume II*, Manila: Historical Conservation Society.

Bibliography

Go, B.J. (1995) 'Ethnic Chinese in Philippine Banking', in Palanca (ed.) *China, Taiwan and the Ethnic Chinese in the Philippine Economy*.

Go, B.J. (1996) *Myths about the Ethnic Chinese 'Economic Miracle'*, Manila: Kaisa Para Sa Launlaran.

Guerrero, M. (1969) 'The Political Background', in Felix (ed.) *The Chinese in the Philippines*.

Hsiao, S. C. (1975) *Chinese-Philippine Diplomatic Relations: 1946-1975*, Quezon City: Bookman Printing.

Hutchcroft, P. (1994) 'Booty Capitalism: Business-Government Relations in the Philippines', in A. MacIntyre (ed.) *Businesss and Government in Industrialising Asia*, Sydney: Allen & Unwin.

Hutchcroft, P. (1998) *Booty Capitalism: The Politics of Banking in the Philippines*, Ithaca: Cornell University Press.

Jiang, J. (1974) 'The Chinese and the Philippine Political Process', in McCarthy (ed.) *Philippine-Chinese Profiles: Essays and Studies*.

Laohoo, W. (1995) 'Filipino Reactions to Philippine Chinese Investments in China', in Palanca (ed.) *China, Taiwan and the Ethnic Chinese in the Philippine Economy*.

Liao, S. (1964) *Chinese Participation in the Philippine Culture and Economy*, Manila: Bookman.

Liu, M.C. (1994) 'The Impact of Taiwanese FDI in Philippines' (in Chinese), paper presented at the workshop on 'Taiwan's Small and Medium-Sized Firms' Direct Investment in Southeast Asia', held by Chung-Hua Institute for Economic Research, November 18–19, Taipei.

McBeath, G. (1975) *Political Integration of the Philippine Chinese*, Berkeley: University of California Press.

McCarthy, C. (1971) *Philippine Chinese Integration: The Case for Qualified Jus Soli*, Manila: Pakakaisa.

McCarthy, C. (ed.) (1974) *Philippine-Chinese Profiles: Essays and Studies*, Manila: Unity for Progress.

McMicking, R. (1967) *Recollections of Manila and the Philippines During 1848, 1849 and 1850*, Manila: Filipiniana Book Guild.

Medrana, S.H. (1975) *People's Republic of China-Philippine Relations and the Local Chinese Community*, Makati: Medrana.

Omohundro, J. (1981) *Chinese Merchant Families in Iloilo: Commerce and Kin in a Central Philippine City*, Quezon City: Ateneo University Press.

Omohundro, J. (1983) 'Social Networks and Business Success for the Philippine Chinese', in Lim and Gosling (eds) *The Chinese in Southeast Asia: Volume 1*.

Pacho, A. (1981) 'Policy Concern and Priorities: The Ethnic Chinese in the Philippines', *Philippine Journal of Public Administration* 25.

Pacho, A. (1983) 'The Naturalization Process and the Chinese in the Philippines', *Philippine Journal of Public Administration* 24 (3).

Palanca, E. and T. Ang See (1990) *The Chinese in the Philippines: A Bibliography*, Manila: De La Salle University Press.

Palanca, E. (1995a) 'An Analysis of the 1990 Top Corporations in the Philippines: Economic Position and Activities of the Ethnic Chinese Filipino and Foreign Groups" in Palanca (ed.) *China, Taiwan and the Ethnic Chinese in the Philippine Economy*.

Bibliography

Palanca, E. (ed.) (1995a) *China, Taiwan and the Ethnic Chinese in the Philippine Economy*, Manila: Philippine Association for Chinese Studies.

Palanca, E. (1995b) 'Chinese Business Families in the Philippines Since the 1890s', in Brown (ed.) *Chinese Business Enterprise in Asia*.

Quisumbing, P.V. (1983) *Beijing-Manila Detente: Major Issues – A Study in ASEAN-China Relations*, Quezon City: University of the Philippines Law Center and Foreign Service Institute.

Rivera, T.C. and K. Koike (1995) *The Chinese-Filipino Business Families Under the Ramos Government*, Tokyo: Institute of Developing Economies.

See, C. (1981) 'Chinese Clanship in the Philippine Setting', *Journal of Southeast Asian Studies* XII (1).

See, C. (1988) 'Chinese Organizations and Ethnic Identity in the Philippines', in Cushman and Wang (eds) *Changing Identities of the Southeast Asian Chinese Since World War II*.

See, C. (1985) 'Education and Ethnic Identity among the Chinese in the Philippines', in Carino (ed.) *Chinese in the Philippines*.

See, C. and T.A. See (1990) *Chinese in the Philippines: A Bibliography*, Manila: China Studies Program, De La Salle University.

Sussman, G. (1976) 'Chinese Schools and the Assimilation Problem in the Philippines', *Asian Studies* 14.

Tan, A. (1972) *The Chinese in the Philippines, 1898-1935: A Study of Their Awakening*, Quezon City: R.P. Garcia.

Tan, A. (1981) *The Chinese in the Philippines During the Japanese Occupation, 1942–1945*, Diliman: University of the Philippines Press.

Tan, A. (1985) 'Chinese Mestizos and the Formation of Filipino Nationality', in Carino (ed.), *Chinese in the Philippines*.

Tan, A. (1988) 'The Changing Identity of the Philippine Chinese 1946–1984', in Cushman and Wang (eds) *Changing Identities of the Southeast Asian Chinese Since World War II*.

Tan-Co, F.V. (1993) '1.17 B-Strong Consumer Market Provides Motivation to Invest in Mother China', *Business World Sixth Anniversary Report* (27 July), Manila.

Tan, S. (1994) 'The Tans and Kongs of Sulu: An Analysis of Chinese Integration in a Muslim Society' in Ang See and Go (eds) *The Ethnic Chinese: Proceedings of the International Conference on Changing Identities and Relations in Southeast Asia*.

Tang Tack (1988) *Wo Zai Shang Zhong Shanshi Nian* (My Thirty Years with the Federation), Manila: Federation of Filipino-Chinese Chambers of Commerce and Industry.

Tilman, R. (1973) *Ethnicity and Politics: The Changing Political World of Philippine Chinese Youths*, New Haven: Yale University Press.

Van Der Kroef, J. (1967) 'Philippine Communism and the Chinese' *China Quarterly* 30, April–June.

Wang, H.S. (1995) 'Philippines: The New Frontier for Foreign Direct Investment from Taiwan', in Palanca (ed.) *China, Taiwan and the Ethnic Chinese in the Philippine Economy*.

Weightman, G. (1960) The Philippine-Chinese: A Cultural History of a Marginal Trading Community, Ithaca: Cornell University Press.

Bibliography

Wickberg, E. (1965) *The Chinese in Philippine Life, 1850–1898*, New Haven: Yale University Press.

Wickberg, E. (1988) 'Chinese Organizations and Ethnicity in Southeast Asia and North America Since 1945: A Comparative Analysis' in Cushman and Wang (eds) *Changing Identities of the Southeast Asian Chinese Since World War II*.

Wickberg, E. (1992) 'Notes on Contemporary Organizations in Manila Chinese Society, in A.S.P. Baviera and T.A. See (eds) *China Across the Seas: The Chinese as Filipinos*.

Wickberg, E. (1992) 'Chinese Organizations in Philippine Cities Since World War II: The Case of Manila', unpublished paper presented at the 'Luo Di Sheng Gen' Conference, University of California, Berkeley, 26–29 November.

Yung, L.Y.W. (1996) *The Huaqiao Warriors: Chinese Resistance Movement in the Philippines 1942–1945*, Manila: Ateneo de Manila University Press.

Yoshihara, K. (1985) *Philippine Industrialization: Foreign and Domestic Capital*, Quezon City: Ateneo University Press.

Yoshihara, K. (1994) *The Nation and Economic Growth: The Philippines and Thailand*, Kuala Lumpur: Oxford University Press.

Indonesia

Ahok, P. (1988) 'Kembalinya Pengusaha Cina di Banda Aceh' (The Return of Chinese Businessmen to Banda Aceh), in Kuntjoro-Jakti (ed.) *Perdagangan, Pengusaha Cina, Perilaku Pasar* (Trade, Chinese Businessmen, Market Behaviour).

Alisjahbana, I. (1996) 'Persoalan-Persoalan Pembangunan Manusia Indonesia Menghadapi Masa Lepas Landas (Suatu Pengamatan Filosofis Terhadap Pembangunan Manusia Beserta Alamnya)' (Human Development Problems in Indonesia Towards the Take-off Era: A Philosophical Observation), in *Etika Bisnis Cina: Suatu Kajian Terhadap Perekonomian di Indonesia* (Business Ethics of Chinese: A Study of the Indonesian Economy).

Amir M., S. (1997) 'The Non-Pribumi and Social Justice', in Chalmers and Hadiz (eds) *The Politics of Economic Development in Indonesia: Contending Perspectives.*

Anspach, R. (1963) 'The Problem of a Plural Economy and its Effects on Indonesia's Economic Structure: A Study in Economic Policy', PhD diss., Ann Arbor: University Microfilms.

Anwar, R. (1991) 'Pembauran dan Kewiraswastaan Umat' (Assimilation and Entrepreneurship), in Jahja (ed.) *Nonpri Dimata Pribumi* (Ethnic Chinese in the Eyes of Ethnic Indonesians).

As'ad, M. (1988) 'Kota Sinabang: Studi Tentang Perdagangan Dalam Perspektif Sejarah' (The City of Sinabang: A Historical Study of Trade), in Kuntjoro-Jakti (ed.) *Perdagangan, Pengusaha Cina, Perilaku Pasar.*

Assegaff, D.H. (1991) 'Taipan-Taipan Baru' (New Tycoons), in Jahja (ed.) *Nonpri Dimata Pribumi.*

193

Bibliography

Bahar, S. (1996) 'Mitos Keunggulan Bisnis Etnik Cina, Masalah Kultur, Manajemen Atau Politik?' (The Myth of Ethnic Chinese Excellence in Business: A Matter of Culture, Management or Politics?), in *Etika Bisnis Cina: Suatu Kajian Terhadap Perekonomian di Indonesia.*

Berger, M.T. (1997) 'Post-Cold War Indonesia and the Revenge of History: The Colonial Legacy, Nationalist Visions and Global Capitalism', in M.T. Berger and D.A. Borer (eds) *The Rise of East Asia: Critical Visions of the Pacific Century*, London: Routledge.

Blusse, L. (1991) 'The Role of Indonesian Chinese in Shaping Modern Indonesian Life: A Conference in Retrospect', *Indonesia.*

Bratanata, S. (1997) 'We Need New Policies to Help the *Pribumi*', in Chalmers and Hadiz (eds) *The Politics of Economic Development in Indonesia: Contending Perspectives.*

Carey, P. (1984) 'Changing Javanese Perceptions of the Chinese Communities in Central Java', 1755–1825', *Indonesia* (37), April.

Castles, L. (1967) *Religion, Politics, and Economic Behavior in Java: The Kudus Cigarette Industry*, New Haven: Yale University Southeast East Asia Studies.

Cator, J.W. (1936) *The Economic Position of the Chinese in the Netherlands Indies*, Oxford: Basil Blackwell.

Chalmers, I. and V.R. Hadiz (eds.) (1997) *The Politics of Economic Development in Indonesia: Contending Perspectives*, London: Routledge.

Coppel, C.A. (1976) 'Patterns of Chinese Political Activity in Indonesia', in Mackie (ed.) *The Chinese in Indonesia.*

Coppel, C.A. (1977) 'Studying the Chinese Minorities: A Review', *Indonesia* (24), October.

Coppel, C.A. (1983) *Indonesian Chinese in Crisis*, Kuala Lumpur: Oxford University Press.

Coppel, C. (1989) 'Liem Thian Joe's Unpublished History of Kian Gwan', in Yoshihara (ed.) *Oei Tiong Ham Concern: The First Business Empire of Southeast Asia.*

Daulay, A.H., et al. (1994) *William Soeryadjaya Kejayaan dan Kejatuhannya: Studi Kasus Eksistensi Konglomerasi Bisnis di Indonesia* (The Rise and Fall of William Soeryadjaya: A Case Study of Indonesian Conglomeration), Jakarta: Bina Rena Pariwara.

Dewanto, A.B. (1993) 'Etik Bisnis dan Keberagaman Kelompok Kristen dalam Perspektif Sosiologis' (Business Ethics and Diversity in Christian Denominations: A Sociological Perspective), PhD diss., Bandung: Universitas Padjadjaran.

Feith, H. (1995) *Soekarno-Militer Dalam Demokrasi Terpimpin* (Sukarno-The Military In Guided Democracy), Jakarta: Pustaka Sinar Harapan.

Fernando, M.R. and D. Bulbeck (eds) (1992) *Chinese Economic Activity in Netherlands India: Selected Translations from the Dutch*, Singapore: Institute of Southeast Asian Studies.

Fromberg, P.H. (1926) *Verspreide Geschriften* (Miscellaneous Writings), Leiden: Leiden Leidsche Uitgeversmaatschappij.

Furnival, J.S. (1939) *Netherlands India: A Study of Plural Economy*, Cambridge: Cambridge University Press.

Gitosardjono, S.S., et al. (1993) *Bisnis dan Pembangunan Ekonomi* (Business and Economic Development), Jakarta: Haji Masagung.

Bibliography

Hadiz, V.R. (1997) 'The Economic Democracy Debate: Conglomerates and *Pancasila*', in Chalmers and Hadiz (eds) *The Politics of Economic Development in Indonesia: Contending Perspectives*.

Hadiz, V.R. (1997) 'Pribumi-Chinese Relations', in Chalmers and Hadiz (eds) *The Politics of Economic Development in Indonesia: Contending Perspectives*.

Hamzah, A. (ed.) (1998) *Kapok Jadi Nonpri: Warga Tionghoa Mencari Keadilan* (Fed Up With Being Nonpri: Ethnic Chinese in Search of Justice), Bandung: Zaman.

Handoko, T.H. (1996) 'Tradisi (Manajemen) Dagang a la Tionghoa' (Tradition of Business Management a la the Chinese), in *Penguasa Ekonomi dan Siasat Pengusaha Tionghoa* (Economic Power Holders and the Strategy of Chinese Businessmen), Yogyakarta: Lembaga Studi Realino.

Hasjim Ning (1997) 'The Struggles of a *Pribumi* Entrepreneur', in Chalmers and Hadiz (eds) *The Politics of Economic Development in Indonesia: Contending Perspectives*.

Heidhues, M.F.S. (1996) *Bangka Tin and Mentok Pepper: Chinese Settlement on an Indonesian Island*, Singapore: Institute of Southeast Asian Studies.

Husodo, S.Y. (1985) *Warga Baru: Kasus Cina di Indonesia* (New Citizens: The Case of Chinese in Indonesia), Jakarta: Lembaga Penerbitan Padamu Negeri.

Irwan, A. (1995) 'Business Networks and the Regional Economy of East and Southeast Asia in the Late Twentieth Century', PhD diss., Binghamton: State University of New York.

Irwan, A. (1996) 'Cina dan Etnis Cina di Asia Timur dan Tenggara' (China and Ethnic Chinese in East and Southeast Asia), *Warta Ekonomi* VII: 44, March.

ISEI-Association of Indonesian Economists (1997) 'The Principles of Economic Democracy', in Chalmers and Hadiz (eds), *The Politics of Economic Development in Indonesia: Contending Perspectives*.

Ismail, E.E. (1988) 'Perdagangan Cina dan Kegiatan Jengek di Pelabuhan Bebas Sabang' (Chinese Trading and *Jengek's* Activities in the Free Port of Sabang), in Kuntjoro-Jakti (ed.) *Perdagangan, Pengusaha Cina, Perilaku Pasar*.

Jackson, J.C. (1970) *Chinese in the West Borneo Goldfields: A Study in Cultural Geography*, Hull: University of Hull.

Jahja, J. (ed.) (1991) *Nonpri Dimata Pribumi* (Ethnic Chinese in the Eyes of Ethnic Indonesians), Jakarta: Yayasan Tunas Bangsa.

Jahja, J. (1991) 'Epilog/Kesimpulan: Pribumi Kuat, Kunci Pembauran' (Strong Pribumi is the Key to Assimilation), in Jahja (ed.) *Nonpri Dimata Pribumi*.

Jahja, J. (1993) *Sekitar Konvensi Pengusaha Cina Sedunia* (Around the Chinese Businessmen's World Convention), Jakarta: Institute for Studies on Ethnic Chinese Assimilation in Indonesia.

Joesoef, D. (1996) 'Sistem Sosial Budaya dan Pengaruhnya Terhadap Bisnis Cina' (Socio-Cultural Systems and its Impact on Chinese Business), in *Etika Bisnis Cina: Suatu Kajian Terhadap Perekonomian di Indonesia*.

KADIN (1997) 'To Become Masters of Our Own Economy', in Chalmers and Hadiz (eds), *The Politics of Economic Development in Indonesia: Contending Perspectives*.

Bibliography

Kasali, R. and W. Bob (1988) 'Entrepreneurship in Indonesian Chinese Business Organizations', *Majalah Management & Usahawan Indonesia* XVII: 8.

Kuntjoro-Jakti, D. (ed.) (1988) *Perdagangan, Pengusaha Cina, Perilaku Pasar* (Trade, Chinese Businessmen, Market Behaviour), Jakarta: Pustaka Grafika Kita.

Kuntjoro-Jakti, D. (1991) 'Cukong & Praktek Percukongan' (Cukongs & Their Practices), in Jahja (ed.) *Nonpri Dimata Pribumi.*

Kwik, K.G. (1996) 'Etika Bisnis, Sistem Ekonomi dan Peranan Pemerintah' (Business Ethics, Economic System and the Role of Government), in *Etika Bisnis Cina: Suatu Kajian Terhadap Perekonomian di Indonesia.*

Kwik, K.G. (1997) 'The Myth of Chinese Economic Dominance', in Chalmers and Hadiz (eds) *The Politics of Economic Development in Indonesia: Contending Pierspectives.*

Kwik, K.G. (1997) 'A Scientific Basis for Economic Democracy', in Chalmers and Hadiz (eds) *The Politics of Economic Development in Indonesia: Contending Perspectives.*

Kwik, K.G. (1999) *Ekonomi Indonesia Dalam Krisis dan Transisi Politik* (Indonesian Economy in Crisis and Political Transition), Jakarta: Gramedia.

Kuntjoro-Jakti, D. (1988) 'Pengantar' (Introduction), in Kuntjoro-Jakti (ed.) *Perdagangan, Pengusaha Cina, Perilaku Pasar*, Jakarta: Pustaka Grafika Kita.

Laanen, J.T.M. van (1988) 'Di Antara de Javasche Bank dan Ceti-Ceti Cina: Perbankan dan Kredit di Indonesia Pada Zaman Kolonial' (Between the Javasche Bank and Chinese Cetis: Banking and Credit in Indonesia During the Colonial Period), in A. Booth, W.J. O'Malley and A. Weidemann (eds) *Sejarah Ekonomi Indonesia* (History of Indonesian Economy), Jakarta: LP3ES.

Liem, T.D. (1995) *Perdagangan Perantara Distribusi Orang-Orang Cina di Jawa* (Chinese Middlemen in Java) (originally published in Dutch in 1926), Jakarta: Gramedia Pustaka Utama.

Liem, T.L. (1979) *Raja Gula Oei Tiong Ham* (Sugar King Oei Tiong Ham), Surabaya: Liem Tjwan Ling.

Liem, T.L. (1989) 'Sugar King: Oei Tiong Ham', in Yoshihara (ed.) *Oei Tiong Ham Concern: The First Business Empire of Southeast Asia.*

Lohanda, M. (1996) *The Kapitan Cina of Batavia: 1837–1942*, Jakarta: Djambatan.

Lombard, D. (1996) *Nusa Jawa: Silang Budaya Kajian Sejarah Terpadu Bahagian II: Jaringan Asia* (Historical Study of Asian Networks) (A translation of *Le Carrefour Javanais: Essai* d'histoire *Globale II, les Reseaux Asiatiques*), Jakarta: Gramedia Pustaka Utama.

Moch Sa'dun, M. (1999) *Pri-Nonpri: Mencari Format Baru Pembauran* (Pri-Nonpri: In Search of a New Format of Assimilation), Jakarta: Cides.

Mackie, J.A.C. (ed.) (1976) *The Chinese in Indonesia: Five Essays*, Melbourne: Thomas Nelson.

Mackie, J.A.C. (1976) 'Anti-Chinese Outbreaks in Indonesia, 1959–68', in Mackie (ed.) *The Chinese in Indonesia.*

Mackie, J.A.C. (1990) 'Property and Power in Indonesia', in R. Tanter and K. Young (eds) *The Politics of Middle Class Indonesia*, Clayton: Monash University.

Bibliography

Mackie, J. (1991) 'Towkays and Tycoons: The Chinese in Indonesian Economic Life in the 1920s and 1980s', *Indonesia*.

Magenda, B. (1991) 'Masalah Tionghoa: Ekonomi dan Sosial' (The Chinese Problem: Economic and Social), in Jahja (ed.) *Nonpri Dimata Pribumi*.

Magenda, B.D. (1996) 'Bisnis Cina Sebagai Salah Satu Pola Integrasi Bisnis di Indonesia: Beberapa Catatan' (Chinese Business as a Pattern of Business Integration in Indonesia: Some Notes), in *Etika Bisnis Cina: Suatu Kajian Terhadap Perekonomian di Indonesia*.

Majid, M.D. (1988) 'Pasar Angkup: Studi Kasus Perilaku Pasar' (Angkup Market: A Case Study of Market Behaviour), in Kuntjoro-Jakti (ed.) *Perdagangan, Pengusaha Cina, Perilaku Pasar*.

Manajemen (1992) 'Cina Perantauan Sang Supreme Deal Maker' (Chinese Overseas the Supreme Deal Makers)', May–June.

Maulana, I.B. (1997) 'Chinese Connection', *Sinar* (V: 1, 20) September.

McBeth, J. (1996) 'Astra at the Apex: Car Maker Accelerates Into First', *Far Eastern Economic Review* (28 December).

Muhammad, F. (1997) 'The Task for Business: To Promote Economic Equity', in Chalmers and Hadiz (eds) *The Politics of Economic Development in Indonesia: Contending Perspectives*.

Naveront, J.K. (1994) *Jaringan Masyarakat Cina* (Chinese Networks), Jakarta: Golden Terayon Press.

Nawawi, H.M.B. (1996) 'Bisnis Cina Sebagai Salah Satu Pola Integrasi Bisnis di Indonesia' (Chinese Business as a Pattern of Business Integration in Indonesia), in *Etika Bisnis Cina: Suatu Kajian Terhadap Perekonomian di Indonesia*.

Oei, H.L. (1989) 'Reminiscences', in Yoshihara (ed.) *Oei Tiong Ham Concern: The First Business Empire of Southeast Asia*.

Oetama, J. (1991) 'Momentum Kepeloporan Pengusaha Swasta Nasional Dalam Pembangunan' (Momentum of the Pioneering Role of National Private Businessmen in Development), in Jahja (ed.) *Nonpri Dimata Pribumi*.

Oetomo, D. (1989) 'The Ethnic Chinese in Indonesia', in Suryadinata (ed.) *The Ethnic Chinese in the ASEAN States: Bibliographical Essays*.

Ong Eng Die (1943) '*Chineezen in Nederlandsch-Indie – Sociografie van een Indonesische bevolkingsgroep* (The Chinese in the Netherlands-Indies – A Sociography of an Indonesian Population Group), PhD diss., Assen: Van Gorcum en Comp.

Onghokham (1989) 'Chinese Capitalism in Dutch Java', in Yoshihara (ed.) *Oei Tiong Ham Concern: The First Business Empire of Southeast Asia*.

Palmer, I. (1978) *The Indonesian Economy Since 1965: A Case Study of Political Economy*, London: Frank Cass.

Pangestu, M. and H. Soesastro (1999) 'The Role of the IMF in Indonesia: Crisis and Recovery', a paper presented at a conference on 'Asia in Economic Recovery: Policy Options for Growth and Stability', organized by the Institute of Policy Studies, 21–22 June 1999, Singapore.

Panglaykim, J. (1988) 'Family Businesses in Indonesia', in Cushman and Wang (eds) *Changing Identities of the Southeast Asian Chinese Since World War II*.

Panglaykim, J. and I. Palmer (1989) 'Study of Entrepreneurship in Developing Countries: The Development of one Chinese Concern in

Bibliography

Indonesia', in Yoshihara (ed.) *Oei Tiong Ham Concern: The First Business Empire of Southeast Asia*.

Pour, J. (1998) *Jakarta Semasa Lengser Keprabon: 100 Hari Menjelang Peralihan Kekuasaan* (Jakarta in the Period of the Resignation: The Last 100 Days), Jakarta: Elex Media Komputindo.

Prawiro, R. (1991) 'Bidang Ekonomi Hendaknya Menjadi Sasaran Utama Proyek Perintis Pembauran' (The Economy Should be the Main Target of Assimilation Pioneering Projects), in Jahja (ed.) *Nonpri Dimata Pribumi*.

Rahardjo, D. (1996) 'Pengembangan Sumber Daya Pengusaha Indonesia: Untuk Mencapai Etika Bisnis Indonesia' (Human Resource Development of Indonesian Businessmen: To Achieve Indonesian Business Ethics), in *Etika Bisnis Cina: Suatu Kajian Terhadap Perekonomian di Indonesia*.

Raybeck, D. (1983) 'Chinese Patterns of Adaptation in Southeat Asia', in Lim and Gosling (eds) *The Chinese in Southeast Asia: Volume 2*.

Robison, R. (1986) *Indonesia: The Rise of Capital*, Sydney: Allen & Unwin.

Robison, R. (1992) 'Industrialization and the Economic and Political Development of Capital: The Case of Indonesia', in McVey (ed.) *Southeast Asian Capitalists*.

Robison, R. (1996) 'The Middle Class and the Bourgeoisie in Indonesia', in R. Robison and D.S.G. Goodman (eds) *The New Rich in Asia: Mobile Phones, Mcdonalds and Middle-Class Revolution*, London: Routledge.

Ropke, J. (1988) *Kebebasan Yang Terhambat: Perkembangan Ekonomi dan Perilaku Kegiatan Usaha di Indonesia* (A translation of *Die unterentwickelte freiheit: wirtschaftliche entwicklung und unternehmerisches handeln in Indonesien*, 1982), Jakarta: Gramedia.

Rush, J.R. (1990) *Opium to Java: Revenue Farming and Chinese Enterprise in Colonial Indonesia, 1860–1910*, Ithaca: Cornell University Press.

Sato, Y. (1993) 'The Salim Group in Indonesia: The Development and Behaviour of the Largest Conglomerate in Southeast Asia', *The Developing Economies*, December.

Schijf, H. and B.A.M. Teh (1992) 'Chinese Doctors in the Dutch East Indies: Social Mobility Among an Ethnic Trading Minority in a Colonial Society', *Indonesia* (53) April.

Schwartz, A. (1994) *A Nation in Waiting: Indonesia in 1990s*, St. Leonards: Allen & Unwin.

Seda, F. (1997), 'The Impact of the Tapos Summit', in Chalmers and Hadiz (eds) *The Politics of Economic Development in Indonesia: Contending Perspectives*.

Shin, Y.H. (1989) 'Demystifying the Capitalist State: Political Patronage, Bureaucratic Interests and Capitalists-in-Formation in Soeharto's Indonesia', PhD diss., Yale University.

Siahaan, H. (1974) *Golongan Tionghoa di Kalimantan Barat: Tinjauan Ekonomis Historis* (Chinese in West Kalimantan: An Economic-Historical Review), Jakarta: LEKNAS-LIPI.

Siauw, T.D. (1999) *Siauw Giok Tjhan: Perjuangan Seorang Patriot Membangun Nasion Indonesia dan Masyarakat Bhineka Tunggal Ika* (Siauw Giok Tjhan: The Struggle of a Patriot to Build the Indonesian Nation and the Bhineka Tunggal Ika Society), Jakarta: Hasta Mitra.

Sinergi, Media Sinergi Bangsa, November 1998–April 1999.

Bibliography

Sjahrir (1997) 'Changing the Image of Indonesia's Conglomerates', in Chalmers and Hadiz (eds.) *The Politics of Economic Development in Indonesia: Contending Perspectives.*

Soeharto (1997) 'The President's Instructions for Outlining Economic Democracy', Chalmers and Hadiz (eds) *The Politics of Economic Development in Indonesia: Contending Perspectives.*

Soekisman, W.D. (1975) *Masalah Cina di Indonesia* (Chinese Problems in Indonesia), Jakarta: Yayasan Penelitian Masalah Asia.

Soemitro (1991) 'Dialog Presiden Dengan Pengusaha Besar' (Dialogue Between the President and Leading Businessmen), in Jahja (ed.) *Nonpri Dimata Pribumi.*

Soetriyono, E. (1989) *Kisah Sukses Liem Sioe Liong* (The Success Story of Liem Sioe Liong), Jakarta: Infomedia.

Suhanda, W. (1996) 'Etika Bisnis Cina Dalam Konteks Budaya, Sifat dan Sumbangannya Pada Perekonomian Nasional' (Chinese Business Ethics in the Context of its Culture, Nature, Contribution to the National Economy), in *Etika Bisnis Cina: Suatu Kajian Terhadap Perekonomian di Indonesia.*

Sulaiman, I. (1988) 'Pengusaha Cina dan Pengusaha Aceh di Kota Madya Banda Aceh' (Chinese and Aceh Businessmen in Banda Aceh), in Kuntjoro-Jakti (ed.) *Perdagangan, Pengusaha Cina, Perilaku Pasar.*

Supreme Advisory Council (1997) 'Applying the Family Principle to Build a Common Economic Purpose', in Chalmers and Hadiz (eds) *The Politics of Economic Development in Indonesia: Contending Perspectives.*

Supriatma, A.M.T. (1996) 'Bisnis dan Politik: Kapitalisme dan Golongan Tionghoa di Indonesia' (Business and Politics: Capitalism and the Chinese in Indonesia), in *Penguasa Ekonomi dan Siasat Pengusaha Tionghoa,* Yogyakarta: Lembaga Studi Realino.

Suryadinata, L. (1995) *Prominent Indonesian Chinese: Biographical Sketches,* Singapore: Institute of Southeast Asian Studies.

Suryadinata, L. (ed.) (1997) *Political Thinking of the Indonesian Chinese 1900–1995: A Sourcebook,* Singapore: Singapore University Press.

Susanto, B. (1996) 'Rekayasa Kekuasaan Ekonomi (Indonesia 1800–1950): Siasat Pengusaha Tionghoa' (Engineering Economic Power: Chinese Businessmen's Strategy), in *Penguasa Ekonomi dan Siasat Pengusaha Tionghoa,* Yogyakarta: Lembaga Studi Realino.

Tan, G.L. (1963) *The Chinese of Sukabumi: A Study in Social and Cultural Accommodation,* Ithaca: Cornell University Press.

Tan, M.G. (ed.) (1981) *Golongan Etnis Tionghoa di Indonesia* (Ethnic Chinese in Indonesia), Jakarta: Leknas-LIPI dan Yayasan Obor Indonesia.

Tan, M.G. (1987) 'The Role of Ethnic Chinese Minority in Development: The Indonesian Case', *Southeast Asian Studies* 25: 3, December.

Tan, M.G. (1995) 'The Ethnic Chinese in Indonesia: Issues and Implications', in Suryadinata (ed.) *Southeast Asian Chinese: The Socio-Cultural Dimension.*

Tan, M.G. (1995) 'Market Expansion and Social Integration', a paper prepared for the seminar on 'The Cultural and Social Dimensions of Expanding Markets', organised by the Goethe Institute and the University of Bielefeld, in Labuan, Malaysia, 16–17 October 1995.

Bibliography

Tan, M.G. (1996) 'Dimensi Sosial Budaya Berbisnis Pengusaha Etnis Tionghoa' (Social Cultural Dimension of Chinese Business), a paper presented for the seminar on 'Relevansi Etika Bisnis Dalam Era Globalisasi', organised by Pusat Pengembangan Etika Atma Jaya Universitas Katolik Atma Jaya, Jakarta, 19 June 1996.

Tan, M.G. (1996) 'Feng Shui and the Road to Success: The Persistence of a Traditional Belief System in the Face of Market Expansion', a paper presented at the third seminar on 'The Social and Cultural Dimensions of Market Expansion', organised by the Goethe Institute in cooperation with the University of Bielefeld and Gadjah Mada University, Yogyakarta, 26–27 August 1996.

Tan, M.G. (1996) 'Usaha Ekonomi Etnis Tionghoa di Indonesia: Suatu Tinjauan Sosiologis' (Chinese Business in Indonesia: A Sociological Review), in *Etika Bisnis Cina: Suatu Kajian Terhadap Perekonomian di Indonesia*.

Tan, M.G. (1997) 'The Ethnic Chinese in Indonesia: Issues of Identity', in Suryadinata (ed.) *Ethnic Chinese as Southeast Asians*.

Tan, M.G. (1998) 'Agama dan Hubungan Antara Kelompok Etnis di Indonesia' (Religion and Inter-Ethnic Relationship in Indonesia), a paper presented at a seminar organised by the Institute for the Study of Religion and Philosophy, in Jakarta.

Tan, M.G. (1999) 'The Ethnic Chinese in Indonesia: Trials and Tribulations', a paper prepared for a lecture program at the invitation of the US-Indonesia Society (USINDO) of Washington, DC and presented at a number of universities and academic institutions in the US, March–April 1999.

Thomas, K.D. and J. Panglaykim (1976) 'The Chinese in the South Sumatran Rubber Industry: A Case Study in Economic Nationalism', in Mackie (ed.) *The Chinese in Indonesia*.

Tjoa, S.T. (1989a) 'The Lawsuit Against Oei Tiong Ham Concern', in Yoshihara (ed.) *Oei Tiong Ham Concern: The First Business Empire of Southeast Asia*.

Tjoa, S.T. (1989b) 'One Hundred Years of Oei Tiong Ham Concern', in Yoshihara (ed.) *Oei Tiong Ham Concern: The First Business Empire of Southeast Asia*.

Twang, P.Y. (1979) 'Political Attitudes and Allegiances in the Totok Business Community, 1950–1954', *Indonesia* 28, October.

Twang, P.Y. (1987), 'Indonesian Chinese Business Communities in Transformation, 1940–1950', PhD diss., Australian National Univeristy, Canberra.

Vleming, J.L., Jr. (1926) *Het Chineesche zakenleven in Nederlandsch-Indie* (Chinese Business in the Netherlands-Indie), Weltevreden: Dienst der Belastingen in Nederlandsch-Indie.

Waldron, S. (1995) *Indonesian Chinese Investment in China: Magnitude, Motivations and Meaning*, Queensland: Centre for the Study of Australia-Asia Relations, Faculty of Asian and International Studies, Griffith University.

Wibisono, T. (1997) 'Peta dan Anatomi Konglomerat Indonesia' (Map and Anatomy of Indonesian Conglomerates), *Kompas* 13, 14 and 15 October.

Bibliography

Wibisono, C. (1995) 'The Economic Role of the Indonesian Chinese', in Suryadinata (ed.) *Southeast Asian Chinese and China: The Politico-Economic Dimension.*

Wibowo, I. (1999) *Retrospeksi dan Rekontekstualisasi Masalah Cina* (Retrospection and Recontextualization of the Chinese Problem), Jakarta: Gramedia.

Widyahartono, B. (1989) *Kongsi & Spekulasi: Jaringan Kerja Bisnis Cina* (Kongsi & Speculation: Chinese Business Networks), a paraphrase of *Het Chineesche zakenleven in Nederlandsch-Indie,* by J.L. Vleming, Jr., 1926), Jakarta: Pustaka Utama Grafiti.

Widyahartono, B. (1996) 'Etika Bisnis Sebagai Ketanggapan Sosial, Sistem Ekonomi dan Peranan Pemerintah' (Business Ethics as Social Response, Economic System and the Role of Government), in *Etika Bisnis Cina: Suatu Kajian Terhadap Perekonomian di Indonesia.*

Williams, M. (1991) 'China and Indonesia Make Up: Reflections On a Troubled Relationship', *Indonesia.*

Willmott, D.E. (1960) *The Chinese in Semarang,* New York: Cornell University Press.

Yan, Jiann-fa (1997) 'Coping with Corruption in Indonesia: The Perspective of Taiwanese Business', paper presented at the workshop on 'Ethnic Chinese Business Research in Southeast Asia', 17–18 November, organized by Program for Southeast Asian Area Studies, Academia Sinica, Taipei.

Yoon, H.S. (1991) 'The Role of Elites in Creating Capitalist Hegemony in Post-Oil Boom Indonesia', *Indonesia.*

Yoshihara, K. (ed.) (1989) *Oei Tiong Ham Concern: The First Business Empire of Southeast Asia,* Kyoto: Kyoto University.

Yudohusodo, S. (1991) 'Kelompok Bisnis Dalam Proses Politik di Indonesia' (Business Groups in the Indonesian Political Process), in Jahja (ed.) *Nonpri Dimata Pribumi.*

Zain, W. (1991) *Biaya Sosial Om Lim* (Social Cost of Uncle Lim), in Jahja (ed.) *Nonpri Dimata Pribumi.*

Zamroni, A. and M. Andin (eds) (1998) *Pahlawan Reformasi: Catatan Peristiwa 12 Mei 1998* (Heroes of Reformation: Notes on the Event of 12 May 1998), Jakarta: Pabelan Jayakarta.

Zhong, W.P. (1996) 'Etika Bisnis Cina Ditinjau Dari Sudut Agama dan Filsafat Konfusius' (Chinese Business Ethics From the Point of View of the Religious and Confucianism), in *Etika Bisnis Cina: Suatu Kajian Terhadap Perekonomian di Indonesia.*

Index

Acer, 13, 167
Alliance, 65–66, 107–108, 110
Allied Banking Corporation, 106, 119
Asia Trust Group, 90
Astra Group, 13, 30, 31, 131
Aw Boon Hwa, 21, 23

Baba community, 6, 63, 102, 167
Backman, M., 55–56
Ban Hin Lee Bank, 23, 82
Bank Bali, 136, 173
Bank Central Asia (BCA), 10, 136, 168
Bank of Ayudhya, 29, 90, 171
Bangkok Bank, 3, 8, 29, 90, 93–95, 171
Bangkok Mercantile Bank, 90
Bangkok Metropolitan Bank, 21, 29, 171
Barisan Nasional (National Front), 66, 70–71
Barito Pacific Group, 30
Benteng program, 128, 142, 172
Berjaya Group, 10, 29, 70, 168
Biggart, N.W., 17–18, 167–168
Bob Hassan, 3, 10, 30, 131
Bulakun Group, 89–90, 171

Cantonese, 7–8, 64, 81, 86, 103–104, 167, 169
Cator, J.W., 126
Chan Kwok Bun, 3, 11, 46, 56

China Banking Corporation, 104
Carino, T.C., 15, 33, 166
Charoen Phokpand (CP) Group, 3, 25, 28, 29, 32, 34, 93–95, 99
Chearavanont family, 3, 29
Chearavanont, Dhanin, 25, 27, 28, 93–94
Cheng, William, 4, 10
Chiang Kai Shek, 152
Chinese conventions and conferences, 2, 15, 143, 166
Chinese Exclusion Act, 103
Chinese mestizo, 6, 7, 102
Chuan, Dee C., 110
Chung Thye Phin, 65, 169
Clammer, J.R., 45–46, 169
corporatization movement, 33, 67–68, 79–80
Christianto Wibisono, 13, 138
Chua family, 23
Chung Khiaw Bank, 21, 169
Chung Thye Pin, 21
Creative Technology Ltd, 28, 31, 32, 58–59
crowding-out effect, 51, 52, 56–57, 60
Cushman, J., 88
Cycle & Carriage Group, 23

Daim Zainuddin, 71
Dirlik, A., 19–20
Dual Nationality Treaty, 129

Economic Development Board, 43, 44
Ekran Group, 10, 70
Eu Tong Sen, 65, 169

Far East Organisation Group, 23, 31, 50
Federation of Filipino-Chinese Chambers of Commerce and Industry (FCCCI), 106, 112–114, 115, 120
First Pacific Group, 25, 123
Foochow, 8, 82
Fromberg, P.H., 126
Fukuda, S., 103–104
Fukuyama, F., 19, 49

Gale, B., 78–79
Gokongwei, John, 3, 10, 31, 32, 106, 107, 108–109, 110, 114, 115, 116–117, 119
Goody, J., 20
Gomez, E.T., 13, 26, 79–80, 167, 168, 170
Gotianun, Andrew, 3, 31, 114
Gotianun family, 109
government-linked corporations (GLCs), 38, 39, 42, 49, 51, 52, 57, 58, 59, 168
guanxi, 19, 48, 52–56, 57

Habibie, B.J., 133, 135, 136, 168, 173
Hainanese, 7–8, 9, 64, 86, 169
Hakka, 7–8, 9, 46, 64, 81, 86, 104, 167, 169, 171
Hara Fujio, 3–4, 26, 78
Haw Par Group, 23
Henderson Land, 4
Heng Pek Koon, 3, 26, 69–70, 78, 79, 81–82, 169
Henghwa, 8, 169
Hiscock, G., 55
Ho Kwon Ping, 50
Ho Rih Hwa, 50
Hodder, R., 16
Hokchia, 8, 9, 169
Hokkien, 7–8, 33, 46, 54, 64, 73, 81, 82, 86, 103–104, 167, 169, 173
Hong Leong Group (Singapore), 3, 21–22, 31, 32

Hong Leong Group (Malaysia), 23, 29
Hong Leong Bank, 8, 10, 82
Hong Leong Investment Holdings (HLIH), 22
huaqiao, 7, 46, 73, 140, 167, 170
huaren, 7, 46, 167
huasheng, 73
huayi, 7, 167
huiguan, 53

Indah Kiat Paper & Pulp, 28, 32
Indofood, 10, 28, 32
Industrial Coordination Act (ICA), 67

Jesudason, James, 4, 77–78
Jobilee Foods Corp., 28, 32

Kanjanapas family, 29
Kao, J., 1–2
Khaw family, 21, 64, 88
Khaw Soo Cheang, 89
Khoo Kay Peng, 4, 23, 29, 82, 168, 170
Khoo Teck Puat, 31, 82
Kim Seng Lee, 89
Kotkin, J., 2, 14
Kuok, Robert, 2, 4, 27, 28, 29, 31, 170
Kwek family, 21–22, 31, 168
Kwek Hong P'ng, 21–22
Kwek Leng Beng, 22
Kwik Kian Gie, 138
Kwongsai, 8, 169

Lam, D.K.K. and I. Lee, 24
Lamsam family, 29, 89–90, 96, 171
large-scale enterprises (LSEs), 85, 99, 100, 171
Lau Pak Khuan, 21, 65, 169
Lee Hee Seng, 50
Lee Kong Chian, 21, 30, 65, 169
Lee Kuan Yew, 11, 15
Lee Rubber, 21, 169
Leong Sin Nam, 21
Li Ka-shing, 2, 4, 27
Liem Sioe Leong, 2, 3, 10, 11, 14, 25, 26, 27, 28, 30, 32, 123, 131, 135, 136, 168
Lien Ying Chow, 50

Index

Lim Goh Tong, 4, 28, 29
Lim, L. and Gosling, L.A.P., 18
Ling Liong Sik, 68
Lion Corporation, 10
Lippo Group, 30, 131, 136
Loh Boon Siew, 4, 13, 29, 34
Loke Yew, 65, 169
Lopez, Eugenio, 114

Mackie, J., 76–77
Mahathir Mohamad, 10, 15, 68, 70
Malayan Banking, 8, 33, 82
Malayan Credit, 23
Malayan Chinese Association
    (MCA), 65–66, 67, 68, 69, 78, 79
Malayan United Industries (MUI),
    23, 29, 82, 168, 170
Marcos, Ferdinand, 11, 13, 105–107
McVey, Ruth, 7, 91
Megawati Soekarnoputri, 136
Mercantile Bank of China, 104, 110
Metrobank, 114
Multi-Purpose Holdings (MPHB),
    23, 29, 68. 78–79

Naisbitt, J., 38
National Development Policy
    (NDP), 70–71
New Economic Policy (NEP), 33,
    66–67, 68, 70, 78, 79, 80
New World Development, 4
Ng Teng Fong, 23, 31, 50, 169
Nubla, R., 106

Oei Tiong Ham, 7, 21
Oetomo, Dede, 124
Omohundro, J., 112–114
Ong Eng Die, 126–127
Oriental Holdings Group, 13, 29
Oversea-Chinese Banking
    Corporation (OCBC), 3, 8, 21, 28,
    30, 32, 33, 51, 52, 82, 169, 170
Overseas Union Bank (OUB), 3, 31,
    32, 50, 51, 52, 169

Pacific Bank, 21, 82, 170
Palanca, E., 107, 108, 167
People's Action Party (PAP), 11,
    41–42, 43, 56, 59

Peranakan community, 6, 7, 63, 102,
    139, 167
Philippine-Chinese General
    Chamber of Commerce, 112
Prayogo Pangestu, 3, 10, 30, 31
Public Bank, 8, 29, 33, 82

Quek Leng Chan, 10, 22, 23, 82

Ramli family, 136
Ramos, Fidel, 12, 119
Ratanarak family, 29, 90, 171
Redding, S.G., 16, 19, 49–50, 52
Retail Trade Nationalization Law,
    105, 112, 121
revenue farms, 64–65
Riady, Mochtar, 3, 30, 131, 133, 135,
    136
Riady, James, 131
Riggs, F., 90–91
Rivera, T.C. and K. Koike, 114, 116,
    122
Robison, R., 34, 131
Romulo, Carlos, 114
Rose, M., 20

Salim Group, 10, 13, 26, 30, 123, 131,
    132, 168
Sato, Y., 26
Schwarz, A., 14, 132
Seagrave, S., 118
Shangri-La Group, 28, 32
Shih, Stanley, 13
Shinawatra, Thaksin, 27, 28, 29
Shinawatra Group, 93
Sim Wong Hoo, 28, 31, 58–59
Sinar Mas Group, 13, 30, 136
Sincere-Wing On model, 47
Singapore Chinese Chamber of
    Commerce and Industry (SCCCI),
    41, 46, 54
Singapore Federation of Chinese
    Clan Association (SFCCA), 54
sinkhek, 7, 40, 54
Sjamsul Nursalim, 3, 30
Skinner, G.W., 87–88, 167, 170
small and medium-scale enterprises
    (SMEs), 10, 11, 13, 18, 23–24, 25,
    35–36, 38, 39, 43–44, 49–50, 51,

Index

60, 61, 69, 71, 72, 77, 78, 80–81, 85, 86, 99, 100, 123, 146–147, 148, 149, 151, 152
Soeharto, 10, 11, 14, 130, 131, 132, 133, 135, 136, 172
Soekarno, 130, 133, 142
Soerjadjaja, William, 3, 131
Soerjadjaja family, 30, 31
Sophanpanich family, 2, 3, 29, 94–95, 171
Sophanpanich, Chin, 90, 94–95
Southward Policy, 153
Suehiro, A., 3, 34, 88–89, 171
Suryadinata, L., 76, 124, 142, 171, 173
Sun Hung Kai Properties, 4, 27
Sy, Henry, 3, 10, 31, 32, 106, 108, 110, 114, 119

Tan Chee Yioun, Vincent, 4, 10, 23, 70, 168, 170
Tan Cheng Lock, 7, 21
Tan Kah Kee, 3, 46, 65, 74–76, 169
Tan Koon Swan, 68
Tan Lark Sye, 41
Tan, Lucio, 3, 10, 11, 31, 106, 107–108, 109, 114, 115, 119
Tan Yu, 3, 31, 116
technopreneurs, 39, 56–59
Tejaphaibul family, 21, 29, 171
Teo family, 23
Teochew, 7–8, 10, 46, 64, 86, 167, 169
Thai Farmers Bank (TFB) Group, 29, 90, 93, 95, 96, 171
Thai-Hua Group, 90
Ting Pek Khiing, 10, 70, 170
totok, 7, 139
two-legged policy, 42
Ty, George, 3, 31, 114, 115, 119

United Malacca Rubber Estates, 21

United Malays' National Organization (UMNO), 65–66, 68, 70
United Overseas Bank (UOB), 3, 8, 31, 32, 50–51, 52

Virata, Cesar, 114
Vleming, J.L., 126

Wah Chang Group, 50
Wang Gungwu, 47, 72–74
Wanglee Bank, 8, 90
Wanglee Group, 89–90, 171
Wee Cho Yaw, 50–51
Weidebaum, M and S. Hughes, 2
Whitley, R., 16
Wickberg, E., 74, 112–113, 118
Widjaja, Eka Tjipta, 3, 10, 14, 27, 28, 30, 32, 135, 136
Wing Tai Holdings, 22
Wong S.L., 20, 113, 123

xingyong, 53–56, 57, 59–60

Yeo, Alan, 22–23, 50
Yeo family, 22
Yeo Hiap Seng (YHS) Group, 22–23, 50, 168, 169
Yeo Keng Lian, 22
Yeo Thian In, 22, 50
Yeoh, Francis, 10
Yeoh Kok Kheng, 79–80
Yong, C.F., 74–76
Yoshihara Kunio, 3, 24, 26, 27, 35, 48–49, 56, 76–77, 78, 120–121, 166, 171
Yuchengco, Alfonso, 3, 10, 31, 114, 115, 119
YTL Corporation, 10, 29, 34, 70, 83, 170

For Product Safety Concerns and Information please contact our EU
representative GPSR@taylorandfrancis.com
Taylor & Francis Verlag GmbH, Kaufingerstraße 24, 80331 München, Germany

www.ingramcontent.com/pod-product-compliance
Ingram Content Group UK Ltd.
Pitfield, Milton Keynes, MK11 3LW, UK
UKHW040927180425
457613UK00010B/270